# A Successful MARRIAGE GOD'S WAY

Understanding God's Design for Your Marriage & Applying It *Successfully*...

## YaQuanda Payne McCall, Ph.D

A SUCCESSFUL MARRIAGE: GOD'S WAY
YaQuanda Payne McCall, Ph.D.

www.ispeaksuccess.com (website)
ispeaklife@ispeaklife2u.com (email)
PO Box 14167 Tallahassee, FL 32317 (address)

Published by YaQuanda P. McCall
Printed by Rose Printing, Tallahassee, Florida

Edited by Dee Thomas-Lockley of Thomas Transcription Services, Inc.
www.thomastx.com

Art Direction, Cover Design and Layout by Macork Solutions™
www.macorksolutions.com

ISBN    978-0-9896127-0-8

Copyright @ 2013 by YaQuanda Payne McCall
All rights reserved

This book or parts thereof may not be reproduced in any form, stored in a retrieval system, or transmitted in any forms by any means- electronic, mechanical, photocopying, recording, or otherwise- without prior written permission of the publisher, except as provided by United States of America copyright law.

Unless otherwise noted, all Scripture quotations are from the King James Version of the Holy Bible.

Scripture quotations marked NIV are from New International Version ©1978, 1984 by International Bible Society, Colorado Springs.

Scripture quotations marked NKJV are from New King James Version of The Holy Bible © 1982 by Thomas Nelson, Inc.

Scripture quotations marked NLT are from New Living Translation © 1996 by Tyndale House Publishers, Wheaton, IL.

Scripture quotations marked NCV are from New Century Version ©1991 by Word Bibles, Dallas.

Definitions marked Merriam-Webster are from Merriam-Webster Online Dictionary. Springfield: Merriam-Webster Inc., 2005. <http://www.merriam-webster.com>

Definitions marked Strong's are from Strong, James. The New Strong's Exhaustive Concordance of the Bible. Tennessee: Thomas Nelson Publishing, 1984.

Library of Congress Control Number: 2013911538

McCall, YaQuanda Payne.
A Successful Marriage: God's Way/ YaQuanda Payne McCall
Includes bibliographical references.
ISBN 978-0-9896127-0-8 (paperback)
1.Marriage—Religious aspects—Christianity 2. Spouses—Religious life. 3. Premarital—Religious aspects
XX0000.00.X00 2013
000.0'000—XX00

2013911538

People and incidents in this book are composites created by the author from her experiences in counseling. Names and details of the stories have been changed, and any similarity between names and stories of individuals described in this book to individuals known to readers is purely coincidental.

Printed in the United States
2013—First Edition

# Table of Contents

Foreword: Tommy McCall

Author's Preface

Acknowledgements

Introduction

| | | |
|---|---|---|
| Chapter 1: | The Importance of Beholding Vision and Prosperity | 1 |
| Chapter 2: | Revealing the Best You | 15 |
| Chapter 3: | Let's Get an Understanding of Marriage | 37 |
| Chapter 4: | Success: We Can Do This! | 56 |
| Chapter 5: | Let's Explore Love | 68 |
| Chapter 6: | Appreciating Love and Friendship | 84 |
| Chapter 7: | Enjoying Sexual Love | 92 |
| Chapter 8: | Meeting Your Spouse's Needs | 106 |
| Chapter 9: | Conquering Negative Conflict | 122 |
| Chapter 10: | Comprehending Communication and Commitment | 137 |
| Chapter 11: | Expressing Anger Positively | 155 |
| Chapter 12: | The Necessity of Forgiveness | 168 |
| Chapter 13: | Learning How to Support Your Spouse | 181 |
| Chapter 14: | Appreciating the Process of Victory | 192 |

Bibliography

About the Author

# Foreword

I am blessed and honored to be able to scribe the foreword for this life-changing book. Let me start by sharing a little bit about the author. Ya-Quanda McCall obtained her Computer Information Science Bachelor's degree from Florida A&M University, her Christian Counseling Master's degree from Jacksonville Theological Seminary, and she received her Doctorate degree from Truth Bible College and Seminary. Dr. McCall is also the founder and President of I Speak Life Global Ministries, Inc. She also is a marriage and family counselor. She counsels couples before and after they are married to help them obtain the success this book teaches.

God has favored me to be married to Dr. McCall for 14 years. Notice I did not say 14 illustrious years because there have been good times and not so good times. That is what this book is about, not having an illustrious fairy tale marriage but having a successful marriage the way God intended. This book is for couples that are looking for a blueprint to success not perfection. Having personally read the book, I find myself implementing some changes in my own marriage. I have become enlightened about understanding the different facets of how God sees marriage.

The numerous references to scripture lets me know that Dr. McCall is giving her educated and well qualified perspective on what the Word of God has to say about marriages. While the entire book has nuggets in it for everyone, I must say that my favorite chapter is the one dealing with needs. Pay special attention to this one because if we can meet these needs for our spouses, then the enemy has no room to come in and cause some of the other problems that we see in marriages today. Singles will benefit greatly by reading this book because this teaching will extensively help prepare them for marriage.

With the divorce rate being just as high in the church as it is in the secular world, we need a 21$^{st}$ century approach to deal with the complex issues that rip marriages apart. *A Successful Marriage: God's Way* not only diagnoses the problems that arise in marriage but also offers sound biblically based solutions. *A Successful Marriage: God's Way* is both helpful and quite entertaining as well. Dr. McCall has a beautiful sense of humor and keeps you engaged throughout the entire book. I sincerely believe that your marriage will be enriched and you will be empowered to make your marriage succeed.

Tommy McCall, Pharmacy Consultant, PPSC
Pharmacy Support Solutions, CEO

## *Author's Preface*
## I BELIEVE IN MARRIAGE!

Hello beloved, I am elated that you have chosen this marriage enhancement tool to serve as a road map to the next level of success in your marriage. One of my favorite quotes is, "Success is not the absence of failures but it is the wisdom to pull educational fragments from failures with the intent to try again!" We all make mistakes but we can still have the success we desire if we have the tenacity, resilience and perseverance necessary. Marriage is hard work in itself. With all the pressures of life that we encounter we have to learn how to serve our spouse in a manner that keeps the excitement going. Having success God's way can instill in us the fortitude to handle the vicissitudes of life. We have the proclivity to desire success and today, my friend, you have a tool in your hand that has proven true in my marriage and others marriages as well.

Whether you are newly married, almost married or have been married a long time… this empowerment tool is just for you! I have devoured the principles and established new patterns that have produced results beyond my wildest dreams in my marriage! Marriage is good! Marriage is fun! Marriage is a place where I can explore, explode, exceed and exhale all in one day! Marriage with the proper foundation can be the launching pad of great ideas that in turn produce great experiences, services and products. The power of agreement in marriage causes us to rise above the mundane and cultivate an atmosphere of ingenuity, creativity and unity!

Having had success in many areas, I wanted to extend the invitation to marriages everywhere to experience what God has made beautiful… I want us all to experience marriage His way. Whether you already have a marriage God's way or you are embarking upon this exhilarating journey of allowing God to fabricate His DNA in your marriage; I guarantee you that you will never be the same again after ingesting these principles!

As a Marriage and Family counselor, I have counseled many couples. They have kept me polished with experience and additional educational aspirations. Married couples encounter so many difficult situations and we need access to Biblical knowledge that can help us. I've encountered and empowered couples who were lost, confused and in trouble through Biblical coaching. The Bible has proven true! There are over 200 Bible scriptures referenced in this marriage empowerment and enhancement tool! Success is always at our fingertips when we make room for Biblical instruction.

As a Marriage Ministry leader, I have had the joy of teaching principles and patterns for years with my wonderful husband. Even as we took many trips away to work on this tool just for you, we were learning more about each other. Marriage is not for the feeble because as we encounter situations that could knock us down, we need to be open to allow God to strengthen us through His Word and His presence.

Listen friend, God is for you and He is for your marriage. The marriage you desire is yours as long as you are willing to work, serve, love and apply a lot of grace. I am excited that you are serious enough about the betterment of your marriage to the point you are willing to sow time and resources. You are a winner my friend! I know that you are a winner because there are no losers on my team and if you have this book in your hand, I know we are on the same team! No matter what it looks like, I want to encourage you that you can have a Successful Marriage: God's Way! I believe in Marriage and I believe in you!

# Acknowledgements

First and foremost, I give honor to God my Father, Jesus Christ my Lord and Savior and my very best Friend Holy Spirit. I want to thank my amazing husband, Tommy McCall who made this book possible. Thank you for loving me in spite of me. You are forever my Boothang! To my beautiful children Arielle, Arionne, Tommy Elisha, Timothy Elijah and Travis Paul, thank you for making sure I pray every day! Thank you for not complaining because I had to work on this book and couldn't play the Wii with you. I pray now for your marriages that you will have success God's way. To my Mommy, Vanessa Williams, You believed in me when no one else did. I love you forever Ma Duke! To my Pops, Fred Payne, all of my life you called me a genius and told me I could do anything! Well! I believed you and this is just the beginning! To my little brother Fredrick Payne, always fighting your battles gave me the strength to do this! I love you lil dude! To Junious and Tony, I love you big brothers. To my modern day Naomi, Ladonna Fennell, Thank you for loving me as your very own daughter! You give Mother in laws a good name! To my lil sis Tiffany Mason, I love you!

To Pastors, Joseph and Robbin Davis, thank you for believing in me and not scolding me for traveling so much and missing church! Thank you for trusting us with the people God gave you to lead. I love you TGCC! Thank you TGCC Marriage Ministry for listening to me teach about Marriage Victory! To Bishop Carolyn Love, you gave me Global vision and I love you. To Bishop Keith Johnson, thank you for believing in me and giving me a chance to serve God's people and empower them at the same time. This book was birthed out of Greater Marriage Ministry! To Overseer Gregory L. James, serving in ministry with you was exhilarating! Thank you for allowing me to serve at TLCI! To Pastor Michael Smith, thank you for teaching me that I am my husband's wife and not his counselor. I love you and Katina!

Mega Love and thanks to MaCork Solutions! Sir Michael Cork, you are a Marketing Success Extraordinaire! You know how to make me look good! Thank you to Shemeka Grey and LaShae Roberts for proofreading my book so I sound like I have some good sense. Thank you Lady Dee Thomas of Thomas Transcription Services Inc. for editing this book and helping me sound real real good!

Thank you to Prophetess Dwann and Bishop Harold Rollinson for always believing in me and being available whenever I needed you. Thank you to Pastors Bobby and Angel Thomas for loving me and speaking life over me always. To all my counselees, you are the reason I do what I do. Thank you for allowing me to counsel you and speak words of life to your marriage. To this day, every couple that completed their premarital counseling with me is still married! To God be all the Glory! Successful Marriage done God's way is the best way!

# Introduction

Imagine two people on a ship sailing out to sea. They see a whirlpool in the sea ahead of them. The couple did not prepare for a whirlpool. The whirlpool begins to pull the ship down. The couple holds onto one another while the waves of water knock against the ship. The intensity of the waves has the strength to destroy the ship. The ship is rock solid against the waves. The couple knows they must stay in the ship or they will die. They pray and then they quickly come up with a plan. They run to the wheel of the ship. Together they put enough force on the wheel to cause the ship to turn away from the whirlpool. The couple makes it out of the whirlpool stronger than ever. They have encountered and overcome a situation that had the potential to destroy them.

Let us apply that illustration to marriage. The two people represent the husband and the wife. The ship represents the foundation on which they built their marriage. The ship was rock solid. The Bible shares an instance that reveals the wisdom of building our house upon a rock. "Anyone who listens to my teaching and follows it is wise, like a person who builds a house on solid rock. Though the rain comes in torrents and the floodwaters rise and the winds beat against that house, it won't collapse because it is built on bedrock."[1] God's Word is that Rock. The scripture references a man that ignores God's Word. This particular man built his house on sand. The world offers us a chance to build our marriage upon sand. The way to having a successful marriage, my friend, is to make the Word of God the foundation of your marriage.

The whirlpool represents divorce, hard hearts, unforgiveness, uncontrollable anger, lack of commitment, not communicating, unmet needs, selfishness, unwillingness to work together and other tools the enemy uses to destroy marriage. We are not suffering defeat because the whirlpool is attempting to suck us in. We are not suffering defeat if we begin to sink. Married couples will encounter whirlpool experiences. There will be trials, tribulations and attacks of the enemy in every marriage. There will be times in a marriage when we fail to do the right things. Success is not that we never fail. Wisdom reveals the components of true success in the fragments of our failures. When we fail, we must be tenacious enough to learn from our mistakes. We cannot allow any level of failure to rob us of the victory that comes next. For example, I have failed countless times at being patient. However, after paying attention to what happens, I am now better at being patient. We cannot give up on our marriage, our spouse or ourselves.

The waves of life and the whirlpools of defeat will always reveal the grace of God in marriages. The grace of God is the reason the ship does not sink. That same grace of God is available to marriages. We do not have to succumb to negative situations. We can arise victorious in Christ Jesus in our marriages. The ship aforementioned actually began to sink. It began to sink just as Peter began to sink when he walked on the water with Jesus.[2] Like Peter, marriages have the opportunity at this point to grab a hold of one another and reach to Jesus. Like Peter, we must be willing to cry "Lord, save my marriage".

The couple held onto one another and prayed. Their power to believe came from what they knew about God. They knew He loved them and would take care of them. They knew they may suffer loses but never defeat. Trials will come but these trials should not destroy the marriages that God puts together. They did not stop at praying but by faith, they came up with a plan. They established a vision of success. They did not pray and wait on God to send them something out of the sky. They prayed and implemented the portion of the process for which they were responsible. As we pray for our marriages, we have to be mindful to do our part. Show me your faith and your actions, and I will guarantee your results based on the Word of God.

The water tossing the ship seemed like utter defeat was inevitable. Sometimes life can hit us with situations that feel like utter defeat. It is at that time we must hold onto what we believe. We must allow the Word of God to speak for us. Water can represent purification. Purification is simply removing anything that is impure or unclean. God can always use the trouble we experience to cleanse us. When married couples go through trials, they should draw closer to God and closer to each other. God can use the rough waves of life to purify us. Purification is the prelude to the promises of God.

We will all experience different variations of trials and tribulations. God does not attack us with trouble. God does not put sickness on us to show us He is a Healer. Sickness came because Adam sinned against God. We experience sickness because of the fallen and sinful world that we live in. God gave us the power to overcome sickness and disease by speaking and believing the Word of God in faith. Couples will experience many trials throughout their marriage. Nevertheless, God can use each trial to purify them of doubt, fear or any other impurities. He has given us the power of healing. Godly couples that experience the rough waves of life can find peace in God's Word.

God will make sure that we come through our trials stronger. Couples that go through trials together with God's help always come out better. Life will cause unexpected situations to come. Couples must do their part to remain joined together. God has given us the Word to help us come out victorious. Marriages survive the purification process through prayer, commitment, and living the Word of God. These marriages will always come out stronger. Our strength comes when we acknowledge that the most successful way to stand is to hold on to each other under the Mighty Hand of God. Couples must understand that God is for them and He will hold them up as they hold on to Him.

In order to understand anything there must first be a willful submission. If we ever want to understand how to have a successful marriage God's way, then we must seek God. He knows what each marriage needs. There is no real catchall to marriage because God made us different. The only constant is Him. We are an ever-changing people. Our looks change, our attitudes change and our thinking changes. Yet, God never changes. He is the same yesterday, today and forever![3]

It is wise to look to Him for success in our marriages. He pours out wisdom and unconditional love when we stand under His Word. He pours out what we need to survive and thrive in marriage. We must never accept the world's statistics. As a believer, if you stand under God's Word then your marriage has a one hundred percent chance of being successful. It takes a humbled heart to receive God's teachings. He will correct us individually first, and we must focus on ourselves first. We must understand God's grace for ourselves before we can truly extend it to our spouse. Once we truly grasp just how much we need God's grace, then we can extend it unconditionally to our spouse.

Marriage is God's business. He is the only one who can make it work the way it should. God's purpose for marriage will prevail over the perversion of the world. So often, we look at other couple's marriage as our standard. We look at them and we say that our marriage is not that bad. However, our model must be the one on the heart of God. To look at a couple whose marriage appears to be worse than ours and say we must be doing something right because our marriage is not that bad is erroneous. We must seek God daily for His perfect will and divine wisdom about our marriage. God has a unique and glorious design for each marriage and it includes Him being first. Besides, someone else could be looking at your marriage saying the same thing. Let us look to the Creator for a divine model of what we strive for in our marriage.

I was at McDonald's with my four children and two of my nieces. I saw this police officer there with his two little children. I proceeded to initiate a conversation with him. I began to ask him questions about his job as a police officer and how it affected his marriage. The job was not the problem; it was him. He had decided not to dedicate himself to his wife or his children. He shared with me that he had been married twice and had four children (two from each marriage). Before I judged him, I had to be careful. I quickly remembered the scripture that says, "Do not judge so that you will not be judged."[4]

I allowed the Holy Spirit to edit the words I spoke. That proved to be a sure sign of wisdom. I asked him, rather boldly, considering he was carrying a gun, "What makes you think this marriage is going to be any different from the first two?" He said, "Because I am a believer now and the woman I am engaged to is a believer as well". He said you could not have told him two marriages ago that it made a bit of a difference if God was in your life for a marriage to work. He begs to differ now. He said the difference is God. He said they are doing it right this time. They are not shacking, fornicating or deceiving one another. They are getting to know one another better. They are getting to know God better as well. They decided they would not entertain sin. They decided to follow Jesus. He indicated they would be successful because they were doing it God's way. You can have success in your marriage, too.

If you do not know Jesus, please take the time now to consider where you will spend eternity. Christ died for you to live with God forever. That is eternal life. Eternal life starts now for those who believe in Jesus Christ as their Savior. Jesus loves you. He chose to die for you. He wants to lead you into a life of righteousness. Righteousness is not doing all the right things. Righteousness is having a right relationship with the right God. Your relationship with God through Christ Jesus is what makes you a righteous person. We will not have you pursue a successful marriage without pursuing eternal life first. While a successful marriage requires work, Salvation is a gift from God. Consider the Gospel: We are all sinners and that is why we must accept Christ[5] We cannot save ourselves from sin. We need a Savior.[6] God loved us while we were sinners. He knows we cannot save ourselves from sin. He sent His Son to die for our sins to give us eternal life.[7] God's gift to us is salvation and eternal life.[8] Our gift to our spouse is living for Jesus. Please contact us at *salvation@ispeaklife2u.com* if you want to accept Jesus as your personal Savior. He loves you and He is waiting on you to say yes to Him today. Do not hesitate. Contact us now. We want to pray with you and send you some more information about eternal life through Jesus Christ.

My prayer for your marriage is that Holy Spirit will use the words of this book and the meditations of God's Word to make your marriage as God intended. In other words, I want you to have a successful marriage. This book will help you if you apply what Holy Spirit reveals to you with your whole heart.

# *Chapter 1*
# BEHOLDING THE IMPORTANCE OF VISION AND PROSPERITY

"I changed my mind!" screamed Valerie as she slammed the back door. She and Richard had been arguing over moving to Georgia. At first, Valerie was in favor of moving but fear began to set in. Together she and Richard had written a vision. The vision included short and long-term goals. They both researched the area in which they were moving. Richard communicated with his wife to find out what happened. He found out that her fears came from their past mistakes. Together they worked through all of her fears. They knew that as they relocated from Florida they could encounter unexpected events. They agreed to stick to the plan as much as possible. They understood that the shift would be uncomfortable at first, but chose by faith to launch out into new territory. As a result, their marriage, family and finances prospered greatly. Having made up their minds they refused to let anything deter them from moving forward with their vision.

## THE IMPORTANCE OF VISION IN MARRIAGE

In order to be successful in any field we need to have a vision. Many meanings come to mind when we hear the word vision. Vision is having mental sight, which helps us to be able to reach our goals. In marriage, vision should include a couple having the mental ability to perceive the goals they desire to reach together. Vision is the power of seeing; a mental image; the aptitude to identify with a mental eye something of great beauty.[1] Having the mental ability to succeed is a required component of a successful marriage. Marriages encounter countless types of trials but if we make up our minds and believe we can be successful, we will overcome every trial. Having the power of vision is important when we go through challenges. As we go through the struggles, having a vision of victory will enable us to stand in faith during the trying times. Marriage is a very important part of God's plan for His Church. The statistics state that there is a fifty percent chance of staying married versus getting a divorce. I believe that by faith we have a one hundred percent chance of staying married if we obey God's instructions.

Vision includes having a mental image. The mind is where the battle for our marriages and our lives take place. If we have a vision based on God's Word for our marriage even if things look contrary to that vision we can still aim towards the goals we have established. I believe marriage has been misunderstood. Love is not real love unless it is the love of God. Misuse of the word love has clouded our ability to perceive that we can overcome trials beyond our feelings. We say things like, I love apples. We say I love that color. We say I love those jeans. We say I love that truck. Usually when we say we love something, we are equating that thing we love with a feeling of pleasure. I love what brings me pleasure. Well, marriage will not always be pleasurable. Marriage is for adults; children need not apply! There will be times in marriage that we stay married simply for the sake of our faith. Marriage is not always pretty but it always has purpose.

Because of our erroneous beliefs about love and marriage when hard times come we throw in the towel. Faith will always pick that towel up and throw it back at us to wipe our sweat so we can stay in the game. Faith is like the love of God. They both never fail. We love to get the victory. Victory only comes after a fight. People who do not understand God's love for us are challenging marriages that follow God's way. We cannot be ignorant or naïve to the fact that marriage is being misrepresented. The family unit is the key to any nation. We need marriages to have healthy families. We need successful families to produce successful children. Marriage is important and we must understand its purpose and significance. It is the prelude to family. God created Adam and Eve. Together they produced the first family unit. God blessed the entire world through one family unit. One who appreciates the significance of marriage is wise.

Unfortunately, couples are having weddings but neglecting to build marriages. Marriages built upon a strong foundation will stand. The foundation that a marriage needs to build upon is the Word of God. The Bible shares God's will with us so we can write a vision for our marriage. Our vision should include staying together until death do us part. Statistically, marriages are staying together until conflict about money tears them apart. Trouble is not biased. We all go through hard times at some point. The Bible gives us wise advice, saying it is better that there be two so if one falls, the other one is there to help them up. The verse actually says, "Two are better than one, because they have a good reward for their labor. For if they fall, one will lift up his companion. But woe to him who is alone when he falls, for he has no one to help him up."[2] We should be there for each other no matter what happens. The issue is when one spouse falls and the other spouse is not there for support. Marriage is good. Let us build our marriages on the Word of God.

We must be taught how to sacrifice for the successful of our marriage. Sacrifice is learned behavior. Couples must remember that they are a team because it helps their willingness to sacrifice what they want for the good of their marriage. There have been times when I have had to do what I call, "Take one for the team." This has included many selfless acts where I had to get over myself for the sake of the team. Team players learn how to support one another. If we work together then we win but if we are divided, we will lose.

Having the proper mental ability to perceive that we can have a successful marriage is the prelude to attaining it. Many couples get married but they have different mental pictures of what they expect out of the marriage. Misconceived expectations cause unnecessary conflict that could be avoided with effective communication. Having a vision for your marriage gives you the upper hand. Being able to see your marriage as successful when it resembles failure is valuable. There has to be a mental capacity in both spouses to comprehend that the marriage will work. We have to make sure that we remain on one accord. We have to desire success in our marriage. If we make sure our will is in check, then when trouble comes, we will choose not to give up. "Not my will but Your will be done Lord", becomes our answer. Setting our mind to obey God even in hard times will help us have a successful marriage.

Vision includes seeing mentally something of great beauty. To see your marriage as something of great beauty when it looks very ugly is one of the pillars of success. There were times when my marriage looked like the bottom of a torn shoe but I had a vision that we would stay together successfully. There were times that my husband did not like me and there were times when I did not like him very much. However, we were committed to the marriage even when we had a hard time committing to one another. Let us stop being superficial. Marriage is hard work! You are taking two adult individuals and asking them to allow God to mold them into something that is contrary to the way they have lived in most cases for at least eighteen years. This is not an easy task but it is attainable. There is a specific process afforded to each marriage. Having a vision that includes the components shared in this book will help foster an environment of marital success.

Vision and prosperity go hand in hand. We will discuss prosperity later on in this chapter in more detail but let me share a few points as it relates to vision. Third John chapter one verse two shares a prayer for us. "Beloved, I pray that you may prosper in all things and be in health, just as your soul prospers."[3] This is the key to vision and prosperity in marriage. We can prosper in all things and be in good health if we have vision. Again, vision is the mental ability to perceive and see something with our mind's eye. The soul consists of our mind, intellect, will and emotions. Prosperity starts in our mind and entails mental stability. Prosperity requires us to use our intellect. We must set our will to obey certain principles to be prosperous. Vision is the first step to being prosperous. If I have the mindset of prosperity, then it does not matter where I am in the process because I know prosperity is my portion. As I prosper in my soul, I will exist in a position of prosperity and thus produce prosperity in my life and my marriage no matter where I am. Let us write a vision for our marriage so we can prosper.

Let me share an example of a prosperous mindset. In Genesis chapter twenty-six, we find that God had blessed Isaac. Isaac had a mindset of prosperity. Isaac dug a well that gushed with water. The people around Isaac challenged him about his well. Isaac having a mindset of prosperity did not argue with them about the well. He allowed them to have the well. He went to another place and dug another well. That well began to gush with water as well. Because Isaac has a mindset of prosperity, he knew that wherever he went he would be prosperous. We have to have that same mindset in marriage. We must believe that no matter what we go through in life we will prosper.

The Bible says, "And whatever he does shall prosper."[4] The reason we prosper is that we are relationally obedient to God's Word. Let me add that Isaac was in a place of obedience. Isaac was not perfect. His purpose included his mistakes and flaws. Your purpose includes your mistakes and your flaws as well. He had a right relationship with God. Therefore, when he wrote the vision of digging the wells he had God's promises on his side. You will have God's promises on your side as you write the vision for your marriage. Writing the vision begins with seeing the vision mentally. As you allow God to prosper you there will continually be blessings waiting for you to grab a hold of and enjoy.

The Bible shares in James chapter two verse seventeen, "So you see faith by itself isn't enough. Unless it produces good deeds, it is dead and useless." Our faith to have a successful marriage must produce or it is not God's best. Surely, a successful marriage is a good deed. It is good indeed. As we write the vision by faith, we have to work the vision by faith. Our mindset of prosperity will continually give us creative ways to fulfill our vision and our goals. My friend, let me share this with you, I have to change my mind before I can change my habitual actions. You must allow the Word of God to change your mind to one of vision and success before you can see the continued display of success in your actions. God is faithful to reveal His will for our life and our marriage. We are then encouraged to establish a vision and goals based on His will. We are only able to comply to His will if we know it. Understanding God's plan for our marriage will produce passion in us. Passion will intensify our desire to see that His will be done in every aspect of our life. A key to understanding God's will is realizing that His will is good. God will help us create different visions and goals based on His will for our lives.

Proverbs chapter twenty- nine verse eighteen says, "Where there is no vision, the people perish." We could make this applicable to marriage by saying, "Where there is no vision, the marriage perishes." Having an understood vision is imperative for success in our marriage. We need to have a clear understanding of our goals and plans. We need to know how we are going to accomplish our goals together. We need to know where we are in the plan. We need to know what our next steps are after we accomplish our goals. Goals are an end that one strives to obtain.[5] Plans are a systematic order for doing something. Goals and plans are essential to productive success in marriage.

As we agree in our marriage that God's will is good, we can see His blessing multiplied in our lives. Agreement is a major benefit in our marriage. Amos chapter three verse three asks us a very important question, "Can two walk together, except they be agreed?" I think we have all experienced at some point in our lives the horror of trying to accomplish a task with a person we cannot get along with let alone agree with. Trying to work with someone like that can be difficult. Marriage does not have to be difficult. God has given us order and His ways to see success in our marriage. Couples that learn to agree will always see a greater benefit than couples who fail to agree. The Bible gives us a precious promise if we can agree. This promise is one of the reasons I believe Satan fights marriages so hard. The power of agreement in marriage is magnanimous. It is amazing! The Bible reminds us "If two of you shall agree on earth as touching anything that they shall ask, it shall be done for them of my Father which is in heaven."[6] If we can learn to spend less time bickering about petty things and more time agreeing about major stuff then we can see success. Agreeing with God's will and order will make things easier day to day.

God has a plan for our marriage and us. He said to us in Jeremiah chapter twenty-nine verse eleven, "For I know the plans I have for you," says the Lord. "They are plans for good and not for disaster, to give you a future and a hope." This verse is good news for marriages. We can rest assured that God's plans for our marriage are good, peaceful and full of hope. We have to pray and seek the Lord for His specific instructions for our marriage. For example, if I am seeking God about purchasing a car, then I cannot go to the Bible and look for car. I need to seek God in prayer about that specific instruction concerning the car. Some things are available to us by our will. If I have the means to buy a car then I do not have to go on a three-day fast to ask God if it is ok. God has made us very intelligent people. As long as we are sensitive to Holy Spirit, then we will do well in all things.

Another scripture refers to having counselors around. Proverbs chapter one verse five reminds us that, "A wise man will hear, and will increase learning; and a man of understanding shall attain unto wise counsels:" Trusting God to use His counselors to assist us is a great idea. Commitment is essential to any vision happening. Patience is a key to success in any arena. Be careful not to define your marriage off the mold of someone else's marriage. It is good to glean from what others are doing right. However, we have to be careful to allow God to unravel His plan for our marriage. What may be acceptable in one marriage may not be acceptable in another. For instance, my friend and her husband travel out of the country monthly. That will not work in my marriage right now. I am currently homeschooling my four children. If I tried to follow my friend in that sense, I would become disgruntled. I would be missing a very important season in my life. Trying to be just like someone else robs the world of the authentic flavor you bring to this world. Let us see your marriage flourish as God designed. Learning how to hear Holy Spirit speak to us about our marriage is very important.

Life can hit us with situations that we are not prepared for and are not expecting. The good thing is that God is prepared. He is always prepared. What we are experiencing is never a surprise to Him. We simply have to tap into the provisions that God has set for us. God does not play games with us. Life will not change His mind about His vision for us. We have to make sure we do not allow what we experience to turn us away from God's vision for our marriage.

Writing our vision out is a very good idea. The scriptures remind us to "Write the vision, and make it plain upon tables, that he may run that readeth it. For the vision is yet for an appointed time, but at the end it shall speak, and not lie: though it tarry, wait for it; because it will surely come."[7] Once you see the Vision that God established for you then you will see the importance and

| ONCE A DAY   | Love       | Live     | Laugh   |
|--------------|------------|----------|---------|
| ONCE A WEEK  | Share      | Shine    | Show    |
| ONCE A MONTH | Appreciate | Aspire   | Attend  |
| ONCE A YEAR  | Plan       | Perceive | Prepare |

urgency of building your marriage as a reflection of liberty where people can truly know Christ. Write the vision for your marriage. Try to meet weekly, monthly or quarterly. We must write the vision in order for us to run with it.

Vision planning is important. Let us consider this table for establishing healthy vision meetings.

Once a day, we should strive to express our love for each other. This will allow us to express love in an undeniable way daily. If your spouse likes verbal affirmations then use opportunities everyday to speak life to your spouse. Living is something we only get to do once. We have to daily aim to resist the monotony that sets in and makes us tired of the same ole' things. Laughing together will always help us appreciate the good in life. As we laugh together, we get to enjoy each other more. Let your vision include daily ways you can express love and gratitude to each other.

Once a week, we can share our plans. Weekly, we can share our feelings for certain things. We can schedule a date night where we just share how much we love one another. Learning to shine is important. Shining as the light is a key to showing others the ways of God. Shining in doing marriage God's way is the key to becoming an instrument in revealing God's ways to the lost. People are seeking those couples who are shinning for Christ. Show each other you care. Think of ways to show each other how glad you are to be married to them. Once a month, appreciate one another in a creative way. Monthly aspire to show your spouse that you are on their team and you believe in them. Attend to the dreams and desires of your spouse by doing something for them that conveys that. If your spouse dreams of being a model then set up a runway for her to let her know you believe in her. Finding ways to attend to your spouse will be well worth the time it takes to do it.

Once a year you should plan for the year. Yearly you should perceive that this year you will see many of your goals and dreams happen. Place your expectation on God to do His part and together you do your part. Preparing for results is a sign of faith. As you plan your year, you should dream big. Allow God to show forth His glory in your marriage in a way beyond your own understanding. He is willing and able to do so.

## THE IMPORTANCE OF PERSONAL VISION

The Word gives me hope for a personal vision for my growth in Christ.

Romans chapter three verse twenty-three shows me I have sinned and come short of God's glory in my marriage. That helps me hold up a mirror instead of pointing fingers at my spouse. There are things in me that I need to change. As I learn more about reflection, I work more diligently to change myself. Reflection includes asking my spouse what he sees when he looks at me. The more time I spend working on my reflection gives me less time to work on my spouse. Sometimes I do not see my faults as clearly as I see my spouse's faults. As I see myself more clearly, I realize that I need to change. Some steps to change include:

1. I must acknowledge and see the need to change.
2. I must believe that change is possible.
3. I must want to change.
4. I must agree to allow the process of change.
5. I must change to reflect the image of Christ.

Change means to make different or to exchange. Change is intentional and done on purpose. If we want to change then we can. God takes us from one level of faith to another level of faith. It is a process orchestrated by Him for His glory. He also takes us from one level of glory to another level of glory. He reveals His glory through our marriage and through us in profound and unique ways.

This equation will produce positive results:
"I am willing" + (plus) "God is able" = (equals) "Change in my marriage and me"

My marriage will be changed as I allow God to change me. As a major ingredient in my marriage, what goes on with me goes on in my marriage. Whether what I am experiencing is negative or positive it will affect my marriage. Luke chapter ten verse nineteen gives me authority over the enemy. However, my authority and power is not over my spouse. I have authority and power over the devil, principalities, powers, rulers of darkness, and spiritual wickedness. I can stop them from destroying my marriage. I can especially stop them from using me to destroy my marriage. I have to ask myself:

1. Am I walking in my authority?
2. Am I pulling down strongholds?
3. Am I thinking on things that produce God's glory?
4. Am I speaking life? (I will have what I say.)
5. Am I putting off the old man and his carnal ways?
6. Am I putting on the nature of Christ?
7. Am I living in faith?
8. Am I staying in my lane? (God did not give me dominion over my spouse.)

We have to meditate continually on good reports, honest ideas, pure thoughts and righteous actions. Together my spouse and I can conquer anything. Having a vision for our marriage helps to keep us focused on the right things. As we aim to better ourselves, we can appreciate our spouse more.

Having a vision for my marriage includes having a vision for me. God's vision for us includes eternal life. His Son dying for us depicts his desire for us to have life. God saved us and gave us eternal life. The benefits of eternal life start now. "While we were still sinners, Christ died for us."[8] He did not wait until we got it right because we need Him to get it right. Jeremiah chapter seventeen verse nine shares, "The heart of man is deceitful and desperately wicked; no one can truly know how evil it is?" People can be deceitful, crooked and polluted without God. We need God. It is out of the heart of man that flows sins like: "worshiping false gods, witchcraft, hating, fighting, being jealous, being angry, arguing, dividing into little groups and thinking the other groups are wrong, false teaching, wanting something someone else has, killing other people, using strong drink, wild parties, and all things like these."[9] God sent His Son to pay for our sins with His own life.[10]

Jesus said, no man could take His life but He laid it down himself.[11] He gave His life for us to be saved and know Him. To believe is to commit to, trust in, be faithful to and to be sure, that God will perform is His Word. You have to ask yourself do you really believe. In order to trust Him you have to know Him. We get to know Him and His power by suffering. The Bible tells us to be happy if we suffer for righteousness' sake. "And to rejoice, inasmuch as we are partakers of Christ's sufferings; that, when His glory shall be revealed, we may be glad with exceeding joy."[12] We will suffer because we believe in Him. You must trust Him, commit to Him and be faithful to Him no matter what. He would not have allowed His Son to die if He wanted to destroy you. God is serious about us. He does not want to destroy us. Sin destroys us but if we choose God then He will save us from all evil. "Many are the afflictions of the righteous: but the Lord delivered him out of them all."[13] "We are troubled on every side, yet not distressed; we are perplexed, but not in despair; Persecuted, but not forsaken; cast down, but not destroyed;"[14] God loves us so much that He takes our times of suffering and makes them produce good in our lives. It is not always easy to see this but it is true. God is faithful. Romans chapter eight verse twenty-eight says, "And we know that God causes everything to work together for the good of those who love God and are called according to His purpose for them." Everything includes troubles, trials, afflictions, suffering, pain and tribulations.

He did not say we eventually get eternal life but He said we have eternal life when we believe in Jesus. In order to have life God must increase in us and we must decrease. Life sometimes can make us think we have nothing. On the contrary, if we are in Christ, we have eternal life and eternal life starts now. We can have all the blessings of God. Blessings are not just money but peace, faith, love, truth, hope and every need met. He will meet all our needs. He is everything we need. Yes, the thief comes to steal our peace, to kill our hope, and to destroy what God has for us. However, Jesus came so that we can have life, and have life in abundance. We can have abundance now. We do not have to wait to get to heaven to have good things. We do not have to lack any good thing. When God fills us with His Spirit, we can have love, joy, peace, patience, kindness, goodness, faithfulness, gentleness and self-control. He gives us spiritual blessings. God promises us that no good thing will He withhold from them that walk uprightly.[15] God is good. He has pleasure in the prosperity of His children. Prosperity in life is not just money. It includes health, marriage, relationships, business and life.

## HAVING PROSPERITY IN YOUR MARRIAGE

Prosperity is more than money. God wants to prosper us in the areas of wealth and health. He has given some people the desire to own a business and have several streams of income. Everyone must have some form of income to survive in the system we live in today. The Word helps us understand that He is our source. He gives us the power to get wealth.[16] God wants to teach us how to leave a spiritual legacy and inheritance of generational prosperity. When God prospers us it is not just for us but for the future generations coming after us.

Webster's definition of prosperity is success.[17] The Biblical word for prosperity also includes having wisdom and good success.[18] Wisdom is the prelude and the key to total prosperity because she will lead us in the way of spiritual prosperity (success) and spiritual wealth (increase). Wisdom teaches us righteousness, victory and the right way to obtain riches. Prosperity is wealth and good health through transformation, renewal of the mind, good eating habits and other practical means. Prospering also includes the presence of God, overflow, provision, edification, resilience and release. Allow God to overflow your marriage with His presence. God's presence will always bring an overflow. God's presence brings provision for godly visions. Successful marriage is a godly vision that God is willing to provide for, as we allow the Word to edify us and build us up. Then, we will in return edify our spouse. Life can be unpredictable and uncomfortable but with resilience, we can develop an attitude that we will not give up. God will use our lives to release His glory and light into the lives of many people. We can be prosperous.

## TOTAL PROSPERITY

Total Prosperity is prospering in spirit, soul and body. God wants us to prosper. He wants us to have good success in spirit, soul and body. The first component of "Total Prosperity" is "Spiritual Prosperity". Spiritual prosperity includes prayer, which is successful communication with God. Prayer is two-way communication with God. We pray to God the Father in the name of Jesus by the power of the Holy Spirit. God is a Spirit. We must communicate with Him in spirit and in truth. That means that we cannot approach God as we do everyone else. Those who even talk to God must first believe that He is who He says

He is. My relationship with God depicts my ability to communicate with Him. The more I communicate with Him means the more I learn about Him.

Spiritual prosperity includes faith. Faith believes the spiritual truth or revelation released from God via His Word into our lives. Faith includes us obeying His command. Faith includes believing and responding. Faith takes the truths of the spirit realm and produces or manifests them in the material or natural realm. Faith takes truth we cannot see to produce truth we can see. If God speaks to me and He says that He wants to heal my body that is truth I cannot see yet. If I believe Him, obey His Word and lay hands on myself then healing will come. Healing becomes the truth I can now see. We can apply this principle to our marriages. God's Word will produce His intended results in our marriage and life. If God speaks to me and says, He wants to prosper me financially. That is truth I cannot see at the time He speaks it. This truth predicated on the Word of God says God has given me power to get wealth. If I believe God and operate in the gifts that He has given me then wealth becomes truth that I can see. God is the epitome of success in this life. God wants me to prosper in every area of my life because He gets the glory. Evidence of us prospering in a spiritual aspect is God communicating with us and us being able to hear what He is communicating. The language of the spirit is the Word of God.

The second component of total prosperity is prospering in our soul. Prosperity of the soul is our ability to receive from God and mentally process what He is communicating. The soul consists of mind, emotions, intelligence, will and decision making center. When God releases a spiritual truth to us, we have to be in-sync in our soul. We need to have our soul in a place of subjection to the Spirit of God. God speaks and then my mind, emotions, intelligence, will and decision-making center comply with what He said. Third John chapter one verse two sheds some light on prospering in our soul. "Beloved, I wish above all things that thou may prosper and be in health, even as thy soul prospers." Health and prosperity are products of my mind. I must have an attitude of prosperity. When my soul is prospering then everything else in my life must prosper. Prospering is intentional.

To be prosperous is in an attitude. My attitude determines my altitude, gratitude and magnitude. Our attitude will determine what we will accept as truth. What we will accept determines our actions. Prosperity is a lifestyle. Prosperity is the portion of those in Christ. Galatians chapter three verses thirteen and fourteen says, "But Christ has rescued us from the curse pronounced by the law. When he was hung on the cross, he took upon himself the curse for our wrongdoing. For it is written in the Scriptures, "Cursed is everyone who is hung on a tree." Through Christ Jesus, God has blessed the Gentiles with the same blessing he promised to Abraham, so that we who are believers might receive the promised Holy Spirit through faith." We are sons and daughters of Abraham.

Galatians chapter three verse twenty says, "Now unto him that is able to do exceeding abundantly above all that we ask or think, according to the power that works in us" This verse is a direct correlation that if we prosper in our thinking we will see the abundance of God. I prosper in my will by asking God via prayer. The fact that I choose to ask for blessings shows evidence that my will is in harmony with God's Word that says He wants to bless me. I prosper in my thinking when I think about the blessings of God coming to my life and my marriage. God is going to use the power of the Holy Spirit working in me to produce prosperity in my marriage and every area of my life. Everything God does will have eternal implications.

If my marriage is falling apart and I hear God say He will restore my marriage then I have to receive it and believe it to experience it. I must receive that Word in my spirit (success) and I must choose to believe that Word in my soul (success). The Word of God will always set us free. As we are set free, we can see that fruit in our marriages. I can be set free from lack, poverty and all else that is not God's best for my life. We birth businesses out of prosperity of the soul. As God releases ideas to us, we have to take those ideas and produce them in the natural. Success starts in my spirit. We process success in our soul. We produce success through our body.

The third component of total prosperity is in the body. Prosperity of the body is our ability to obey God. Obedience opens the door for the power of heaven to come to earth. John chapter nine verses six and seven says, "Then He spit on the ground, made mud with the saliva, and spread the mud over the blind man's eyes. He told him, "Go wash yourself in the pool of Siloam" (Siloam means "sent"). So the man went and washed and came back seeing." The scripture is telling me that if I am blind I must receive the Word "That I can see" in my spirit and I must choose to believe that Word "That I can see" in my soul and now I act in obedience to the Word "Go Wash in the pool of Siloam" in my body. The Word will manifest and produce exactly what it said and more. I will come back seeing and more!

## THE PROCESS OF TOTAL PROSPERITY

The Process of total prosperity is in the Life of Christ. Jesus gives us an example of the process we go through to be in place of prosperity. This process changes us and prepares us in spirit, soul and body.

### *Process Step 1:*
The Spirit led Him to the wilderness so that He could have success in His spirit while He was here on earth. The wilderness changed His appetite to the Word of God. When tempted to sin He spoke the Word of God.

### *Process Step 2:*
He chose to go into the Garden of Gethsemane. He submitted His Will (His Soul) to God the Father. His mind, emotions, intellect, will and decision-making

centers all complied with the Will of God. He said to the Father, "Not My will Lord, but Your will be done."[19]

## *Process Step 3:*
He laid His life down in obedience to the will of the Father on the cross. They nailed His body to a tree so that the will of the Father would be complete. He was selfless. He did it for us. He paid a debt He did not owe. We owed a debt we could not pay. We can experience total prosperity in our marriages as we allow God to take us through wilderness experiences to change our output to the Word of God. We also have to allow God to change our will by getting us to a place where we say, "Not my will but Your will be done." Lastly, we have to be willing to carry our own cross to the glory of God.

Spiritual prosperity includes successful prayer and faith to hear from God. Prosperity of the soul includes successful mental abilities to receive from God. Prosperity of the body includes the ability to successfully obey God and see healing, miracles, deliverance, health and wealth in your life and marriage now.

Questions from Luke chapter sixteen verses ten through twelve can reveal where you are in the process of prosperity as well. Can God trust you to be faithful with small things? If not, you can forget bigger things. Can God trust you to be faithful with natural things? If not, you can forget spiritual things. Can God trust you to be faithful with another person's things? If not, you can forget ever getting your own.

God has given each person the capacity to prosper. Your gifts and talents will be the catalyst for your success. Hearing God is spiritual prosperity. He will speak life to your gifts and talents. Believing what God speaks to you is prosperity of the soul. We must believe He will activate our gifts and talents. Obeying God's leading is prosperity of the body. When you obey God, your gifts and talents will produce the wealth of God and the Glory of God at the same time. Total prosperity is yours for the taking. Are you ready friend?

Prosperity is more than money but it does include it. Prosperity has a purpose. God prospers us to establish His kingdom in the earth realm through us. When God makes us successful and wealthy, it is for His glory. He knows what we need to fulfill our individual purpose on earth. Individual purpose always correlates with His kingdom purposes. We are ambassadors here on earth. Prosperity brings responsibility with it. We have a responsibility to know and to do according to God's will. He prospers us to help others. He prospers us to show forth His kingdom. God calls us to operate in prosperity. In order to operate continually in prosperity, we have to affect this world for the good of God's kingdom. Prosperity is not just for us to do as we please. There is always a plan for our lives. God's plans include using our prosperous ways and endeavors to bring glory to Him.

God prospers us to have access to people to lead them to Jesus Christ. Salvation is always on the mind of God. He wants His creation saved. He wants the lost found. We are wise to use our financial prosperity to establish avenues to lead people to Christ. God preordains the purpose of prosperity. He knows we will need money to meet certain needs. He also knows that we can help others know His love by using our money to meet their needs in the name of God. God knows the children that He can trust with riches. We have to be wise. We can use our prosperity to encourage others. As God prospers us financially, we can be a blessing to so many people. We can encourage people by helping them so they know that God loves them. We should be resourceful. That means we should be able to help people deal with problems, issues and concerns. We should use our prosperity to help people see that God has a plan for their lives.

Allowing God to use us requires cleansing from the inside out. Money can become a god. Greed for money can cause us to neglect the kingdom purposes of financial prosperity. As He prepares us for prosperity, we have to submit to His will. As we prosper, we have a mandate to teach others how to prosper. Teaching them how to prosper spiritually is the most important. We have to strive to say Y.E.S. to God. We submit to Him that we are, "Your Eternal Servants". As His servants, we yield every area of our lives to Him. We submit to serve Him in everything including our marriage and our finances.

## GETTING AN UNDERSTANDING

The Biblical word for prosperity is being able to understand. Understanding something includes comprehending it. As we understand the principles found in God's Word, we can apply them and see success in our marriages.

As aforementioned, the Biblical word used for prosperity also includes success. As we prosper in our marriage, we will experience success. We have lined up several components of a successful marriage that you should understand. We believe that the prosperity in your marriage will be the fruit of this book. We believe you can have the successful marriage you desire to have. As you commit to comprehend God's ways and apply them to your life and marriage, you are guaranteed success.

## BECOMING WHAT WE BEHOLD

What we behold is very important. Learning to importance of beholding a proper vision of prosperity is essential to possessing it. Beholding is having a clear idea of what it is you desire or seeing something so often that it becomes your desire. The more you behold something the more you make room in your life for that thing to exist. I implore you to be mindful of what you continuously behold. The mind is so powerful that the Bible says if a man thinks of himself a certain way then he will be as he thinks. The verse actually reads, "For as he thinks in his heart, so is he."[20] The mind is so powerful that we can think a thing and believe it to the point of becoming it. We really do become what we consistently behold. I admonish you to behold success. I beseech you to grasp success in your mind for your marriage, to be willing to work at it and to be ready to prosper in it.

Write the vision for your marriage friend. Seek God and allow Him to show you the purpose He has for your marriage. Apply the principles found in this book and you will see good results.

## Chapter 2
## REVEALING THE BEST YOU

"I just don't understand that man." Tara screamed into an empty room. I have done everything I know to do to please him. Every time I think I have gotten something down pat he changes his mind. I am starting to wonder if he even knows himself.

"What gives?" mumbled Travis to himself with a hint of frustration lacing his words. "I have bent over backwards to please that woman. Every time I share my feelings with her, she blows up. I don't know her at all. I wonder if she knows herself because she sure as heck doesn't know me. If she does know herself then I sure wish she would tell me so I can know!"

Marriage is a learning institution. It includes spending a lot of time getting to know our spouse. We have to be careful not to neglect taking the time to get to know ourselves. We change every day. We change physically, mentally and spiritually. Trying to understand each other can be a lifelong journey. Understanding ourselves can be time consuming as well. The frustration that Travis and Tara are experiencing is a normal part of relationships. Marriage is a relationship. We get out of our marriages what we are willing to put into them. The more we put in them, the more we get out. Getting to know ourselves is a great place to start.

## THE BEST YOU

Every marriage includes three entities, God, you and your spouse. The Holy Spirit has to teach us how to love God. Then you learn how to love yourself. Then you can love your spouse the way God intended. You are a unique individual. You are the best you that this world will ever see. You are important to the plans and purposes of God. God created you with purpose and for a purpose. God handpicked your gifts and talents. He made you to be an extension of His presence in the earth realm. You are on earth because there is purpose in you. You are amazingly wonderful, my friend. God has made you a masterpiece. You are somebody.

Sometimes our past will try to cover the beauty of who God created us to be. God is faithful to reveal the truth that He has infused you with greatness. You have been endued with power from God to produce on a level that only you can. We need you! Your past does not dictate your destiny… God does. He declared your end from the beginning.[1] Nothing about you surprises God. He knows all about you and He is still madly in love with you. Even the love of a mother or father on earth cannot compare to the love of God. His love for you is limitless. He wants to reveal His glory through you. He wants you to know the real you… The "you" He created you to be… The "you" He gave divine release to show forth His glory on earth… The best "you" is being revealed right now!

# PERSONAL SUCCESS

Understanding includes the ability to comprehend something; the capacity to apprehend; the mental agility to make intelligent decisions by applying concepts; agreement; the power of comprehending.[2] As you seek God you will be able to comprehend His purpose for your life. As you comprehend your purpose, you will grab a hold of what He has for you to do on this earth. You have a purpose. Your marriage has a purpose. As you continue in the path that God has established for you, then you will be able to make intelligent decisions by applying Biblical concepts to your life and your marriage. You are the only person that you can change. If you want to improve your marriage then look for ways to improve yourself. The greatest way to improve yourself is to allow God's Word to mold you according to His design for your life.

You can only agree with what you know. As God reveals your purpose to you, you are able to agree with His plan for your life. It is your choice to submit to living your life with purpose. Knowing your purpose will give you passion. Strength comes with knowing that you have greater purpose. What you see now and what you have seen in the past is not all there is to you. There is more to you. As you began to grasp God's purpose for your life, it gives you agility of mind. It gives you a strong willingness to go through the process that God has set for you. You do not mind going through the process when you know that it is going to produce a desired result. God knows you. He knows the plans He has for you. He knows that your life is an avenue for His glory. Let God show you the real you. The old you is the one your past has molded. God takes your past and uses it to show forth the greater purpose He had in you all along.

It is through many trials that God strengthens our marriages and our individual relationship with Him. It is by faith that we can go through hard times and remain in relationship with God as our Father. We must launch out into a deeper relationship with Him on purpose. In order to grow with God we must first allow Him to show us areas in our lives that hinder the growth process. God will reveal sin and weight that is keeping us from growing in Him.[3] All sin is weight but not all weight is sin. For instance, if I lie, then that sin is also weight working against my relationship with God. By the Holy Spirit, I know to confess the lie as sin and alleviate the weight of the sin. However, if I have put my job before my family that may not be a particular sin but it is weight that can come between my family and me. As we continue in our relationship with God, we can see the areas of sin and weight that we are dealing with. To know yourself is one of the greatest gifts you can give to your spouse.

First, you must assess what needs to happen in yourself. Then, you can effectively assess what you need to do personally to enhance your marriage. Remember, the only person you can change is you. Realizing all the faults of your spouse can be detrimental to the growth and success of your marriage, the kingdom of darkness works very hard to get you to see your spouse as the worst person in the world. You must honestly and whole-heartedly seek the Father and ask Him to show you the areas in your life that need healing or deliverance. You have to get to the root of the problem to fix the problem completely. You have to ask yourself, "Why I do what I do when I do what I do?" For example, I am responding in fear when I respond to Tommy in a way that belittles him. The root in that instance is fear. It is fear because faith would push me to build him up instead of tearing him down. Fear tears him down while faith builds him up. Faith always prevails over fear if we believe.

As a marriage counselor, I am quite often in sessions where the spouse in question refuses to deal with the root (why) of a problem. It is not wise to deal with the fruit of a problem while never dealing with the root. I was constantly on the defense with my husband because I struggled with the fear of rejection. I saw every comment he made through the eyes of rejection. If he said, "I like the red shirt better", then I would interpret that as him saying I was an idiot for picking the purple one. He was only sharing his opinion with me about which shirt he liked. It had nothing to do with me personally. It is imperative for couples to get to know themselves first before attempting to "help" their spouses get "right".

I want to ask you a question, "Have you met Truth?" Truth is a person and His name is Jesus. Holy Spirit is the Spirit of Truth. We can better understand by considering the sun. The actual sun would represent God the Father. The rays that emanate from of the sun would represent God the Son. The power of the sun would represent the Holy Spirit. Through God, we come to know the truth. While we have our versions of truth, there is but one truth revealed through the Word via the Holy Spirit. The Word of God is a lamp unto my feet that shows me what I need to see about me. Many times, we are afraid to go to the Word of God because we are afraid to see the reflection of ourselves as we seek the Lord. The more time we spend in the presence of God the more we see ourselves in the light of holiness. Like the prophet Isaiah, we will see how unclean we are in the presence of a Holy God.[4] However, as the Spirit of God reveals truth to us about us, He is building us up. It is not to condemn us. There is no condemnation afforded to us because of Jesus Christ.

The Holy Spirit is a gentleman. He will gently convict or nudge us to deal with those areas that cause conflict in our walk with Him. We live by faith and not by sight.[5] We may see all of our issues. However, by faith we can learn to see ourselves beyond our issues. I may need help with anger but I have learned to see myself beyond my bouts of anger. By faith, I speak life to myself saying, "I am free indeed in Christ from the hold of sin". As the Holy Spirit deals with us about us, we must obey Him and submit to Him. The goodness of God will lead us to agree with Him about us. In addition, His goodness will lead us to change our minds and our ways to fit His mold.

## ORDER: PRELUDE TO SUCCESS

God has made every provision for the success of your marriage. God established the vision for marriage. He will not ever give you a vision without proper provision. God is a God of excellence and order. There is nothing about us that catches Him off guard. He is well aware of our problems, issues, concerns, actions, words and thoughts. He knows all about each of us and He still desires to fellowship with us in His holiness. God set order in the family unit when He set the parents over the children. God gave parents the authority to protect their children. He gave them the means to provide for their children as well. Abuse begins when parents fail to do what God has set them to do. Many children have suffered because of neglect, abuse and negligence. God established the family unit to run according to His divine plan. He has set the husband over the wife and the parents over the children. This is the provision to keep the vision of God established for the family intact. Of course, we know that sin has set in and caused damage to the original plan of God. Abuse is generally due to ignorance. We define ignorance as simply not knowing or being unaware of something. God has afforded us His Word as a provision for success in our marriages. The entire family unit suffers when parents do not do what God has set in order for them to do. While not all parents are married, it is still relevant to understand that God has set provisions in place for your marriage to be successful.

Often we fail to access or use the means, which God has given us for success. He created marriage and He alone helps us develop a unique plan of success for our marriages. He is our ultimate Provider. Subsequently, He has chosen to use the husband to provide for the family and the wife to take care of the home. In the age we live in now, it can be a struggle to comply with the set order of God. He is faithful and full of grace as we stumble through life trying to juggle God's order over the world's standards. At the end of the day, it is God's order that gives us the success and peace we desire in our marriages. God has specific instructions for each family. Through relational prayer, we can stay in the flow of what He has us to do daily. God is progressive and He alone knows what paths we need to take to get to His divinely inspired plan for our marriages. It is through relational praise that we appreciate God for what He has done, is doing and will do in our lives. We praise God because He is worthy. We understand His worthiness based on our relationship with Him as we consider our lives without His grace, mercy, love and power. Relational worship is the opportunity for us to do everything as unto the Lord. Worship is a lifestyle of doing things God's way. The only way to do that is to know His way, which we find in His Word.

Obedience is the way we have access to the provision that God has set for us. There will be many opportunities to obey God's Word in our lives. To be an asset to our marriage we have to take the time to check ourselves and see what God is saying to us about us. As we become good stewards and sow seeds of obedience, we can see God manifest what our marriages need in order to be successful. Our hope is in the Lord. As we stay connected to Him, we can see the manifold benefits expressed in our marriages. Jesus shows us the way to life and truth. He is the Way to success in our marriages and life endeavors. He is the truth reflected through the Word that shows us the areas we need to change within ourselves. He is the life that every marriage needs in order to be successful God's way.

The Bible says that God is Light and there is not darkness in Him.[6] We are no longer able to walk in darkness when we choose to walk with God and obey His commands. Darkness represents sin, areas in need of deliverance and anything not like God. God is the Light of this world and those who follow Him cannot walk in darkness.[7] As a result, those that walk with God will have Jesus shinning from within their hearts. There is no way that we can walk with God and walk in utter darkness at the same time. If we never see the Light, it is because we choose not to see it. After we indulge in a particular sin for a while, the option for us to be selective is no longer available. That sin slowly becomes our Master.[8] We are no longer in control when we fall head first into the sin we chose to indulge. For example, I know that stealing is wrong. However, if I choose to walk in darkness, then I will eventually become a servant of stealing. No person can control sin. Sin causes a slow death. When Adam and Eve sinned and disobeyed God by eating of the tree that God told them not to eat of, they did not die on the spot. The sin they committed caused them to die a slow natural death. Spiritual death set in immediately as they disobeyed God but they did not fall dead. Sin kills us slowly and often so softly that by the time we see it, it has overtaken us. Secret sin, which is no secret to God, will eventually destroy marriages. The spouse may not always know exactly what is going on when sin sets in. However, that spouse may be able to see the change that is due to the hold of sin. It is when we see the hold of sin on our spouse and we need to pray about it so we can see some light in the situation.

Jesus said that those who want to be His disciples must continue in His Word.[9] We must continue in His Word because His Word is the truth. Truth will make us free only if we are knowledgeable of it .Only truth that I know can make me free. If I lock myself in a closet and I do not know that the key is in there with me, then I cannot benefit from the truth that the key is right there. I cannot apply the Word of God to my life if I do not know the Word of God. Only the Truth that I know can make me free. Searching for Truth will send us to the Word. We have to become disciples who will believe in His Word no matter what we go through.

The Word sheds light on forgiveness. When a person has done wrong to us, we must be careful not to hold forgiveness back from them. God has chosen to forgive us of all of our sins against Him. We will all eventually experience a time of reflection, when we remember how God has forgiven us of the sins we have confessed to Him. Those times of reflection can help us remember that we have no right to withhold the same forgiveness that God gives to us freely. All we have to do is ask for forgiveness and God readily gives it to us. God not only forgives us but He justifies us as though we never sinned through Christ Jesus our Lord. Choices, choices, choices…What is your basis for making one? If I choose to ignore my sin and keep living as though I do not have a problem, then eventually that sin will negatively affect my marriage. God's presence will seem far away from me because He is Light and Light cannot dwell in darkness. That should help me seek Him to restore our fellowship. We have to make sure that our relationship with God is priority. Without God being first in my life, I can miss many blessings. If I choose to walk in darkness, I make a dangerous decision.

We came to Christ spiritually dead and bound by our sins. After meeting Him and accepting Him as Lord, we become a new creature in Him. We have to take off the things that keep us bound or have the potential to bind us. We have to put away sin and any weight that keeps us from flowing with God. For example, God wants us to take off things like "anger, wrath, malice, blasphemy, filthy communication and lying."[10] An angry person can lose control when angry. Anger is not a sin. The Bible reminds us not to allow anger to cause us to sin. A person given to wrath could kill someone. A person given to malice could intentionally hurt their spouse to get what they want. We blaspheme or curse God with our actions. We must be very careful to live a life pleasing to God. We know that there will be people who enjoy living in darkness. They do not want nor do they welcome any light to show how wrong they are before God. This is a result of pride. Pride will not allow us to look truthfully at ourselves. We must be very careful and ask God to reveal anything He sees in us. Filthy communication is repulsive and should be to any born again believer.

The Holy Spirit lives in us and our words should be holy too. When we were sinners, we lived in darkness. Now we live in the Light and take off the deeds of the old man. We must kill "fornication, sexual perversion, unnatural affection, wicked appetites and greed."[11] Walking in the darkness of these sins will not only destroy the marriage but destroy us as well. Sin is progressive. It starts small and grows bigger. Eventually it grows bigger than we expect. We have to deal with sin as the Lord reveals it to us in order for our marriages to be successful. God may lead my husband to show me my faults in love. However, if I reject my husband's attempts to help me then I may also be more likely to reject God when He talks to me about them. That is why we must consistently commune with the Holy Spirit. Our carnal nature really does not profit our marriages anything. The Spirit of God gives us power and life in our marriages.

God will reveal anything to us that is not like Him. He will also reveal to us anything specific in our minds that is not like the mind of Christ. We must understand that our thoughts are powerful. The power of the mind is overwhelmingly strong. We must renew our mind daily with the Word of God to overcome erroneous and faulty thinking. The mind of Christ is available to us via the Holy Spirit. He lives in us as Light. He teaches us, guides us, helps us to see truth and gives us the ability to change. Jesus' desire was to obey the Father even unto death. Jesus' desire was to bring the Father glory. Jesus understood that He was a representative of His Father. Having the mind of Christ enables us to walk as Jesus did. Jesus came to serve. He came to save the lost and heal the sick. Jesus came with serving on His mind. In our marriage, we can do well if we seek to serve our spouse opposed to demanding that they serve us. What is God revealing to you about you? Often in marriages, we forget what Jesus said about judging. We can see the tiny particle in our spouse's character but fail to see the giant bolder in our own.

I recall when I made up my mind to follow Christ in full force and submit every area of my life to Him. However, my husband was not ready at that time for that type of commitment. He was saved and very comfortable with his relationship with God at that time. I magnified everything he did but I minimized and spiritualized everything I did. My basis for this lopsided judgment was that I was trying to live more for Christ than he was. My basis and my actions were both very wrong. It was humbling and heart breaking when God began to reveal my heart to me. I realized my heart was utterly deceitful and perverse without the Holy Spirit. There really is a way that seems right to us but it is wrong and eventually can lead to death of a relationship. I was very broken before God as I saw myself. I began to look inward and deal more with my own issues. The more time I spent dealing with my issues the less time I had to judge my husband. I learned how to pray and wait on God to move in my husband. I became more of a light that shinned based on Christ and not based on what I thought I had accomplished in Him. There were many moments that I frustrated grace by trying to help my husband get it right. I was especially "helpful" when it came to times that he had hurt me. Grace and mercy both would send me back to my room to consider the times God had forgiven me. It was amazing how often I forgot how much I had hurt God and needed His forgiveness. As I considered my own sins against God, I realized that I needed just as much grace as my husband.

We must not ever forget that the god of this world (Satan) has the ability (through our carnal nature) to get us (as we cooperate) to neglect seeing our faults. On the contrary, he will help us see the faults of everyone else. This stems from the root of pride. We choose blindness in certain areas of our lives when we give into our carnal nature. For example, I dealt with anger when I was younger. I expressed my anger in a negative way. I did not realize I had a choice in the matter. I did not know I could chose not to express my anger at all until I had cooled down. I was blind in that area. I was ignorant to the power I had to deny anger from spewing out of my life like lava from a volcano. I was blind to the truth. The truth was that if I did not allow God to reveal that problem to me, I could have blown up and did damage that was not repairable. God is light. He will reveal to us every area of our lives that negatively affect our relationship with Him. Generally, what affects our relationship with God will affect our marriage.

## SELFISH VERSUS SELFLESS

We can reflect our relationships with God by the way we treat our spouses. God has commanded light to shine forth in darkness but we keep covering up our lights with our carnal desires and selfishness. If we look deep enough, we will see that selfishness is the real root of many of the sins we commit. We are saying, *I want what I want and I do not care who I hurt.* When we indulge in this sinful behavior and this type of thinking, we destroy the very fibers of a good marriage.

Jesus reminded us that, "there is none good but one, that is, God: but if we will enter into life, [we must] keep the commandments."[12] Jesus was talking to a rich young ruler who kept the Ten Commandments but had a selfish heart. This ruler was not willing to give up all his goods to serve the Lord. There will be constant conflict in a marriage where selfishness rules in the heart of either spouse. Any good we find in marriage comes from God. He teaches us how to be selfless opposed to our nature, which is to be selfish.

We find that, "Those who live following their sinful selves think only about things that their sinful selves want. But those who live following the Spirit are thinking about the things the Spirit wants them to do."[13] Being selfless is a learned behavior. Spending more time with God and receiving His love for us changes us to be more like Him. God is giving. He gave us His very best when we were at our worst. That is how our marriages should look. When our spouse is at their worst, we should serve them in love. "Each of us should please our neighbors for their good in order to build them up. Christ didn't please himself …"[14] Pleasing our spouses is very important in marriage. We seek to please them to build them up. We show forth the love of God in us as we serve our spouses. Exhibiting selflessness increases trust and unity in marriage. Christ gave us an example that we should follow. We must resist the urge to be selfish and serve our spouse in selflessness to the glory of God.

We must understand that there will be seasons in our marriages where we will have to give 100%. Our spouse may not be in a place to give anything for a season. These seasons can be during times of sickness, temporary work loss, new job assignments, etc. We have to be willing to give 100% and follow in the footsteps of Christ. If we treat our spouse the way that God initially intended and expressed in His Word, we will reap the benefits of our obedience. Each time we selflessly do something we are saying, "Lord, I will do without this now to enjoy the blessings You have for me later and I will trust You."

God is after your heart. Whether you believe it or not, your spouse is after your heart as well. Most spouses want to be loved. Not many people want gifts or nice gestures that are not genuine. If you turn your heart from your spouse, most of the time they would rather know the truth. They would rather know the truth than to believe that you care when you really do not. We find that when we turn our hearts from our spouses and they realize it, no matter what we do they do not receive it. Once again, we must be mindful that selfish people do things for selfish gain. However, in a marriage we must be selfless even when a spouse is self-FULL. For example, I remember a time when I offended my husband so bad that he had turned his heart from me for a moment or two. (I knew his heart had turned by the words that he spoke out of his mouth to me about me.) As a result, it was hard for him to accept my attempts to do things for him. I would do little nice things for him but it was like a clanging symbol. I had offended him and we had not dealt with the offense. That is how we treat God. We sin and then without confessing it as sin and repenting from the sin we attempt to come into His presence and do little nice things for Him.

There is a strong correlation between how you treat God and how you treat your spouse. God has given us specific instructions on how to treat our spouse. When we turn our heart fully to God then we will obey His Word and treat our spouses the way He instructs us to in His Word. God made our spouses in His image. We are abusing God when we abuse them. We must daily ask God to keep our hearts right towards Him and our spouse. Our God will never directly offend us but the things we believe He allowed do offend us. We get offended as if we could do a better job at being God. It is much easier to love a perfect God than it is to love an imperfect human being. Yes, we are all flawed human beings that will either say or do something to hurt or offend one another. We must deal with the hurt or offence in a godly manner so that we do not turn our hearts away from our spouse.

Often, we are wrong in our motives, intents and feelings. We do the outward acts to appease the situation instead of dealing with the real issue, which is likely to be impure hearts. No, this is not a free ticket for us to try to "read into" what our spouses "meant" when they did a certain thing. That is the job of the Holy Spirit. However, words are a gateway to actions. If you and your spouse have dealt with the issue take the outward act as evidence of the inside change of heart. For example, if you have not dealt with the conflict and you do something nice your spouse may not receive it. We have to get it ingrained in our minds and hearts that conflict will come but we do not have to act ugly. We do not have to argue, yell or fight. We have to get to the point where we are secure enough in God to deal with our own issues. We have to be transparent enough to share our issues with our spouse. God will reveal our issues to us but we must be willing to do something about them. When we allow God to cleanse us on the inside then and only then do we see true cleanliness on the outside. Love with no fruit is not love at all. Love is what love does. For example, love is kind and does kind things.

## VESSELS OF HONOR

Marriage can be an effective witness tool and should represent the Gospel light of Christ. It should reflect the love expressed from God to us. Unbelievers should look at Christian marriages and see God. Believers and unbelievers experience trouble. How we deal with trouble reflects what we believe. We deal with the same problems in our marriage as unbelievers like finances, communication issues, in-laws, etc. However, we have a marriage handbook called the Bible. If you are experiencing lack, then give as God has instructed in the Bible in Luke chapter six verse thirty-eight. If your sexual or emotional intimacy is not up to par, ask God to give you wisdom in handling it. Yes, we have to deal with tribulation, trials and suffering but we can be of good cheer because Jesus has given us the power to overcome the world.[15] Sadly, if a Christian marriage does not reveal the Gospel, we are hiding the Gospel from those who are lost and need to see God in us. Satan has blinded the lost from seeing the Gospel.[16] Sadly, he uses believers to help him. The lost think spiritual things are foolish. The devil has seasoned their minds with lies so they refuse to accept the Gospel. In spite of this, if a Christian marriage reflects the light of the Word, then God can use our marriages to draw the lost to Him. By taking on the great responsibility of being like Christ in our actions, words and thoughts, sinners will desire to have the joy, peace and love that we possess. Yes, a successful marriage benefits more than just us. It is one of the greatest ministry tools available.

Righteousness is always right. Almost right is always wrong. We must not be phony because our light shines from within. It is our lack of integrity that aides Satan in blinding the unbeliever to the glorious Gospel of Jesus Christ. Our marriage should reflect the image of God. When we are in Christ, a metamorphosis should take place in each spouse. The Gospel and our faith in Jesus Christ will shine forth and destroy the works of darkness. We do not preach ourselves; we preach Jesus. We do not always preach from the pulpit. We can preach daily through our marriages. We are servants. We are followers of Christ and our lives should reflect His teachings. We must allow our marriages to preach the glorious Gospel of our Lord and Saviour, Jesus Christ. If we do not allow our lives to be a witness of Jesus, then we hide the Gospel from the lost. God saves the sinner because He loves him. He commands light to shine in the darkness of the sinner's heart, therefore, causing the sinner to accept Christ. We deny God the opportunity to use our marriages to shine in darkness when we fail to do things His way. We deny God the chance to draw sinners to experience the glory of God through Jesus when we fail to illuminate Him in our marriages. We have a responsibility as believers to do so.

God wants to work through us as earthly vessels of honor. He will use the treasure of the Holy Spirit in us so that the Excellency of His power will shine through us. God is able to shine His powerful light through us. People should not see our carnal ways more than they see evidence of God in us. Marriages can reflect the omnipresence of God. The omnipresence of God indicates that He is everywhere. God is not limited by what we call an "earth suit". He does not have a body. As a result, He can be everywhere and He can see everything.

Yes, we suffer as believers but we can still have joy because God has already played the video of our lives. He knows the end. We are victorious. God is omniscient. The omniscience of God means that He is all knowing. He has already watched our life play out. He knows what we will encounter and He has already given us the tools we need to be successful. We simply have to do things His way. He has attended to every need and given us everything we need to fight and win. We may experience trouble from every source possible but we are not distressed, worried or anxious because of our faith in God. We may be perplexed or baffled at the things that happen in our marriages, but we are not in despair or helpless because we are in right relationship with the Creator of the universe. We may experience persecutions from others. Our spouse may even mistreat us but God will not desert us nor forsake us. We may experience wounds from being cast down but we are not destroyed and neither are our marriages. We must die to our wills, our ways and our desires so that the life of Jesus Christ can illuminate from our marriages.

Jesus will manifest Himself through us if we do our best and follow the Holy Spirit. We cannot do it by ourselves. We need Holy Spirit to be successful. I believe that Jesus gives us access to the truth, the ways and the life of God. I also believe that the Holy Spirit guides us in the way, teaches us the truth and gives the ability to experience this life in the abundance of God's glory. It is impossible for us to live holy or for us to connect to God without the Holy Spirit. He is a present help in the time of trouble in our marriages. He is the counselor that knows the heart of God and the ways of men. He will never be biased or take sides. I believe that the Holy Spirit is the one counselor that will always be on the side of the marriage. We need Him to lead us daily.

We find that the fight we are fighting is not with flesh and blood. This is also true about our marriages. We do not fight each other. There will be times my husband may hurt me. Nevertheless, I must learn to war against the evil spirit that is trying to use the situation to destroy us. We must stay prayed up. It is not easy because we cannot see or feel the evil spirit but we can see our spouses. Nevertheless, if I neglect to obey the Holy Spirit, then in my anger I am going to be just as guilty. I have had the grand opportunity to work with sarcastic and negative people. As the supervisor, I had two options when they would attack me with their sarcasm or negativity. I could war after the flesh and cut them down to nothing with my words or I could zoom in on the real issue of low self-esteem or insecurities. I wish I could say I have always taken the high and humble road but many times the low and prideful road was overwhelmingly tempting. In fact, I have experienced temptation and lunged head first into a situation I would rather have avoided. I did confess and repent but I had damaged my witness. I had to go back and apologize for my actions without mentioning theirs. That is what we must learn to apply in marriage.

People cannot make me speak negatively to them. I chose to do it. When our spouse has a flesh moment, we must pull back and not respond in the flesh. If we are the spouse having the flesh moment, we must humble ourselves and ask for forgiveness. We must admit that we were wrong without mentioning anything they did. Ungodly sorrow says, "I am sorry I did that but you made me do it." Godly sorrow says, "I was wrong for what I did and I am sorry I hurt you." Pride will definitely destroy any marital success. Humility is a work of the Spirit and is a very intricate and important part of marriage. We do very well to stay humble before God. Our marriages are the first place to apply our humility before God.

There is a war going on inside of us. The war between our carnal nature and our spirit man is intense. We know our spirit man can win because our weapons are mighty through God.[17] God has given us the power of the Holy Spirit and the full armor of God. The fruit of the Spirit are love, joy, peace, longsuffering, gentleness, goodness, faith, meekness and temperance.[18] They are some of the greatest weapons we have to walk in victory over our carnal nature. The carnal man does not desire to love due to past hurts. The carnal man would rather keep fighting and arguing rather than exhibiting self-control. The fruit of the Spirit are also tools we can use to keep peace flowing in our marriages. The fruit of the Spirit will always lead us to consider others over ourselves. We do not have to adhere to the dictatorship of our carnal nature. It is imperative that we understand that we do not have to fight with our spouses. Our battle is not with our spouses. Our battle is with the enemy of our souls. That same enemy desires to destroy our marriages.

    God has given us weapons but we must use them as He has instructed us to in His Word. We have the weapons of prayer, fasting, speaking the Word, speaking life, faith and so much more. God has secured our victory in Him. We really do win. We have to correct issues within ourselves to walk in victory. We have to pull down personal strongholds that we built up in our minds with erroneous thinking. Once we walk in victory over mental battles, then we can help our spouses. We must first cast down our own vain imaginations and then we can help our spouses walk in that victory. We must cast down everything that attempts to lead us to disobey the Word of God in our marriages. We must bring every thought into captivity to the obedience of the Word of God so our marriages will be successful.[19] Every thought that comes to us is not to be entertained. We must reject certain thoughts and stamp them "Return to Sender". We can use the full armor of God to win the battles waged against our marriages by the enemy. We must never forget that we are not fighting our spouses. We are not fighting in the natural but this is a spiritual war. We are fighting those principalities that seek to destroy our marriages.

    Let us consider the following example to illustrate how the full armor of God works in our marriages. Ephesians chapter six verse fourteen through seventeen show us the contents of the full armor of God and I paraphrase, "Stand therefore, with your waist girded with the truth, with a breastplate of righteousness, and your feet shod with the preparation of the Gospel of peace, the shield of faith, the helmet of salvation, and the sword of the Spirit, which is the Word of God;"

## SITUATION:

Johnny comes home from work and finds that his house is not cleaned up the way he likes and dinner is not ready. He is already upset from working in a stressful environment. He looks for Shelby and realizes that she is sound asleep. Shelby had a long day and she slept very little the night before. Little Johnny is teething and has a very bad cold. Johnny wakes Shelby up and yells at her out of his frustration that stemmed from work. He calls her lazy and has little understanding about her stressful day.

## *How the full armor of God can work:*

The *Belt of Truth replies*, "I know that I deserve a nap and I do not feel guilty for taking one. I did not do anything for him to treat me this way. Nevertheless, I refuse to retaliate because God has given me His Word to sustain me. I am not going to yell back at him because he is not my enemy. I am going to speak kindly to him instead."

The *Breastplate of Righteousness* replies, "I know I am the righteousness of Christ. This fellow is not being nice right now. Nevertheless, I will not allow him to pull me into an argument. I will stand for righteousness by getting up and tending to his needs in spite of how I am feeling right now."

The Peace that I walk in replies "The best way to handle this is not to respond hastily. I will be slow to speak and slow to anger. I will follow peace with this man even in the midst of this adverse situation."

The *Shield of Faith* replies, "Eventually I will see the fruit of my prayers in this guy. I have been praying for his temper and his unkind words. I know the Lord will show up on my behalf soon. For me to respond in anger says that I do not trust God to deal with my husband. I know He will convict him so I will by faith choose not to respond to him in a negative manner."

The *Helmet of Salvation* replies, "His names do not hurt me because I know who I am in Christ. I am the apple of God's eye. He knows that I work very hard as a mother and wife. I am the righteousness of God and I will not allow this situation to cause me to display behavior that does not represent Christ."

The *Sword of the Spirit* replies "Let not your heart be troubled daughter. God will take care of you and fight your battles. You do not need to fight with your husband because we do not fight flesh and blood. However, you can pray under your breath in the spirit and command that spirit using him to decease and desist in Jesus Name."

If you are anything like me, you are still trying to figure out how in the world the armor is going to have time to say all of this. Time cannot bind our spirit man but our body is subject to time. As a result, the Holy Spirit has already deposited the responses that you need to counterattack the attacks of the enemy. Satan launches these attacks to make us act out of the character of God. We take care of our natural man but usually we starve our spirit man. We feed our natural man three times a day with snacks in between. Sadly, we fail to realize the importance of feeding our spirit man just as much if not more. The more you feed your spirit man then the more he will grow. It is not easy to respond to natural negative occurrences with positive spiritual responses. The natural man usually has a way of responding in a manner that does not line up with the character of Christ. It is possible to walk in a manner that enables us to respond to negative situations with faith, power and love. Shelby could have told Johnny off from A to Z.

However, she would have scarred her witness as a believer. She gently responded to Johnny with kind words seasoned with grace. As a result, she turned away his wrath with her kind words. He apologized and asked her to pray with him about his job. He also confided in her in a way that showed he felt he could trust her with his heart. The Holy Spirit is always working on our behalf. We simply must choose to follow Him into peace and righteousness. In all of our getting, we must get an understanding because wisdom is one of the most important tools we have when we are seeking to build our marriages God's way.

## TEMPTATION AND MARRIAGE

Yielding to temptation can produce negative results in marriage. Temptation is defined as a strong desire to do something wrong or unwise. Husbands and wives both can be tempted. Being tempted is not a sin. Yielding to the temptation is the sin. For example, I may be tempted to steal my neighbor's car. If I never steal the car then I have won over temptation. We have to be careful not to allow our mind to wander. Our mind can become the enemy's playground if we do not take control of our thoughts. Some battles are lost and won in my mind before I ever encounter them. Some of the temptations we deal with are, adultery, eating disorders, Internet based addictions (i.e. Facebook), pornography, gambling, overeating, alcoholism, drug addiction, stealing and lying.

The pornography industry makes billions of dollars each year. They entice us through our unmet needs at home. They draw us in with pop-up ads. They know men are sight stimulated. They are making a lot of money perverting that fact. Marriages are being torn apart daily by Facebook addictions, credit addictions, pornography addictions, shopping addictions and television addictions. Couples are losing the battle to remain married because they have not taken the time to know themselves. To know myself is the beginning of my quest for doing things the right way. We all sin consistently in some way, shape, or form. Sin is simply all the bad things we do. Understand, my friend, that righteousness is not doing all the right things. Righteousness includes having a right relationship with the right God because His Son did the right thing to die for us. God gives us the right motives and the power to do the things that benefit our family and us.

Our selfish nature desires the things that are not healthy for us. Our natural man desires things it cannot have. This can be proven by simply adding a "Do not touch" sign to something no one ever touches. Their carnal nature will push them to touch it anyway. This is simply because the desire to touch it increased when you denied them the right to touch it. The Law is the same way. In the Bible, Paul shared with us that the Law or the Ten Commandments showed us that we could not obey them. God gave us the Law so that we would realize our need for a Savior.[20] No one has been able to live a sinless life besides Jesus Christ. He alone has given us the power to overcome the temptations to sin.

A very important question is who tempts us? I have had people respond to that question with God, Satan or flesh. The Bible sheds light on that for us. James chapter one verse thirteen says, "And remember, when you are being tempted, do not say, "God is tempting me." God is never tempted to do wrong, and He never tempts anyone else." We must be careful not to blame God for our temptations. It does not begin with God. However, it can end in victory with God. God does not need to tempt us because He knows our struggles. Temptation simply reveals desires in us.

Our next question is, "Where is temptation initiated?" I have had people share the heart, the body or the mind as answers. We find that every temptation starts in the mind. It starts with a desire. James chapter one verses fourteen and fifteen say, "Temptation comes from our own desires, which entice us and drag us away. These desires give birth to sinful actions. And when sin is allowed to grow, it gives birth to death." This scripture helps us to understand that temptation comes from our own desires. Something that I do not desire cannot be a temptation for me. That is why knowing myself is so important. If I know what I like then I have the upper hand to stay away from that particular thing. Men who know they like women with a particular characteristic need to stay away from places where they can initiate an improper conversation with them. Ladies who like men with triceps and biceps need to stay away from the gym until they have tapped into the power of God that gives them strength to resist the temptation to lust.

Yes, Satan knows that we are weak. The Bible helps us understand that our spirit man is willing to do what is right but our carnal man is weak. That is why we have to guard our heart. Mark chapter fourteen verse thirty-eight says, "Watch ye and pray, lest ye enter into temptation. The spirit truly is ready, but the flesh is weak." Prayer will guard us from entering into temptation because our spirit and not our flesh will lead us. If Satan can get us to indulge in temptation then he knows he can try to destroy our marriages. If a husband consistently gives in to the temptation to have an affair then eventually his marriage will fall apart. Sin destroys lives and marriages. We will not have the marriage that God designed if we continue to habitually sin. Again, being tempted is not the sin. Giving into the temptation and sinning is the issue. Taking time to read the Word will help us combat those crazy temptations that attempt to lure us away from God's best.

Another question I like to ask is, "Who is predisposed, likely or prone to be tempted?" I have had people answer, "Sinners and saints". The truth is that we are all tempted at some point. Jesus was tempted. We will be tempted, too. Jesus desired for the Father to rewrite His destiny by not sending Him to the cross. His flesh was weak but His Spirit was willing. Jesus did not succumb to temptation. He had victory and so do we. The Bible helps us understand the struggle. Paul says,

> *"I have discovered this principle of life—that when I want to do what is right, I inevitably do what is wrong. I love God's law with all my heart. However, there is another power within me that is at war with my mind. This power makes me a slave to the sin that is still within me. Oh, what a miserable person I am. Who will free me from this life that is dominated by sin and death?"*[21]

Reading that verse made me feel hopeful because I realized I was not alone in my struggles. Paul was showing us that we cannot overcome the flesh by sheer willpower. We need God's help to overcome a life that is dominated by sin and death. I remember having a life that was dominated by sin and death. I was ignorant to God's purpose for my life. I realized one day that I could not free myself. I was stuck like Chuck. I was in like Flynn. I could not stop sinning. Sin was in me like gas in a moving car. I was on my way to a place of judgment. I was not enjoying God's best. However, one day my Answer came.

I hear you screaming to know, "Who rescued you?" I also hear you asking, "Who can rescue me?" Again, the Bible helps us to understand where our victory comes from. "Thank God. The answer is in Jesus Christ our Lord. So you see how it is: In my mind I really want to obey God's law, but because of my sinful nature I am a slave to sin."[22] This verse shows that Jesus is the Answer to my sinful nature. His death on the cross has freed me from sin's death grip on my life. I cannot tame or save my sinful nature. I must deny my flesh. I must not allow the flesh to control me. That is where the Word of God, the Holy Spirit and a sold-out heart comes in. It is in you to sin, my friend. God knows you need His help. He is offering it to you right now. It is up to you to take it and overcome sin in your life. It happens daily. Each day you grow stronger in your ability in Christ to resist temptation. The closer you draw to God keeps you closer to the Help you need.

I do feel the need to warn you though. We never need to get to a place where we think we have arrived. This walk is a daily walk with Christ. Daily we must acknowledge that we need Him. He is our victory.

> *"So watch yourself. The person who thinks he can stand against sin had better watch that he does not fall into sin. You have never been tempted to sin in any different way than other people. God is faithful. He will not allow you to be tempted more than you can take. But when you are tempted, He will make a way for you to keep from falling into sin."*[23]

## WAYS TO OVERCOME TEMPTATION:
1. I must be real with myself.
    a. Get to know yourself and the truth about your struggles.
2. I must stay away from those situations that cause me to struggle.
3. I must expose it.
    a. You cannot eradicate what you will not expose.
4. I must confront it.
    a. You cannot conquer what you will not confront.
5. I must be accountable to someone with integrity.
6. I must apply the Word of God liberally to my life.
    a. The Word only works if you work it.

7. I must get help if I need it.

    a. Humbling ourselves is the key to victory.

The Bible gives us the truth we need to overcome temptation. "And (*Jesus*) said unto them, Why sleep ye? Rise and pray, lest ye enter into temptation"[24] If we rise and pray, then prayer can keep us from entering into temptation. Temptation comes to prove by solicitation to sin what your desires are. Temptation tests you with the purpose and intent to cause you to fall. God will never tempt us because He already knows what is in us. Our own fleshly lusts tempt us. (*See James 1:13-15*) Satan will tempt us by trying to use our weaknesses to destroy us. Prayer can preserve us during times of temptation. We find that these times of temptation show us just how much we need God, how much we need to pray and how much we need to stay spiritually strong.

## GETTING BEYOND OFFENSE

As we conclude this section on understanding yourself, I want to leave you with a very important revelation. We have many chances daily to be offended. In fact, offense is one of the enemy's greatest tools to get married couples to throw in the towel and walk away from their God ordained marriage. A person that has offended someone is referred to as one who is counted as guilty of doing something wrong. This person has missed the mark and caused a negative response from the other person involved. We are easily offended because of our selfish nature. When someone causes us to have to entertain something that we do not desire to entertain, we count that person as one who has done something wrong to us. Husbands and wives find themselves daily in the position to miss the mark and offend their spouse. Offense is one of the many causes of conflict in relationships. Communication is the antidote to clearing up any offense. Through the process of clearing up offenses, we must be willing to commit to the betterment of the marriage. If a wife offends her husband, she must allow God to reveal her error to her and then do as God has instructed her to do in His Word and vice versa. When we find we have offended our spouse, we must go to our spouse and ask for forgiveness. Marriage is for mature adults. There will be times you will offend your spouse by something you did. Your spouse may be offended even though you were not being malicious. It is at that time that as a mature adult we must indulge our spouse's heart and apologize to them. Your ability to say you are sorry when you know you have not done anything per say is an indication of your ability to be like Christ. He never sinned but He did bear the sins we committed on His body. He suffered for us and we must be willing to suffer and submit to His way and apologize to keep the peace.

Being easily offended gets us off track with the flow of God. We must stay in a place in God that allows us to keep our carnal nature under subjection to the Word of God. We must not allow people to cause us to be offended. We must get in a place of being un-offend-able. The person that walks with the Lord closely is able to see what is going on behind the scenes when the opportunity to be offended comes about. This person is able to pull down the tactics the enemy uses to cause problems in the marriage. We have to get to the place where we trust our spouses so much that they cannot offend us. When you know a person's heart is right towards you, then you know that they are not trying to hurt you. Many times, we get offended because we have issues we need to deal with within ourselves.

We must be very careful not to take offense by the truth that God reveals. We must allow the truth He reveals to change our lives. Meekness is a sure weapon of victory against being offended. The fruits of the Spirit also are essential to having victory against the wiles of offense. Offenses can cause us to stumble away from the will of God. You can love your spouse when they miss the mark. You can walk in peace when it looks like you are about to get offended. You can walk in self-control when you start thinking about something your spouse said that possibly could offend you. There are some ways to overcome offenses. These ways include: Having a love for the Word; Having the Love of Christ; Being a servant; Praying always; Giving good for evil; Not fighting against flesh and blood; Not being intimidated but walking in the power of God; Forgiving quickly and agreeing quickly with them and apologizing as necessary for peace. We ultimately have to be in a posture of humility and ask God to create in us a clean heart. We have to stay in a place of prayer where we can walk in the power of not being offended by our spouse.

Finally, you must know who you are in Christ Jesus. According to the Word of God, you have many blessings afforded to you because of salvation. You are a child of God. You have been redeemed from sin and death. You are forgiven. You are saved by Grace through faith. You are justified. You are sanctified. You are a new creature in Christ Jesus. You are a partaker of God's divine nature. You are redeemed from the curse of the law. You have been delivered from the power of darkness. You are led by the Spirit of God. You are a son of God as the Spirit leads you. You are protected. God meets all of your needs. You can cast all your cares on God. You must be strong in the Lord and in the power of His might. You are an heir to the blessings God released to Abraham. You must know who you are but I admonish you to know who God says you are and line your life up with what the Lord has said about you in His Word.

## THE PROCESS

The process of going from carnally minded to spiritually minded takes time. It is intentional. God monitors every detail. He is so intent on helping us that He orders our steps. He maps out our paths. He uses everything we encounter to make us more like Christ. Understanding yourself is not as easy as it sounds. I found that I had become what everybody else said and desired me to be. At first, I thought I had lost myself. Then I realized that I had never known my true self. I had never really come to know the person that God had called me to be. If I can share a portion of my process then I think it will shed some light on how God is so amazingly attentive to every detail of our lives. How he loves us so much. How He cares about us. How in spite of our issues and faults He still chooses to love us and bless us.

My elementary life was not the best. The spirit of perversion was unleashed upon me like hungry lions on their prey. I struggled in middle school with homosexuality because a teenage girl molested me when I was five years old. I had a boyfriend and a girlfriend in middle school. I did not want to be gay. It was wrong and I knew it. I struggled to the point that I tried to kill myself. I remember that day very well. I took every pill I could find in my mother's medicine cabinet. As I was dying, I heard a voice say, "Do you really want to die?" I did not know it then but I know now it was the voice of the Holy Spirit. Immediately, I called my mom and she called the ambulance. They pumped my stomach but failed to pump my life. We never dealt with my issues. I was so afraid to tell the truth about my life that I said what I needed to say to the caseworker to go home. I did not die that day but I lived a very suicidal life. I stopped wrestling with homosexuality but promiscuity became a stronghold. Understand this, my friend, just because we no longer wrestle with a certain issue does not mean we have experienced true deliverance. We have to deal with the root. Sadly, we give up bad habits and think we are free. If I give up one bad habit just to pick up another bad habit then I am still bound.

At that point, I looked for love in all the wrong places. As I reflect back, I was certainly heading for a life of sinful indulgences. I could roll a joint (marijuana) by the time I was in first grade. I knew the difference between "top shelf" liquor and "rot gut" liquor. I was exposed to a lot of perversion. I was exposed to pornography at an early age. I was reading sexually explicit novels in the fourth grade. I still remember reading the book, *Wifey*. There was nothing in that book about sugar, spice or anything nice. That was not a good book for a little girl to read. I did not love myself so I indulged in sin without hesitation. My parents were present in my life and they were as attentive as they could be at that point in my life. I never did those things in front of them. They had the philosophy of "Do what I say and not what I do." I did what they did anyway. I had a boyfriend or two that dealt heavily in dealing drugs. In fact, if I had stayed connected to him, there is a huge chance that I would have served several years in a federal prison for associating with the wrong crowd. Our connections can control our paths if we are not careful.

After having several abortions, I almost lost my mind. I would sit in the dark and hear babies crying. It was a very low time for me. I loved the attention of men so I would dress provocatively. It did not matter that they were looking in lust. I just wanted attention. I had become an attention junky. I was addicted to making men look and lust after me. It was a stronghold. I was also very angry. I was constantly fighting and getting into altercations. The fear of rejection rested so heavily upon me that I walked around looking for somebody to say something to me. When they did, I foolishly responded. Let me say this, I grew up in the suburbs. My dad was a top executive for the city government. He was Chief of Minority Business. My mom had a good job working for the state government. We were not poor in the least bit. We had several cars including a Lincoln Continental Mark VII and a nice brick house. We had stuff but we did not have God. I did not want for anything. That is why it was so hard to explain my desire towards being in a relationship with a drug dealer. I can answer it now. I did not know how to love myself. I had to learn to love God in order for Him to teach me how to love myself. We can love to an extent because we have the breath of life in us. However, for us to experience the total benefits package of love we have to know God. Throughout our entire lives, He draws us into a relationship with Him.

As I was pregnant for the fifth time, I realized that abortion was murder. I was devastated. I thought it was a choice. I had been deceived. The pain of my past attempted to destroy me. My boyfriend (my husband now) was caught up in college life and sin. As a result, he fell off from what he knew about God. Together we made some poor choices. As fun as it was the price we paid was far more than we expected. We both went to church. He and I both had experienced baptism. We both knew better. We were not taught how to be disciples of Jesus Christ. We did not know about the power made available to us through Jesus Christ. We did not know ourselves. We only knew what our flesh wanted. When I turned up pregnant, it was not hard to figure out how that happened. My husband being the caliber of man he is, said he wanted to marry me. With my mommy's help, they convinced me to get married before my daughter was born. I was more concerned about being too fat for a wedding dress at that time. To this day, I thank God for my daughters. Their very presence changed my life.

Soon after I was married, I rededicated my life to Christ. It was an easy choice to make that day. It was not an easy choice to maintain. Salvation is more than a choice. Salvation is a lifestyle. I had to learn how to live for Christ. I thank God for my mentor. She helped me learn how to serve my husband and my children. I had to go through detoxification. Detoxifying my life included removing the poison that the carnal mind had established from the ways of the world. I had to learn to live like Christ. I am still learning how to do that. I shared this small portion of my process with you because I want to help you see that I was a mess when I became a wife. Everything I was, did, said, thought, and wanted came with me into the marriage. I had to allow God to show me myself before I could become the best wife for my husband. You too, my friend, brought a lot of baggage into your marriage if you had not allowed God to help you cut the cords of your past. Becoming the best me includes allowing God to show me how to be the best me. I want you to be the best you for your spouse.

## THE SURRENDERING WIFE

God created women to walk in dominion too. Submission is learned behavior. We have to learn how to submit to our husbands. I was a very independent woman when I got married. I had a plan for my career. I was going to finish my bachelor degree. Secure myself an MBA and finish it off with a Doctorate degree. I took my maternity leave after both of my daughters were born. When the leave was up, I went back to work. I was ready to execute my plan. The problem was my prideful attitude and resistance to submitting to God and my husband at this point. After I finished my Bachelors at Florida Agricultural and Mechanical University in Tallahassee, Florida, I prepared to pursue my Masters in Business Administration. However, I found out I was pregnant again with my third child. I felt like my prophecy was, "Unto you a son will be given right in the middle of your plans." I handled it well. I was glad to have this last pregnancy out of the way. I was thrown aback when I found out I was pregnant with my second son. For every ache I gave my parents, my last child would avenge them. My plans were postponed but not cancelled, so I erroneously thought.

As I was praying one day, I heard the Lord impress upon my heart that I should stay home with the boys. I quickly agreed to stay home with them for one year. As I write this book, I have been home almost ten years. My inability to submit to the Word of God and my husband is the reason I believe I had to be at home. I planned to be married forever but just in case it did not work out, I had a backup plan. My stinking thinking was robbing me and I did not even know it. I had a separate account just in case my marriage failed. As I was sitting in front of the television one day, I heard the Holy Spirit impress upon my heart to give God my money I had saved up. I totally discounted that because no way God wants me to be in a sticky situation with no money. Well, it was God and I obeyed Him. I emptied out my savings account of several thousand dollars. It was not the happiest moment of my life. I tried to be a cheerful giver but my cheeriness kept eluding me. I was sick. I kept trying to understand in my mind what had just happened. As I prayed and grew closer to God, I found in His Word that I had to put my trust in Him not my savings account.

*Listen friend, this is my story.* Your story is your own. Never allow someone else's process to be your process. If you submit to God, He will prepare you for your promise. I was prideful, arrogant and selfish. As I gave my all to God, I grew closer to Him. I saw myself in His light. I saw the good, the bad and the ugly in me. I surrendered to God that month. I took my hands off my life, let it go and allowed God to be God in my life. Eventually, because I was home with the kids I learned how to surrender and submit to my husband. I stopped trying to control him. I stopped worrying about the bills and let him take care of me. Until I was willing to submit, I could not receive God's best for my life. As long as I had a backup plan, I made failure an option. I made room in my marriage for divorce. I was very independent and that affected my relationship with God and my husband. I was unruly, unwilling to submit and I had a very bad attitude. I know, I know, it is hard for you to imagine me that way. However, it is true… I was that way… I am much better now thanks to Jesus.

Do you know what God is requiring of you, dear one? Abraham had to offer up Isaac. God did not take Isaac but Abraham had to be willing to give him up. We have to be willing to give up anything that we know could come between God and us. For a man, you may have to submit that thing you desire so badly. For a woman, you may have to submit to allowing God to take care of you His way. However, the Lord calls you to submit I admonish you to say, "Yes, Lord." I did and it has proven to be one of the best choices I have ever made.

Self-esteem includes how a person feels about himself or herself. The best way to feel good about you is to know your "God worth". God loves you so much that if you were the only sinner on earth He would send Jesus to die just for you. That is proof that you are valuable. Trying to find esteem in ourselves outside of God can lead to pride. It is in Christ that we have our true existence. We must look to God's Word to know who we are in Christ. Reinforcing self-esteem includes speaking the Word over our spouses. Knowing who the Bible says we are will always lift our self-esteem because we will see ourselves in Christ. A wise husband will encourage his wife with the Word of God and vice versa. The Word of God should never be used to hurt a person. Truth sometimes does hurt. However, truth shared in love causes our self-esteem to grow. It helps us to submit to the process. The process is necessary for us to grow and be as God designed.

Knowing that God has accepted us for who we are is vital to our self-esteem. Rejection can destroy our self worth. Especially when we are rejected by the ones who are supposed to accept us no matter what. Spouses must communicate acceptance in their words and deeds. Everyone needs to feel accepted and loved. Wise spouses will make sure that the spouse knows without any doubt that they accept them. Spouses should meet the needs they are capable of meeting. Husbands and wives who follow Christ will seek Him to show them how to love their spouse the way they need to be loved. The love we need comes from God. However, the way we need the love expressed is different. A wise spouse knows that God's love is limitless. God is love and He loves His sons and His daughters. Each spouse must allow God to love through them. As we learn more about God, then we learn more about ourselves and then we can learn more about our spouse. As we love God and love ourselves then we can love our spouses. Getting to know God is the prelude to getting to know the real you. Getting to know ourselves is the key to a successful marriage.

# *Chapter 3*
# LET'S GET AN UNDERSTANDING OF MARRIAGE

Kyle and Kristy enjoy a brisk walk along the beach. They hold hands as they enjoy each other's company. They have meaningful conversations as the sand runs through their toes. The twinkle in Kristy's eyes shows how much she adores Kyle. Kyle scoops Kristy up for a fun game of drop and run. He drops Kristy in the sand and runs down the beach laughing. He does not see Kristy as he looks back expecting to see her running behind him. In fact, Kristy has gotten up off the sandy beach and limped back to the car. Kyle runs to the scene looking for any shred of evidence as to where his wife is. He yells her name continually but he receives no reply. He begins to panic just a little. He searches the beach to no avail. Finally, with his shoulders drooped and his head hung low he walks over to the car. He perks up because he sees Kristy in the car. He runs over to car expecting to hear that some horrible mishap forced her to run to the car without sharing it with him. However, Kristy is upset. She is sitting in the car with the music playing loud and tears running down her face. Kyle reaches out for her hand but she snatches it away. Confused and befuddled, Kyle shakes his head in disbelief. "What happened? Are you okay?" he screams over the loud music. Through her tears, Kristy shares that when Kyle dropped her, he hurt her. She limped back to the car in total embarrassment. Kyle did not mean to hurt her so he is more than willing to do whatever it takes to rectify the situation. In marriage, we can go from feelings of happiness to feelings of discontentment quicker than a New York minute. Learning to understand marriage is going to be essential if we desire to have a successful one.

Like Kyle and Kristy, we will experience joy, comfort, adoration, fun, laughter, hurt, fear, sadness, panic, failure, happiness, disappointment, pain, confusion, embarrassment, resentment, compromise, willingness to help, and much more in marriage. Marriage should be a flourishing relationship. Married couples should grow together. Understanding marriage is essential to having a successful marriage the way God intended.

## LET GOD HELP YOU

Everything begins and ends with God. He is the Creator of all things. Our issue is that we seek to find out the purpose of a thing by asking the thing. If we want to know how to put together a lawn mower or a vanity mirror set, we cannot ask the mower or the mirror. We have to ask the inventor. The inventor generally gives us a manual. God has given us a manual for marriage. He knows the purpose of marriage. He knows our individual purpose. He knows how to help us work together. He knows how to make a marriage work right. He knows because marriage is His design. He knows what the output is supposed to look like. We may be able to put a lawn mower together without the manual but it probably will not look as good as the intended design. It can be the same way with marriage. We can do it our way but it will not be like God's intended design. God is the Originator of marriage. Therefore, He is the only One who can give us a full understanding of marriage. We must aim to seek God so that He may reveal to us His truth about marriage. As a result, we can stand under His truths when the world's system tries to get us to compromise and conform to its erroneous ways. We can always stand on the Word of God as we accept His Word as truth. I admonish you to let God help you understand what marriage entails.

## DEFINING MARRIAGE

Understanding marriage will help us prepare for success in our marriage. We cannot be successful in something that we do not have any knowledge about. A definition of marriage is a permanent (until death) and sexually exclusive (forsaking all others) covenant relationship of extraordinary care (love, comfort, keep, support, etc.) between one man and one woman. Marriage is in fact a covenant of ministry. Ministry includes serving one another selflessly. Philippians chapter two verse three sheds light on that for us. It says, "Don't be selfish; don't try to impress others. Be humble, thinking of others as better than yourselves."[1] We should focus on serving our spouse opposed to thinking they should serve us. As we honor God's Word, we will see fruit in our lives. We should serve our spouse as an expression of our love for God. We must, "Work willingly at whatever you do, as though you were working for the Lord rather than for people."[2] As we serve our spouse we will be pleasing the Lord. We are wise to seek to please God. Our spouse may not always deserve our best but neither do we. As we serve each other as unto the Lord, we are then able to reap the rewards that God's Word produces.

My dictionary defines marriage as the state of being united to a person of the opposite sex as husband or wife in a consensual or contractual relationship recognized by law. The only issue I have with this definition is that marriage done God's way is not contractual. Marriage is a covenant that a man and a woman make with God. Covenant includes agreement, vows, a promise and generally a witness or two. Contracts by definition include an "if-then-else" clause. If you do your part then I will do my part or else, I will not do my part because you did not do your part. Covenant says that even if you do not do your part I will still do my part. There is evidently a greater commitment required for a covenant opposed to a contract. Covenant is permanent, includes some type of sacrifice and includes freedom from being controlled by the erroneous expectations of someone. Covenant also requires us to be obligated to one another. Covenants are intentional. Covenants promise to love unconditionally, readily offer forgiveness, consistently display hope, supply comfort and continual respect. Contracts are generally for a specific purpose and are not permanent. Contracts can be a part of marriage. However, the marriage itself is a covenant.

Adam was Eve's husband. Eve was Adam's wife. God came up with the concept of marriage, which includes a husband and a wife. God created Adam and gave him a job to do. Adam was a man with purpose before he became a husband. God noticed that Adam had no one that looked like him. He had no one to help him or meet his needs. As a result, God put Adam to sleep and took out of him what he needed to make his life complete. God took Eve out of Adam. Everything Adam needed to make him complete as a husband was wrapped up in Eve. God performed the first marriage Himself. God referred to Eve as a help meet. Her purpose included helping Adam fulfill his God given destiny. Eve did not come into the marriage with family issues. Her dad did not fail her. Her mother did not abuse her. Eve came into the marriage whole. In that respect, women of today must do the same thing that Eve did by coming into their marriage whole. Whole in the sense of knowing who they are in Christ. That way they can help their husbands reach the goals that God has set for them.

We have to be careful not to allow our lives to get overloaded. If we get in overload, we may start neglecting our spouse and other relationships. Marriages need appropriate time, energy, attention and willingness to sacrifice. As believers, we have an opportunity to love our spouse as an extension of our love for Jesus. Sometimes when we read scriptures about loving our neighbor, we forget that our spouse is our closest neighbor. Our spouse should get the greatest benefits of being in the family of God with us, seeing as we spend so much time together. Certainly, we have the most opportunities to be kind to one another. Spending appropriate time together is vital to establishing a protective atmosphere for success in marriage. We give our time to the things that we value the most. We value our livelihood so we give our time to work to be paid. Our time and our money can really show us where our heart is. I found out that my heart was in my stomach at one point. I checked my bank statement to find that I spent most of my money on food. We have to be mindful of where we spend our money, what we spend it on and to whom we give our time. Time is the most precious asset because we cannot get it back once we have used it. Giving our marriage the appropriate time is essential.

I had to ask myself if I had given myself totally to my spouse. It was not as easy to answer as I thought it would be. Love in marriage is essentially giving yourself to your spouse. Love includes sacrifice and attentiveness. God shows us the greatest example. He loved us (attention) enough to give His best for us (sacrifice). We can learn a lot from the Most High God.

Pastor Rick Warren informed us that we are here on earth for a reason. He let us know we are here for worship, fellowship, discipleship, to serve and do missions.[3] We can apply these same purposes to marriage. As we learn how to worship God, He teaches us how to love our spouse. As we fellowship with our spouse we learn how to help each other face the many trials we encounter as a couple and as individuals. As we submit to the process of becoming a true disciple, we learn how our faith in God can help us grow in marriage. We learn how to serve one another better as we grow in ministry together. In fact, our first ministry after God is our spouse. We can see our gifts expressed at home sometimes before we see them in other areas. For example, I am a teacher. Therefore, I take time to teach you how to do something opposed to just telling you what to do. That gift was evident at home before I started teaching in other arenas. Sharing our faith together can help us appreciate the good in each other. As we go out to tell others why we believe, we will remember the Christ-like qualities in our spouse.

Marriage gives us the greatest opportunity to experience life together as a team. In marriage we can serve each other, we can sacrifice for each other, we can comfort each other, and we can share our hearts and our stuff with each other. In marriage, we have to be able to be ourselves. One of the hardest things to endure is to have to be pretentious and fake around our spouse. Marriage should reflect the acceptance of Christ. We have to be open, humble and honest. That includes being vulnerable. There can be no true intimacy where there is no mutual and genuine sharing. Marriage is the place where we can communicate our hurts, share our feelings, admit our failures, release our thoughts, acknowledge our fears, disclose our weaknesses, ask for help and request prayer. If we really want to find out how healthy our marriage is, then we should ask our spouse how freely they are able to share the above list with us. We can ask ourselves how freely we can share with our spouse. Working on these areas is a good place to start in building our marriages to reflect a true connection.

Marriage can be the greatest forum for us to get past our fears. An atmosphere of healing flows when two people serve one another the way God intends in marriage. As a result, we can heal from past hurts, failures, disappointments, rejections and fears. Together couples can operate in faith. Faith is the antidote to fear. Faith comes when we believe in the truth of God's Word. Fear comes when we believe the lies of Satan's deceit. The lie that we cannot move beyond our past is prevalent amongst believers. This lie works against our faith because we believe that Christ died for our sins. If we believe He died for our sins then a lie about God not forgiving us will not cause us to doubt the validity of God's Word. To risk rejection, ridicule or being hurt again requires faith. The Word of God will always give us the boost in faith we need to believe in our spouse, our marriage and ourselves.

Marriage can also be the platform that God uses to help us fulfill our yearning to be understood and valued. We spend a lot of time looking for significance and validation from other people. Once we find our purpose and significance in God, we can stop searching for it in other people. God often uses marriage as an opportunity to show forth His love for His children. In marriage, we can be understood and be accepted for who we are. In marriage, we can also be valued and wanted. Even if we did not choose our spouse as in some cultures, we can still choose to accept them and value them. Receiving sympathy, kindness, patience and gentleness can help us grow in our appreciation of God's goodness shown through our spouse. Even when we make mistakes in life, we can still receive the benefits of a godly marriage. Instead of revenge or retaliation against one another, we can resolve for restoration. God faithfully helps us overcome trials. We should do the same in marriage.

People often get married hoping that their spouse will make them whole. It does not happen that way. Married couples need to be "made whole" in Christ before they can be joined together the way God intended. Couples who get married before they come to know Christ miss the benefits afforded them through salvation. Unbelievers are always candidates for conversion. Once an unbeliever accepts Christ then they can win their spouse to Christ by their actions. God can take that union and show forth His love. It is by His power that married believers become one. We become one in Him. God is extending the same invitation to unbelievers that He did to the paralyzed man in the Bible. The question to be asked now is "Wilt thou be made whole?"[4] There is something that being made whole requires. Jesus says, "If thou canst believe, all things are possible to him that believeth."[5] He also says, "For God so loved the world that He gave His only begotten Son, that whosoever believeth in Him should not perish but have everlasting life."[6] God is calling all unbelievers to accept His Son Jesus as their Savior.

Divorce was never God's intention and neither was sin. In order for two people to have a successful marriage, they must both be "made whole" in Christ. Being "made whole" in Christ does not mean we will not make mistakes. However, we are new creatures in Christ Jesus. We are no longer servants of sin because we now serve God. Being "made whole" is a process that Holy Spirit initiates and completes until Christ returns. God has released His Spirit and His Word to perfect us and make us whole. The essence of being whole is following the Spirit of God and obeying His commands.

God gives us point by point, as to what we need. Here are four examples of the necessary components for a successful marriage as the Scriptures reflect:

Loving God is a first component to a successful marriage. Marriages who do not know God may appear to be successful but really they are not. The prophet said in Jeremiah chapter seventeen verse nine, "The heart is deceitful above all things, and desperately wicked: who can know it?" Following our own hearts will not work for our good. Following God is the gateway to success in all that we do. "Jesus said unto him, Thou shall love the Lord thy God with all thy heart, and with all thy soul, and with all thy mind. This is the first and great commandment."[7]

The second component is to love our spouses as ourselves. If we love our spouses the way we want them to love us in return, then success is obtainable. It is just as much hard work to keep success as it to obtain success. We must intentionally love our spouse as ourselves. "And the second is like unto it, Thou shall love thy neighbor as thyself."[8]

The third component is commitment. The husband has to leave his parents and cleave to his wife as he and his wife become one flesh. Before the couple even gets married, the understanding of these Scriptures is vital to the success of the marriage. "Therefore shall a man leave his father and mother, and shall cleave unto his wife: and they shall be one flesh. And they were both naked, the man and his wife, and were not ashamed."[9]

The fourth component is true intimacy. True intimacy is being open and not being ashamed. True intimacy gives each couple the chance to share their inner feelings without the fear of rejection. Being naked includes sharing your heart with your spouse about anything.

There are many other components but these are essential and scripturally sound. Trying to be successful in marriage God's way without knowing what the Word says is equivalent to a blind man driving a Mack truck… destruction is inevitable.

God created marriage to bring Him glory. There are many types of marriages. We will look at a few of them from a Biblical perspective. Common-law marriage is defined as "a marriage recognized in some jurisdictions and based on the parties agreement to consider themselves married and sometimes also in their cohabitation".[10] The world recognizes two people living together as a type of marriage. God considers two people who are living together, sin. Co-habitation is a sin before God. Fornication was never God's plan for humanity. In fact, fornication is a sexual sin that destroys marriage. When couples fornicate before they get married, it is harder to connect as one. They experience difficulty having a marriage the way God intended but it is obtainable as they put God first. Couples who honor God can have God's best in spite of their past. Sin destroys lives. We must learn to tell our flesh no. God will trade our worldly desires for godly ones if we want Him to. He will give us abundant life if we walk with Him according to His purposes for our lives.

The enemy tries to steal our joy, kill our commitment and destroy our marriages. If we keep reading, we find that Jesus said that He came to give us life and life that is more abundant at that. As if life was not enough, God gives us abundant life in Christ Jesus. Our marriages can thrive if we obey God. God created marriage to be a wonderful experience between a woman and a man. Within that experience, the virgin woman and the virgin man can come together and experience the joy of making love for the first time with one another. We can consider ourselves whatever we want but we need to check the Word to see what God says about our actions. Just because the world recognizes two people living together as a married couple does not mean it is such.

God makes matrimony holy. He sanctifies our lives and our marriages. Sanctify means to set apart. God sets apart what He makes holy. Sin destroys lives. Two people living together cannot enjoy the full blessings of marriage. Common law does not constitute marriage. God constitutes marriage. God's plan is for the believer to marry another believer. We are wise to follow God's precepts. We will find life in them.

Open marriage is an agreement between a married couple, which allows each spouse to have sex with other people. This is not God's best. God designed marriage when He joined Adam and Eve together and anything less than His design is perversion. To have sex with other people while we are married is sin. God never intended for a husband and wife to have sex outside of their marriage vows. He created Adam and Eve. He could have created several people and instructed Adam and Eve to pick a few to have fun with on the weekends. He did not do that. God's original plan for marriage included one woman and one man. We are very wise to follow the plan set by the Originator.

Another type of marriage is a shotgun marriage. The definition of a shotgun marriage is "a marriage forced or required because of pregnancy."[11] God can redeem any marriage as long as we allow Him to be first in our lives. I know God will honor those who honor Him. My marriage was a shotgun marriage. I was eight months pregnant with my first daughter when I got married. We had a small wedding at St. Mark Church. My mom, dad, aunt, uncle and my husband's uncle were the only ones there. My husband and I were in a sinful situation and as a result, I got pregnant. We were not ready for what was required of us because of the pregnancy. I was not ready to get married. I still wanted to party and have a good time. However, I believe the Lord was breaking that generational curse off my life. I believe His plan included me marrying the father of my child. I believe God knew that "baby mama" was not a good fit for me. I believe God knew I would submit to Him and accept His Son as my Savior for real. I believe God wanted what was best for me even though I was struggling with sin at that time. I believe the same thing for you.

The wages of sin is still death and I paid the price in my marriage for not adhering to the righteousness of God. I was never prepared to be a wife. I brought so many issues into the marriage with me. I had been in relationships before but I had never experienced real love. Yet, my husband loved me in spite of me. The time he spent in church and in Christian school was beneficial for me in our relationship. I had a lot of residue from the pain of the past in my heart. It was hard to trust him. I suffered from the fear of rejection. If he did anything contrary to what I wanted, I deemed it rejection. I wanted my marriage to work so bad that slowly pleasing my husband became more important than pleasing my God. I paid dearly for that mistake because my husband's love has limits. God's love is limitless. Only Jesus can know all my faults and still die for me. The fact that I had a shotgun marriage stopped me from going through weeks or even months of counseling before I got married. The abuse I suffered and the choices I made left me damaged. I needed healing administered before I said. "I do".

The great thing about God is that He designed marriage to bring two people together and make them one. His original plan includes the two people coming together in holiness. The omniscience of God is great. As God began to deal with me, I realized that I did not know Him. If only wives could get to know their Father in heaven before they get married. Shotgun marriages rob couples of the opportunity to get to know each other. Premarital counseling is serious. Christian counselors have the responsibility of ushering couples into the marriage that God intended based on His Word. It may mean that the couple needs a few more sessions. Changing the wedding date is a small price to pay to make sure that a couple is ready. Wisdom and knowledge are major factors when it comes to accepting someone as our partner for life. Nevertheless, our marriage will prosper and be successful if we allow God to be the true Head of our marriage.

Honoring God is a very important key to having the life and marriage He wants us to have. Even if a marriage starts out in sin, we can still honor God by adhering to His Word. Some couples shack up and deny each other the full benefits of marriage. As we begin to honor God, we will see His promises happen. Therefore, friend, if you are in a sinful situation, now is the time to honor God. I guarantee you that if you honor God now you will see the benefits. You will be very glad that you did. God is a faithful friend to us. As you give Him true access to your life, you will enjoy the blessings of His presence.

The importance of husbands and wives submitting to one another is worth reiterating. The husband carries the weight and responsibility of the marriage and family unit. God came looking for Adam when he and Eve sinned by disobeying Him.[12] A wife should have no problem submitting to her husband if he is doing what God has instructed him to do. In the event the husband is doing what God commanded and his wife is still neglecting to obey the Word of God, there is a remedy in the Bible called pray, hope and wait. Husbands have the responsibility to carry their wives. Submission is easier when the husband is doing what God commanded. In some instances where the wife will not submit, we find that the husband is still learning how to cover her as God commanded him to or the wife has issues with authority.

The perversion of our carnal desires is challenging marriage God's way. God created Adam and then He created Eve. He made them with purpose. God could have created Adam, Steve and Eve and told Adam to pick one but He did not. He could have created Eve, Eva and Adam and told Eve to pick one but He did not. God never intended for a man to be with another man. He never intended for a woman to be with another woman. God created a man and a woman to be joined together as one in holy matrimony. The law of the land is always changing. We have to carefully consider God's Word and use it as a basis for our decisions. Some states have agreed to recognize homosexual marriages. This is not God's best nor His will. It was never God's plan for the laws of the nations to override His Word. The laws of the nations are supposed to be established upon God's Word. The Bible shows us that unless we allow God to build our nations, no matter what we do, it will be in vain and unsuccessful. Regardless of what the world does, we as believers must use the Bible as our road map in life. God's Word will never lead us astray. God created marriage and therefore He is the One to show us how it works.

## THE HUSBAND

The husband is the protector, the provider, the priest, the prophetic voice and the king of his house. The husband protects his wife through his relationship with God. As he seeks God in all things, God will reveal to him all the areas of access the enemy has to his wife and family. God has given the husband authority and power to stop the enemy from destroying his family. Men are physically stronger. The husband's strength enables him to protect their family from all sorts of dangers.

As the provider, God has instructed the husband to work. The Bible reminds us "… if any would not work, neither should he eat."[13] The Bible also lets us know that if a man does not take care of his family he is worse than a sinner that does not even know the Lord Jesus.[14]

As the priest of his house, the husband blesses his children and his wife. He is able to speak the blessing found in Numbers chapter six verses twenty-three through twenty-six, "The Lord bless you and keep you; the Lord shine His face upon you and be gracious unto you; the Lord lift up His countenance unto you and give you peace." God will honor the words of the husband. As a result, all husbands must learn to speak life. He should only speak into existence what he wants to see.

As the prophetic voice of the family, the husband should hear from God about the direction the family is to go. The prophetic is simply repeating what God already said. God will speak the vision to the husband. As a result, the husband is responsible for making sure the vision is written. He has to make sure his family understands the vision so they can do their part. God will also speak to the wife about the vision and direction of the family. Both the husband and wife should respect one another and run with the vision that God gives them. The prophetic voice can also speak life into the family unit. As the husband walks as the prophetic voice of his house, he is able to establish and prosper his family God's way. The gifts of the Holy Spirit include many avenues by which the husband can lead his family. For instance, a word of knowledge, a word of wisdom or the gifts of faith and healing is valuable in the family unit. It is available especially when the husband lines up with God and His Word.

Being the king of the house can be amazingly wonderful. The family will honor and respect the king in his castle. In addition, whatever the king decrees must go forth. The wife would be wise to honor her husband and adore him as the king of her house. Kings take responsibility for their kingdom and make sure that it runs according to the vision. Husbands are a very important part to the success of any marriage or family unit. God sheds light on a husband's responsibility in the Bible.

> "Husbands, go all out in your love for your wives, exactly as Christ did for the church—a love marked by giving, not getting. Christ's love makes the church whole. His words evoke her beauty. Everything he does and says is designed to bring the best out of her, dressing her in dazzling white silk, radiant with holiness. And that is how husbands

*ought to love their wives. They're really doing themselves a favor—since they're already "one" in marriage. No one abuses his own body, does he? No, he feeds and pampers it. That's how Christ treats us, the church, since we are part of his body. And this is why a man leaves father and mother and cherishes his wife. No longer two, they become "one flesh." This is a huge mystery, and I don't pretend to understand it all. What is clearest to me is the way Christ treats the church. And this provides a good picture of how each husband is to treat his wife, loving himself in loving her, and how each wife is to honor her husband."*[15]

One of the first commands God gives to the husband is to love his wife. In order for the husband to love his wife, he must have the love of God in him. God is so specific that He goes on to say that the husband should love his wife as Christ loves the Church. He did not say for husbands to love their wives like their dad loved their mom. God gave us the perfect example in Christ's love for the Church. Christ died for the Church. He suffered the horrible death of the cross for the Church. Husbands must be willing to die to their fleshly desires. They must desire to love their wives over all except God. A husband must be open with his wife. Christ reveals many mysteries to His Bride, the Church. Obeying God's commands is not a matter of our feelings. God's commands are not a matter of whether or not the person deserves it. Husbands must obey the Word of God and love their wife.

If the husband has a problem with loving his wife then he will have to look to God for more grace in that area. Love is not that gooey feeling. God is love and He gives us the wherewithal to love as He does. The husband must understand that Christ loves the Church enough to give His precious life to save it. He gave all that He was on earth to save that, which was precious to Him. Husbands should learn how to rescue their wives from the wiles of life. Christ saved the Church from death, humiliation, sickness, shame, the devil and a host of other things. The husband must do the same for his wife. Just as Christ saved us from death, the husband can help his wife grow more in Christ. The husband can save his wife from humiliation by honoring her. The husband can save his wife from shame by respecting her. The husband can protect his wife from the enemy by pleading the shed blood of Jesus over her. The husband and wife must do as God commanded. God knows that for a marriage to work both parties must do what He said to do. To enjoy the true blessings of God in the marriage both parties must be willing and obedient.

The Bible says that the husband should love his wife and give himself for her like Christ. The husband can set apart and cleanse his wife with the Word of God. Speaking life is a way the husband can wash his wife with the Word. If his wife is dealing with depression, the husband can speak life to her with Psalms twenty-three. If his wife is sick, he can speak life to her with Isaiah fifty-three. If the wife is on the brink of death, he can speak life to her with John chapter ten verse ten. God has given the husband the power that he needs to do what God purposed him to do. Jesus is the Living Water. The husband himself must know who Jesus is before he can speak life to his wife. The husband himself must be in good standing with God before he can sanctify or cleanse his wife by speaking life to her. God's plan is perfect. When the husband does his part to sanctify and cleanse his wife God opens up the wife's womb so that rivers of living waters gush out. A woman who has life spoken to her will produce life. She will be able to do all that God has called her do.

    A husband that speaks life to his wife will reap many benefits. One of the benefits is "she does not walk in the counsel of the ungodly, nor stand in the way of sinners, nor sit in the seat of the scornful. But her delight is in the law of the LORD; and in His law does she meditate day and night. And she shall be like a tree planted by the rivers of water, that brings forth her fruit in her season; her leaf also shall not wither; and whatsoever she does shall prosper."[16] This wife is blessed because she has been washed by her husband. She understands that she should seek godly counsel and advice about her marriage. This wife does not hang out with sinners nor does she commit habitual sins. This wife does not hold grudges. This wife is delighted to follow God's way. Her husband speaks life to her in the Word and she loves it. She meditates trying to figure out ways to please her God and her husband. This wife's has planted her roots in God's Word. She knows that God has set her seasons in life so she does not get jealous when others are blessed. The life-speaking wife will prosper. God knows the power of love. The life-speaking wife who has a husband who loves her as Christ loved the Church will fulfill her purpose. She will not stop until all is well in her house. A husband who speaks life to his wife will have a peaceful home.

    The Lord explains why the husband should do what He commanded. The husband obeys God so that he can have a generous wife with no blemishes or signs of death. In addition, the wife will be holy and faultless by way of the cross. The way the husband gets this result is by obeying God's command. Jesus died so that marriages can flourish and grow. Jesus never intended for marriages to end in divorce. God did not leave us without instructions. The path of God leads to life. The path of life leads back to God. When a husband loves his wife, he loves himself because she is bone of his bone and flesh of his flesh.[17] When a husband nourishes his wife, he is nourishing himself. When a husband cherishes his wife, he is cherishing himself. The husband is able to do this because Christ does it for him. Believers are flesh of Christ's flesh and bone of Christ's bone and we must obey Him. Christ always teaches by example. The Christ and His body are one. The bridegroom and the bride are Christ and the Church. Just as the Church and Christ are one, so are the husband and the wife. The husband must cleave to his wife. It takes an awesome God to take two whole people and make them one. Husbands must do whatever they have to do to love their wives.

    God said the husband is the head.[18] He did not say that the husband tries to be the head. A husband is the head of his family just as much as he is a man. Some husbands like to say their wives will not let them be the head. The wife has no more control over the husband being the head than a lion has control over being a lion. She can be a stumbling block if she has issues with submitting to the order of God. The husband is the head and must learn what that means to God. It does not mean dictatorship. The wife should serve her husband out of love and respect for God's Word. The husband is the earthly protector of his wife. He protects her from all sorts of perils whether real and imagined. Christ saved the Church with His life. A husband should protect his wife from things that may cause her harm as well. Ultimately, God is Savior of all. Nevertheless, He has given husbands the ability and responsibility to protect their family.

The Bible says that wives are subject to their husbands in everything.[19] To be clear, the husband is the spiritual authority in the family. God placed him in that position and to reject him is to reject what God has put in place. The husband has the final word on all issues that pertain to the family. God speaks to the husband and the wife, but the husband is responsible for the Word that God gave the family. Being the head is his responsibility. Husbands are responsible for their wives and their children.

God gave the Church to Christ just as He gave the wife to her husband. Jesus told God that He did not lose any of the people that God gave Him except the one who chose to obey the devil.[20] Husbands are to be responsible for everything that God entrusts them with. Husbands are to be good stewards with what the Lord has blessed them with, including their wives. The Bibles says, "Likewise, husbands dwell with your wife according to knowledge, giving honor unto your wife, as unto the weaker vessel, and as being heirs together of the grace of life; that your prayers be not hindered."[21] Husbands are commanded to dwell with their wives by what they know about them. Each wife has dislikes and likes. A wise husband will take the time to get to know his wife for God commands that he know her. Wives are beautiful, delicate and easily broken if mishandled. The husband and the wife are children of God together in Christ. They both have to extend grace to one another just as Christ does for them. The wise husband that follows God's commands will have his prayers heard and answered. A husband that does not follow God's commands can pray to God but his prayers may be hindered by his disobedience. God does not even entertain our prayers when we have sin in our heart.

It is beneficial for a man to have a mentor. Integrity, character and valor are learned behaviors. Every man should have a godly example of a husband that is Christ-like to model that behavior for him. For example, my sons are learning right now how to behave from their father. They are learning the importance of being a man of your word because they want their dad to keep his promises to them. Being a man of your word is evidence of being more like God. God is not fickle. He is the same always. Jesus served as a mentor to the disciples. He taught them how to keep the commands of God. He taught them how to pray. He modeled the behavior He wanted them to exhibit. Like Christ, husbands must be willing to commit to prayer. Prayer is the vehicle God uses to do mighty works in the earth realm. Just as Jesus intercedes on behalf of the church, the husband must consistently intercede for his wife. Jesus gives us the ultimate example of how to live as children of God. Here are some of the commands that God gave the husband: (1) To love his wife; (2) To give himself for his wife; (3) To sanctify and cleanse his wife; (4) To wash his wife in the Word; (5) To present his wife as glorious and holy; (6) To nourish and cherish his wife; (7) To leave his mother and father; (8) To cleave to his wife; (9) To be one flesh with his wife;[22] (10) To dwell with his wife according to knowledge; (11) To give honor to his wife; (12) Be heirs with her of the grace of life; (13) Do what God says so prayers are not hindered;[23] God knows what it takes for a marriage to work. Following God's plan will work every time.

## THE WIFE

Submission is learned behavior. God created the man and woman to walk in dominion. Nevertheless, God has set the husband as head over the wife. A godly wife will search her heart and seek God to reveal and deal with any areas of her heart that keep her from fully obeying Him. God gave the wife specific commands just like the husband to ensure success in the marriage. The Bible remits, "wives are to submit yourselves unto your own husbands, as unto the Lord. For the husband is the head of the wife, even as Christ is the head of the Church: and he is the savior of the body. Therefore, as the Church is subject unto Christ, so let the wives be subject to their own husbands in everything."[24] The Bible calls for wives to submit to their own husbands. Wives must reverence their husbands without putting him before God. Wives must prefer their husbands to all else except God. Women can be great worshippers. A wife must reverence her husband in a similar manner in which she does God. It is easy to love God because He is always worthy. However, loving and submitting to a flawed human being can be difficult and challenging to say the least. Love must be pursued on purpose because no spouse is perfect. Therefore, all of us need grace and need to give grace to our spouse in abundance. A wife who wants to please God will do all she has to do to make sure she venerates, obeys, worships, honors and encourages her husband.

The wife is to make sure that she reverences her husband. Wives are to respect their husbands simply because they are married to them. Respect is required whether wives feel like their husband deserves it or not. Jesus died for him and as a result, he deserves all God has for him. God set the husband as head of the family and a wife that walks with God will honor him simply because God commanded her to. Feelings are fickle and change as quickly as the fleeting of blinking eyelashes. However, relationship requires obedience to God's Word regardless of our feelings. As wives seek to please God they will obey His commands and submit to their own husbands. There have been many instances reported where a wife will submit to another man quicker than she will her own husband. In this instance, this wife is out of line and must allow Holy Spirit to correct her behavior. The Word of God said that wives are to be subject to their own husbands in everything. This command is to set order in the marriage and family unit. God has given husbands spiritual and natural headship and authority in the marriage and the family.

 A wife who follows God's commands is a wise wife. A wise wife will have a heart that is not corruptible. The only way for her heart not to be corrupted is to put God's Word in her heart. A wise wife knows that calling her husband lord, as Sarah called Abraham is the way to create an atmosphere conducive to success in her marriage. A wise wife has is humble, meek, has a quiet spirit and will subject herself to her husband. "A virtuous woman is a crown to her husband: but she that makes her husband to be ashamed is as rottenness in his bones."[25] Wives should be crowns to their husbands. Foolish wives bring shame to their husbands. We all have been foolish at some point in our lives. Even the most beautiful woman can have a rotten heart if she does not have a relationship with God. A disease that rots away the bones is deadly. The enemy tries to use wives who do things to shame their husbands to rot away marriages. Nevertheless, Jesus can heal anything. God can heal those rotten marriages. They must submit to the teachings of Jesus and then the healing will flow.

 A virtuous woman will study her husband to find out what it takes to keep her man happy. A virtuous woman knows how to do right by her man. A virtuous woman is the joy of her husband's life. She pleases him in all that she does. She is priceless, trustworthy, faithful and good. She is a hard worker, giving, respected, smart and a leader. She is also God-fearing, honored and blessed. She is the woman found in Proverbs chapter thirty-one. The virtuous woman is all that and more because she fears God. Her reverence for God keeps her in a place for Him to prosper her and all she sets her hands to do. Being a wife of excellence is included in God's plan for the wife in a successful marriage. Wives must not sit around complaining about their husbands. They should focus more on things that make their husbands smile.

 If a wife sows love into her husband, she will reap love. Whatever a wife wants to see in her husband she must sow it. Wives are to be their husband's good thing. That includes being so good to him that it blows his mind as to how good God is for giving him such a great wife. A praying wife is a good thing because she will pray for her husband and not just for herself. She brings favor in the marriage. Favor increases because of her relationship with the Lord. The favor of God can take a husband where money cannot. God has set the wife in a place in the marriage that gives her the opportunity to be there for her husband and see him succeed in all his godly endeavors. A godly wife will be a helpmeet and not help beat their husband down. God gave the wife to the husband to be his helpmeet. A wife is to complete him and support him as he follows Christ. A wife's greatest gift to her husband is her prayer life. As she prays for her husband to be successful in the way God intended, she will reap the benefits.

The Bible gives the wife commands that she must follow. If she follows these commands there are some results she will be able to enjoy. Here are some commands God gave the wife: (1) Wives must be subject to their own husbands in everything; (2) Obey the Word; (3) Win the husband over with conversations not the constant clanging of the scriptures; (4) Live so their husband will see their reverence for God; (5) Let her beauty be an inner beauty not make-up & jewelry; (6) Put on a meek and humble spirit (7) Be holy; (8) Trust God; (9) Be her husband's help meet; (10) Respect her husband.[26]

In marriage, wives have to learn to respect the position of the husband. God gave the husband the position as the head of the family. The position of the husband needs to be honored. There may be times that a wife has to honor the position because she is having a problem with the person. David recognized Saul's position as the king. David honored Saul as king even though he was acting like a foolish wild man. Wives must understand that if they were not married then they would not be a wife. His position as the husband gives her the position as the wife. Respecting each other's God given position and purpose is a key to success. Wives must walk along side their husbands. Wives should encourage husbands to experience growth in their relationship with God. That growth will affect both of their lives for the good. As couples walk together through life, they learn how to relate to each other better. Being patient and supportive will foster an environment that gives both parties courage to change for the good.

Wives have to learn to be thankful and see the glass half full instead of half empty. Being optimistic helps marriages flourish. Wives have to make a decision that they want their marriage to do well. We are constantly bombarded with movies that make us believe that the grass is greener elsewhere. The truth is that we can have green grass in our marriage if we want it. Wives have to learn to train their minds to think about their spouse in a positive manner. Wives create an atmosphere of desire for their husband when they take time to think good thoughts about them. Wives have to appreciate their husbands and see him as an asset. Wives have to work on not rejecting any of her husband's advances for sexual attention. Wise wives learn how to divert his attention without rejection. Wives can set a later time for coming together sexually after they have had a chance to prepare themselves. Keeping healthy sexual expressions alive is essential to marriages. Remembering to be friends again is the key to proper connection. Learning to celebrate whatever efforts your husband puts toward doing things together is important. Showing him appreciation for helping out around the house is a key to enjoying one another. Even if it is not what you would do or how you would do it, please celebrate your husband for his efforts.

## A STRONG MARRIAGE

There are certain characteristics that contribute to the strength of the marriage. Questions that the husband and the wife should think about are; 1. Is my spouse my best friend? 2. Do I like my spouse as a person? 3. Do I believe that marriage is a long-term commitment? 4. Do I believe that marriage is sacred? 5. Can we agree on aims and goals? 6. Is my spouse growing more interesting to me? 7. Do I want this marriage to succeed? 8. Is our marriage helping or hurting our social stability? 9. Do we laugh together? 10. Am I proud of my spouse's achievements?[27]

Asking these questions will open up much needed dialogue. Attending to these questions will pinpoint any areas that need to be corrected. Focusing on solutions will prove to be more valuable than focusing on the problem.

Marriage vows are very important. A sample of marriage vows is, "Will you have this woman to be thy lawfully wedded wife, to live together after God's Ordinance in the holy estate of matrimony? Will you love her? Will you comfort her? Will you honor and keep her in sickness and in health and forsaking all others keep thee only unto her so long as ye both shall live?" We write out own vows these days. However, while writing our vows we need to remember that marriage is a covenant. Even if my spouse does not do his part, I am still required to do my part because I made a vow. A vow is a promise to do a particular thing. I made a covenantal vow with God to love my spouse. I did not put any stipulations on it during the wedding and I should not put any on it now. I vowed to love my spouse in spite of himself. He vowed to love me in spite of myself. That is essential to a lasting successful marriage.

God uses hard times, trouble, trials and suffering to help us become better husbands and wives. During these times of trouble, we are more open to submit to God because we desire to get out of the situations that are causing us the pain. God does not always remove us from the situations but He will help us grow pass them. Spending time with God makes us spiritually tougher and allows us to rise above things that used to trip us up. When a man finds himself unable to take care of his family, he can be very open to hear what God has to say. He is interested in what God wants him to do. He allows God to teach him how to be a husband. Women suffer through things and find that they are more focused on their family than themselves. They ask God for help. He teaches them how to be wives and mothers by teaching them how to serve their husbands and raise their children. Trouble will run us to the Word of God for help. We are wise to allow God to use any and everything to help us grow into the person and spouse He knows we can become.

## COMPONENTS OF A SUCCESSFUL MARRIAGE

Components of a successful marriage include *sympathy, acceptance, grace, affection, love, appreciation, hope, approval, faith, attention, comfort, forgiveness, encouragement, respect, security and support.* Sympathy includes having compassion for your spouse. Having someone to share your suffering or troubles with is a benefit of marriage. Acceptance is your ability to receive your spouse unconditionally even though they are not perfect and their behavior reflects that imperfection. Acceptance says even though you make mistakes I am not going to tear you down but I am going to build you up based on what I know about you. The Bible reminds us to give grace to others as we have received grace.[28] As freely as God has given grace to us, so we also need to give grace to others. The Bible also admonishes us to season our words with grace.[29] Speaking to our spouse in a godly manner will increase effective communication. Grace is undeserved favor. As God has given us grace, so we need to give it to our spouse. We can express affection as we show our spouse we care. We express affection by doing things that say, "I love you". Affection is expressed when I send you an email that says, "Honey, I am plum crazy about you and I can't wait to see you at dinner tonight or something like that."

Love is important. Learning to love our spouses the way they need it is vital. Each spouse should ask, "Teach me how to love you." Appreciation is telling our spouses thank you and praising them. We will encounter trouble in marriage but having hope will help us focus on the good in our marriage. Each spouse should be able to share hope in times of need. Approval is building our spouse up. It is speaking words of life to them that we confirm by our actions. Approval is expressed when we affirm our spouse and make sure they know how important they are to us. Attention is letting our spouse know they are a very important part of our lives. Attention is expressed when we take the time to consider our spouses above ourselves. Attention says, "How was your day today? Just talk to me because I am concerned about you." Faith is necessary to please God. As we have faith in our marriages, we see the results. Faith says I believe what God's Word says even if I do not see it yet. Faith says I love you as God loves you even if you are not acting in a godly manner.

Comfort is when we are there for our spouses when they need us to be there for them. Comfort is expressed when we do not ignore but respond in a godly manner to our spouses' feelings, hurts, pain or grief. Learning to forgive is necessary and important. There will be many opportunities for us to forgive. Encouragement is learning how to stimulate our spouses and push them into the destiny that we know God has set for them. Encouragement is responding to our spouses the way they need that will push them into the place we know God has prepared for them. Encouragement says, "I believe in you, dear. I know you may not be able to see how great you are right now. But I do and I want you to know that you are very special to God and to me."

Respect is expressing to our spouse through our actions that we value them and hold them in high esteem. Respect is what we do when we are alone. We can express respect in how we talk to each other. Respect is reverencing the God on the inside of someone else. Respect is honoring your spouse and treating your spouse with the utmost regards. Security is relying on the fact that our spouse will not harm us or do anything to destroy what God has set for us intentionally. Security is having peace in our marriage to the point that no matter what it looks like we know that our spouse has our back. Security says, "I see people getting divorced on every corner but my spouse loves me and will be here for me as God has ordained". Support is when we are in the position to express to our spouse that we are here for them and will assist them in all of their endeavors. Support says, "I am here for you, dear. I will do whatever it takes to help you make your dreams come true according to the will of God."

## WHEN THINGS AREN'T IN ORDER

As I prepare this chapter, I am not ignorant to the fact that some wives and husbands have spouses that do not obey God. As the saved spouse, you should be given to prayer and fasting for the salvation and well-being of your spouse. Learning how to pray for your spouse will be the key to victory in your marriage. I want to encourage you to trust God to speak clearly to you about your spouse and your family. God will speak especially to you about you. I want to implore you to remain in a place of expectation. Expect God to call your spouse into a relationship with Him through His Son Jesus. Treat your spouse as if they are already who you know they can be in God. Treat your unsaved husband like a true man of God. Treat your unsaved wife like a woman of God. As you sow these seeds by faith, you are giving God access to your spouse. God will always honor our faith. By faith, you will have all God's best for you and your marriage. As you lift Jesus up in your life and marriage, He will draw your spouse close to Him. Our witness and testimonies can draw our spouses closer to God. Living for Christ before your spouse will show them the nature of God. Loving them in spite of all their faults will reveal God's grace to them. The saved spouse has a responsibility to win their unsaved spouse to Christ.

Sometimes we find ourselves in marriages that are not experiencing God's best. If couples find themselves in a marriage that is not God's best due to sin then they must trust God by honoring their spouses anyway. The vision of God is seeing their spouse where God can take him and not where they are. There will be times when a spouse realizes that he/she is married to a fool. A fool despises instruction, runs to evil, hates knowledge, hates truth, hates the Word, delights in mocking others, and does not fear God. [30] A wise spouse must seek the counsel of Almighty God to help his/her spouse instead of tearing him/her down. A woman in this situation must seek to be his wife and not a knife. She will build him up and not cut him down. A man must use his power and authority to build his wife and encourage her to be all that God has for her to be.

## MARRIAGE MATTERS

The Bible uses the analogy of marriage to reflect God's relationship with Israel in the Old Testament. God said that He is married to His people.[31] This is an example of Him referencing marriage in a positive manner. The New Testament uses the same analogy to reflect Christ's relationship with the Church. [32] God created marriage. He has placed a lot of power in the family unit. A marriage in God creates children in God and these children go on and on for generations to come. Marriage is an effective tool for God to use to draw His people back to Him. These Scriptures are living proof that God intended for marriages to work to His glory. They also help us not to be ignorant of the enemy's plan to destroy marriages. The thief will do his job and try to steal, kill and destroy our marriages, but we have overcome him in Christ Jesus. The thief is a defeated foe as long as we are on the Lord's side. A successful marriage may come under fire but will not suffer defeat because the Lord is for your marriage. Your marriage will not falter but prevail in total victory because you have allowed God to help you strengthen your marriage. Marriage is a very important entity of God's divine plan for humanity. You are too, friend…

# Chapter 4
## SUCCESS: WE CAN DO THIS!

Bella could not believe it. She had gotten the raise she desired. She had to lie, cheat and steal to get it but it was hers. After a while, Bella began to feel guilty about the people she had to tell lies on to get in her new position. She was the boss now. It really did not matter though because everyone knew what she had to do to be the boss. Bella told her mom what happened. She could not bear to tell her husband what she had done. Her mom told her she would need to right her wrong. She would need to confess and repent. Bella laughed in her mom's face. Bella did not realize her so-called success was a failure until her husband James saw Karen in the supermarket. Karen was one of the people Bella told lies on to secure her new position. She cried on James shoulder because she was so hurt. She trusted Bella. James was furious. He told Bella that she was wrong. He asked her to confess what she had done to her supervisor and deal with the consequences. Bella complied and lost her job. After being unemployed for a year, the company opened a new department. The supervisor remembered Bella's confession and called Bella in to supervise the new department.

## THE BENEFITS OF SUCCESS GOD'S WAY

God shows us His way by His actions. To see the will of God we should look at the life of Christ. Jesus said that He did what He saw His Father do.[1] The more we learn about God, the more we can walk in His ways. We have to know His ways in order to benefit from them. He loves us so much that He gave His best when we were at our worst. We must submit to allowing God to disciple us to the point that we look like Him. That means we let go of everything and grab hold of God. We cannot go forward while holding on to the past. We cannot become who God is molding us into if we hold on to who we were. We must empty ourselves so that God can fill us with His Word. When we confess and repent, we are emptying ourselves. We agree that who we were in the past was not God's best. We turn from who we were to who He designed us to be in Him by faith. Getting what we want is not always an indication of success. Good success is when you can feel good about something because you have followed the ways of God. Bad success is obtaining something in your own strength while neglecting to honor God. God has a way of doing things. He shares His ways in the Bible. Following God is the best way to obtain a success you can hold on to and feel good about it.

"Way" is a course of action leading in the direction toward a desired result. Way is defined as the manner in which we do things or a habitual series of actions.[2] God's way includes following His Word as a course of action so we can have a successful marriage. God gives us directives. He is faithful to reveal His ways to us. Once we know His way then we are required to operate accordingly. As we respect God's design for marriage, we will see good results. Obeying God becomes a life-long habit and desire as we see the benefits of following Him, and there are many.

The Bible teaches us that we should obey God, walk in His ways and fear Him.[3] We learn that He requires us to live in a way pleasing to Him, love Him and serve Him with all of our heart and soul.[4] The Bible shows us how God desires for us to hold tightly to Him.[5] We find great benefits in walking in God's ways because if we love Him and keep His ordinances then He promises to bless us, increase us and protect us.[6] Humility is the way of the Lord. God will bless those who humble themselves. Marriage includes submission. As we humble ourselves before God, He teaches us how to live right and do things with the right motives.[7] We can make a declaration when we follow in God's way. We can declare that we have kept the ways of the Lord by the power of Holy Spirit and we have not turned from God to follow evil.[8] We all should realize that we will make mistakes. However, as we keep the ways of God that we find in the Word of God we can see the results in our marriage. We may not always know the way but we can pray and ask God to teach us how to live and ask Him to lead us along the paths that bring Him glory.[9] Joy is a benefit of following the ways of God. We need joy in our marriages because we encounter manifold situations that can attempt to depress us. As we reverence God and welcome Him to lead us in our marriages and our lives, we find that He gives us joy that supersedes any situation we encounter. We can truly say, "How joyful are those who fear the Lord and follow His ways".[10] God's ways are good to us and they are good for us.

## UNDERSTANDING SUCCESS

In order to truly understand or comprehend something you must be willing to submit to what you have learned. In order for knowledge to benefit me, I must adhere to it. If you tell me that I have one million dollars in my room in the form of a check, then I need to submit to that truth and go get my check. The Bible reminds us that in all of our getting we must get an understanding of what is being instructed.[11] Truth edifies us and builds us up. We will not be able to reap the full benefits of success in our marriages if we do not submit to Bible truths. The greatest truth that we can receive is when the truth aids us in improving ourselves. We must have an understanding of why we do what we do. If we neglect to grasp truth, after time, we will revert to our erroneous ways. The fact is that there has to be a desire to understand how to have a successful marriage God's way. If that desire is intact, then we can seek God through the truths depicted in His Word. God loves us. The Bible will show us how to apply Biblical principles of success to our marriage. If you will submit to Truth, then Truth will set and keep you and your spouse free. It is in that freedom that you will be able to enjoy success in your marriage.

Success is defined as "the favorable or desired outcome, the attainment of wealth, favor or eminence."[12] A successful marriage is generally the favored or desired outcome of those getting married. The process of success is what we neglect to consider sometimes. Wealth is not just a lot of money. Wealth is also having an abundance of something. I am sure we would all like to have an abundance of success in our marriage. We can have that abundance. We can have favor and eminence in our marriages as we allow the Bible to guide us. The favor of God is available for us. The eminence we will have will be to show forth the magnificence of our God. As we submit to the leading of God, we will have the desired outcome of a successful marriage. Success is not the absence of failures. True success is launched from the education we have gained when things did not turn out well.

It is not likely that a person gets married desiring or hoping to have an unsuccessful marriage. Most people get married hoping that their marriage will be successful. Some couples do not really think about the components that make up a successful marriage. They come into the marriage desiring success but do not understand that the success of the marriage requires them to work hard and to put forth effort. It is rare that people just wake up successful. Successful business owners will tell us that they had to work hard to get to the level of success they have obtained. They will also tell us that not only did they work hard to obtain success, but they have to be focused and intentional to maintain that success.

When seeking to have a successful marriage we must be motivated. The best motivation I have found is a promise. Not just any promise but a promise from God. A promise I live by is about giving. If I give then I can expect to receive a blessing given to me in good measure. I will receive a blessing that is pressed down, shaken together and running over.[13] This is especially true in my marriage. As I give love to my husband, I get love back from him in abundance. As I give peace in times of turmoil, I receive manifold blessings because the Word of God is truth. The Word will always produce. By faith, we have to expect God's Word to manifest and look for it. Look for joy in your marriage. Look for peace in your marriage. Look for financial increase in your marriage. Give and it will always be given back to you in greater capacity than when you gave it. God gave His Son to die for us. As a result, the whole world has the opportunity to choose to be in a relationship with Him through His Son. Find a promise in God's Word and sow it into your marriage, my friend, and you will see results!

The Bible is full of promises. We find in John chapter fifteen verse five, if we abide in Christ and He abides in us we can have marital success because with Christ we can do anything. With that promise, we can abide in Christ and allow Him to abide in us and see the fruit of success bloom in our marriages. Another good promise is that if we abide in Him, then we can ask what we will and it shall come to pass.[14] Abiding in Christ is a great promise to build a marriage on. Abiding means, we will remain in relationship with Christ and the Word of God. We know that all things will work out to our good as we stay connected to Him and as God's Word abides in us. Finding out about the promises of God has changed my life. As I meditated on the truth that I am more than a conqueror,[15] I tapped into the power of God to be able to overcome any obstacle that comes my way.

We may experience some problems in our marriages, but those problems will only make us stronger as we work together to solve them. The Bible reminds us that we will suffer in this life because of our commitment to Christ. However, we do not have to allow suffering to open the doors of defeat in our marriage. Suffering can bring spouses closer to one another. On the other hand, suffering can cause us to be black-balled, rejected, or even fired because we refuse to engage is some immoral act on our jobs. There may be some backlash when we stand for righteousness. In the Bible we find that people mistreated Jesus Christ because of righteousness. If we should encounter any level of suffering, we should be able to go to our spouses during that trial. Our spouses at that time should try to comfort us. Ultimately, God will comfort us. We can trust Him to do that.

God created marriages to be successful. We can have the desired success of God in our marriage by attaining the wealth of love, joy, and peace. We can let the favor of God shine through our marriage like the sun if we learn His ways. If we abide in Christ, then we can have a successful marriage God's way. Only a big God can take two people and make them one in Him. When God has joined two people together and they choose to separate, I wonder if when He looks at them, He sees one-half of "the one" flesh He joined together. I can imagine it is like having two pieces of me being in separate places. We cannot be whole outside of the will of God. We must learn to seek Him about His plan of success for our marriage. In God, all things are possible for His children. Nothing is impossible to those of us who believe Him and take Him at His Word.

## MODELS OF SUCCESS

There are two different models of success. The first model of success is worldly success. Worldly success consists of principles that the world has set. Worldly success includes the works of the flesh. We find the works of the flesh in the Bible "… are … adultery, fornication, uncleanness, lasciviousness, idolatry, witchcraft, hatred, variance, emulations, wrath, strife, seditions, heresies, Envyings, murders, drunkenness, revellings, and such like: …"[16] Worldly success proclaims that adultery is acceptable as long as you do not get caught. Worldly success states that fornication is acceptable as long as you wear a condom.

Worldly success decrees that unclean hearts and impure thoughts are acceptable as long as you dress them up in a four-piece suit. Worldly success says that lasciviousness is acceptable as long as it is done behind closed doors. Worldly success asserts that idolatry and witchcraft are okay if you go to church on Sunday. Worldly success expresses that hatred, discord, rivalry; rage and strife are acceptable as long as you put a smile on your face when it counts. Worldly success imparts that murdering an unborn baby is acceptable as long as you call it choice or deem it an accident. Worldly success says that drunkenness is acceptable as long as you can stop whenever you want. Following worldly success will lead a person away from God's best. Being married with worldly standards as a basis can cause marriage to be harder to endure. It is hard to have a loving environment when sin has such a free reign. There is a better way.

The second type of success is Biblical success. Biblical success entails principles that the Spirit of God reveals. Biblical success includes the fruit of the Spirit. We may think we are doing things God's way. However, we need Holy Spirit to help us. The Bibles says, "the fruit of the Spirit is love, joy, peace, longsuffering, gentleness, goodness, faith, Meekness, temperance:… And they that are Christ's have crucified the flesh with the affections and lusts."[17] Biblical success asserts that we love our spouses even when they are not lovable. Biblical success decrees that we have joy in our hearts even when our spouses are wrong. Biblical success states that we have the peace of God that transcends the problems of life. Hallelujah!

Biblical success says that we are to be patient with our spouses and help them reach their goals. We are to be gentle and good-natured when our spouses are hard and mean. Biblical success demands that we have faith that God can do just what He said in His Word. As husband and wife, we should be kind to one another and behave in a controlled manner. When a couple works toward Biblical success, they can crucify the flesh. Biblical success enables us to live in the Spirit and walk in the Spirit. We can live in the Spirit knowing that God is in control. We can walk in the Spirit knowing that the Holy Spirit will guide us into all truth and righteousness. This success allows us to denounce wanting the glory of being right all the time. As we grow spiritually, we will not provoke our spouses and we will not envy what God allows them to do in life. Instead, we will support them and encourage them to be all that God has called them to be.

Just because people call something successful does not mean God does. The Bible reveals the nature and will of God. Anything done against the nature of God is going to fail. We are bound to fail when we attempt to do something contrary to what we were created to do. Failure is eminent when we attempt to do marriage any other way then the way He designed. God created marriage and if it is done His way, it will be successful. If it is not done His way, it will not be successful. Following our carnal mind leads to corruption. We must remember to, "be not deceived; God is not mocked: for whatsoever a man soweth, that shall he also reap. For he that soweth to his flesh shall of the flesh reap corruption; but he that soweth to the Spirit shall of the Spirit reap life everlasting."[18] Good things happen to bad people and vice versa. We all have problems that we must solve. The difference is that the people who believe in Christ live by faith. By faith, we look at the problem but we see it through the eyes of the Problem Solver. Our Problem Solver is God. Believers know that whatever we are dealing with is temporary and shall pass. We must not forget that we are victorious in our marriages because of our relationship with God.

Some couples do not allow other people to see what they deal with in their marriages because they are ashamed. For some reason they think if they "act" like all is well it will be. No, we do not have to air our dirty laundry in testimony or "telli-mony" service. "Tellimony" service is telling all of our business with the wrong motives. Testifying can help couples who are going through difficult times. However, there will be times that we need help and we must be willing to ask for help. Asking for help is important. We just need to ask the right people. A Christian couple or a Christian marriage counselor would be the best option. As a result, all parties (the husband, the wife and God) are represented in the counseling sessions.

Marriage is an atmosphere of sowing and reaping. We are encouraged to plants seeds of love, kindness, joy, patience and goodness in our marriages. Whatever seeds we plant with our words and actions will spring up as fruit in our marriage. Planting an apple seed does not produce an orange. An apple seed produces a tree full of apples. To plant one seed of lying sets you up to receive a tree full of lies. We must follow the Biblical model of success. We do not want to reap the corruption that comes with sowing seeds of the flesh. Most people desire to have a harmonious relationships with their spouses. All marriages in Christ should yield the fruit of the Word of God.

## ASPECTS OF SUCCESS

There are three different aspects of success in marriage. The three aspects of marriage are just staying married, staying happily married and staying joyfully married.

The first aspect is just staying married. Just staying married without the fullness of God's promises is not God's best for marriage. Some people just stay married while sleeping in separate rooms and living separate lives. They never communicate beyond greeting one another and having necessary conversations. They never get to know their spouse or they forget what they ever learned about them on purpose. They are married only because they share the same last name and a piece of paper says so. A person who wanders aimlessly through life will not fulfill his destiny. Just staying married for the sake of marriage and not working towards betterment of the marriage is the lowest level of success that is possible. To be candid, success requires work and there is more to marriage than just staying married.

The second aspect of success in marriage is staying happily married. This aspect involves the emotion happiness. The only problem with this is that happiness is based on what is happening. This aspect of success says that as long as things are the way I like, then I am happy in my marriage. Unfortunately, things do not always happen the way we plan, expect or want. We must not base the success of our marriage on the things that are happening around us or even on the things that are happening in our marriage. We must look for the better way.

The last aspect of success in marriage is staying joyfully married. Joy is a fruit of the Spirit and it transcends what is going on around us. It enables us to be kind to our spouse regardless of how things look in our marriage. Joy helps us look beyond the faults of our spouse because we expect God to set them free, and it enables us to look at ourselves when things go wrong instead of blaming our spouse. Joy reminds us that God will never allow life to be more than we can bear. To be joyfully married is to be Spirit led in our marriage. The Spirit will lead us to life in our marriage the way Jesus intended when He said we could have life more abundantly. No one really wants a dead marriage. We want a marriage that is living and growing. We can experience joy in our marriages because we expect God to bless us. We never have to look at our situation and sulk because we can rejoice over what we expect God to do in our marriages. We can find absolute joy in our faith. The couple in Christ must live by faith and not by what they see. What we see is usually temporary and subject to change. However, what we do according to God's Word has a lasting effect. As we obey God, we see the lives of others benefiting from our obedience. God can use our marriage to reflect His goodness and love. Couples in Christ will see God's righteousness revealed in their marriage from one level of faith to the next.

## OVERCOMING SUCCESS BLOCKERS

Many issues block the success of a marriage. Sometimes we love our spouses the wrong way and if we want to love them the right way, then we need to take the time to get to know them. We need to learn what they like. If we sincerely work at this, then we will see success in our marriages. Loving our spouses the way he or she needs us to includes putting forth effort on our part. The Bible says that husbands must dwell with their wives according to knowledge.[19] To love a person the way they need to be loved requires us to know what they need. Only God can meet certain needs. Our spouse is not our source. God is our source. He allows our spouse to be a resource. If we look to our spouse to meet all our needs then we are setting ourselves up for failure. Only God can meet all our needs.

I remember when I looked to my husband for the level of love, affirmation and acceptance that only God could give me. He would say, "I cannot win with you." He would feel like nothing he did was good enough. I realized that I was sucking the life out of my marriage with my selfish demands. I soon realized that I was my biggest problem and hindrance to victory in my marriage. Learning to love our spouse God's way takes dedication and desire. God has given us marriage as a blessing. We do well to bless each other, as we grow old together.

Sin is another issue that blocks the success of marriage. Sin is simply all the bad things we do. Our nature is to sin. That is why we need a Savior. We need a Savior to save us from ourselves. A successful marriage requires that sin be quickly exposed and dealt with Biblically. We must never cover up the sin of our spouse with lies and deceit. The only covering appropriate for sin is prayer. Sin can destroy marriages. We are reminded that, "… out of the heart of men, proceed evil thoughts, adulteries, fornications, murders, thefts, covetousness, wickedness, deceit, lasciviousness, an evil eye, blasphemy, pride, foolishness: All these evil things come from within, and defile the man."[20] We have to allow God to reveal to us anything that is blocking us from being all that He created us to be. It is not always easy to see our issues and ourselves. However, it is always worth it to allow God to help us eradicate these things out of our lives and our marriages. We must grasp that sin attempts to destroy us from the inside out. We must guard our hearts with the Word of God.

    We learn from the Word that marriages can be destroyed as the result of sin living in our hearts. Whatever is in our hearts will come out. When our heart is full of sin, we do sinful things. Evil thoughts will cause a husband to abuse his wife. Adultery will destroy the bond of intimacy that God intended for the married couple. Fornicating before marriage opens up the door of comparison. The wife with murder in her heart will abort her husband's unborn child. The husband with murder in his heart will beat his wife to death because she came home from work late again. The thief will steal from his job, get thrown in jail, and leave his wife to raise the family alone. The spouse who covets is never satisfied with what he or she has. The spouse who deceives others will eventually deceive his or her spouse. The spouse dealing with lasciviousness will eventually cheat on his or her spouse and destroy the fiber of a successful marriage. The spouse that speaks blasphemy against God needs help. The power of a praying spouse will show them the way. When we pray for our spouses, God allows us to see our spouse the way He does. It is at that point that we realize that our spouses need Jesus just as much as we do. That is when we stop judging and start covering our spouses in love and in prayer.

    Pride will destroy a marriage. The spouse with pride never does anything wrong and blames the other person for everything that goes wrong. The foolish spouse says hurtful and thoughtless things to his or her spouse. Sin comes from the heart, defiles the individual, and affects his or her spouse. Sin is the way of the world. No couple living in sin can have God's best. Living in sin is a choice and couples who want success God's way must choose to live free of habitual sin. We will mess up but our messing up should be the exception and not the rule. Habitual sin and faith cannot dwell in the same marriage. At some point, one cancels the other out. I pray your faith will pulverize your desires to live a sinful life. The Holy Spirit can help and He wants to help. We just have to ask Him and He will answer. I was at a point one time where all I could scream in prayer was "Help" and Holy Spirit did just that. Trust in God and He will come through for you.

    I came from a background of habitual sin. I was not a miserable sinner. I enjoyed sinning because it was my nature. There were moments I wanted to do right. Nevertheless, for the most part, I enjoyed sinning because at the time it was fun. Sin was a stronghold in my life. I was wrapped-up, tied up and tangled all up in sin. I was in trouble. It is sad when someone needs help but he or she does not know it. Eventually, I grew tired of the fun. It became less and less appealing. I started getting to know God better. I started spending more time with God. I began to hate what He hates. He hates sin but He loves the sinner. I began to hate the sinful nature I possessed. I asked God daily, "Please deliver me from this stronghold of sin". He did deliver me because He loved me. It is not hard to grasp how God hates sin and loves the sinner. We have people in our family that do bad things. We do not hate them but we hate what they do. God will help us if we ask Him to.

We are reminded, "Do not love this world nor the things it offers you, for when you love the world, you do not have the love of the Father in you. For the world offers only a craving for physical pleasure, a craving for everything we see, and pride in our achievements and possessions. These are not from the Father, but are from this world."[21] This Scripture tells us that we must not love the world nor the things of the world including the world's version of success.

Without having the love of God the Father, it is impossible to fully love our spouse. The world tries to tempt us by enticing us with the cravings for physical pleasure. Our five senses are bombarded daily with temptations for more pleasures. Sadly, we are embarking upon a generation that says if it feels good then it must be good. Unfortunately, we find out the hard way that this is not true.

The world also tricks us into craving everything we see. We see things that seem desirable to us but they are in fact death to our marriage. We cannot run behind every pretty thing we see. God made men sight stimulated. I believe God gave it to Adam so he would not get caught up in naming the animals in the Garden and forget to know Eve intimately. Knowing Eve would begin to fulfill the command to procreate. The enemy of our marriage always seeks to pervert the things that God creates. As a result, daily husbands are overwhelmingly tempted by evil sight-stimulators. To maintain a healthy conscience, husbands have to do like Job. They have to make a covenant with their eyes to refuse to look at another woman in the wrong manner. Job said, "I made a covenant with my eyes not to look with lust at a young woman."[22] Job knew that he needed to train his eyes not to lust after other women. I remember a time when my husband and I were walking in the mall together. We were best friends before we got married so we had some liberty in the beginning. I would see a nice looking chick and tell him to look too so we could laugh. I knew all too well the attention we look for when we dress a certain way. I know now that doing so was not wise. I should not have called his attention to other women knowing that he was likely to lust after the women we saw. Unfortunately, some women will dress scantly and provocatively around married men. Learning from Job is the key to victory. I like the saying that if I look once shame on you but if I look twice shame on me. Husbands have to resist the urge to look and lust. We all have to train our eyes not to lust after what we see.

The pride in our achievements and possessions is another way the world tries to destroy our marriage. Success can cause us to forget how much we need God. Sometimes, we forget how much we need and love our spouse when we are busy trying to be successful first. There is nothing wrong with us having things. Our issue stems from things controlling us. We have a real problem when our desires for things supersede our desire for God or our spouse. Pride puffs us up to think we are better than others are. Pride always seems to suggest we take the best seat in the house. Pride will trick us into thinking we deserve to be treated better than people we deem beneath us. We tend to forget that our spouse has been there for us in the beginning. Pride makes us have the false belief that we do not need anyone. Sadly, pride robs us of so much. It does not take a rocket scientist to figure out that we do need God and the people He has placed in our lives. Pride will not let us apologize. One of the indicators of maturity is our ability to apologize when we have not done anything wrong. We can apologize for the friction that the incident caused. Pride must be dealt with quickly. We must be humble before God and submit ourselves to Him and our spouses.

Unless we are walking in the Spirit, even when we think we are right we still can be wrong. We find, "there is a way which seems right unto a man, but the end thereof are the ways of death."[23] We may not die but our marriages can die if we do not follow God. We must never put all of our trust in ourselves. Only in God can we do the right things consistently with right motives. We must, "Trust in the LORD with all our heart; and lean not unto our own understanding. In all our ways acknowledge him, and he shall direct our paths. Be not wise in our own eyes: fear the LORD, and depart from evil."[24] Learning to trust God takes careful commitment. God will direct the paths of our marriage if we lean on Him. We may be tempted to follow our own understanding but the flesh will never lead us right. God knows the thoughts He has for our marriage. These thoughts are peace and to give us the expected end that He knows we can have.[25]

A successful marriage is a marriage where two people walk in the fruit of the Spirit because they are Spirit led. Two people walking with God fret not because they stand on the Word of God. The Bible reminds us that, "And we know that God causes everything to work together for the good of those who love God and are called according to his purpose for them."[26] We know that our marriage will work out for the good because we love God. We know we have success because we follow the principles that He has set for marriage. We must stand, "being confident of this very thing, that He which hath began a good work in you will perform it until the day of Jesus Christ."[27] We know that God has begun a good work in our marriage. We know if we follow Him, then He will make sure that things will work out to His glory. We also know that God has a purpose for our marriage. He will enable us to walk in victory. We have confidence in God. We know His ability is not limited by our inability. Success demands that we rely solely on God to lead us and strengthen us to do what He has already declared for us to do.

A successful marriage includes God's way of doing things. Any other way can lead to the death of a marriage, which does not actually have to be divorce. There are married couples that are divorced in their hearts. God knows when we have a hard heart. He knows all things. He wants to help us. The Bible tells us that the only reason God allowed divorce in the Old Testament was because of hard hearts.[28] Divorce is and never was God's intention for marriage. Not all unsuccessful marriages end in the act of divorce. However, some couples stay together but both parties are miserable. Successful marriages are done God's way. His way is reflected in His Word. To understand success is to understand God's Word. In order to be enlightened we must pick up the Bible and ask Holy Spirit to give us understanding of the Word. To experience the Word is a life-changing experience. Holy Spirit is always successful in revealing the will of God the Father. We have to comply with the appropriate actions to what He reveals. We give way to abuse and perversion when we neglect to obey God's way. A successful marriage takes dedication, desire and grace. God is for our marriage. We can have a successful marriage… God's way.

To depict the success found in doing things God's way, let us look at the tables below to see a few comparisons of options we have.

## SITUATION:
Adam had everything set up by the power of God for Eve by the time he got her.

| God's Way | Man should be established, have a job and be responsible prior to getting married. |
|---|---|
| Man's Way | Just get married and figure it out as we go. |
| Woman's Way | Get him and marry him before somebody else does. |

## SITUATION:
God gave Eve to Adam when they were both ready. Adam found Eve after God presented her to him.

| God's Way | Seek God and allow Him to lead you as you find your wife for life. |
|---|---|
| Man's Way | Pick who I want and ask God to fix her after I neglect to seek Him for His counsel prior to marriage. |
| Woman's Way | Find a husband instead of allowing God to help my husband find me. |

## SITUATION:
Adam took Eve as his own flesh and was prepared to take care of her, protect her, provide for her and love her.

| God's Way | Take the wife I have given you and take care of her as you would yourself. Follow My example and be a godly husband. |
|---|---|

| Man's Way | I do not have to take care of her. I am not her daddy. She needs to get a job just like me and work. |
|---|---|
| Woman's Way | I am my own woman. I do not need him to do a thing for me. |

## SITUATION:
Adam and Eve were instructed not to eat the forbidden fruit.

| God's Way | Be obedient and do not eat the fruit. |
|---|---|
| Eve's Way | Disobey God, yield to temptation and misuse her influence. |
| Adam's Way | Disobey God and cause sin to separate all humanity from God. |

## SITUATION:
Adam did not take responsibility for his actions when God gave him the chance to repent.

| God's Way | Agree with God that you have sinned via confession. Repent by changing your actions and your mind. |
|---|---|
| Man's Way | Blame Eve because she made me do it. |
| Woman's Way | Blame the serpent because he tricked me. |

As you can see by looking at these tables, God's way is the best way. It is in the best interest of our marriage to follow Him and His Word into Total Victory.

# Chapter 5
## LET'S EXPLORE LOVE

"I love that man!" Catherine yelled to her mom. Catherine's mom grinned with delight. She quickly remembered the tough situations that Catherine and Karl had just overcome. Karl's business partners were engaging in several illegal business deals. Karl had not directly participated but he had suspected something was wrong. He was not completely surprised when the cops came in to close the business down. He was, however, surprised when they charged him equally. Catherine was a stay-at-home mom. She had recently given her life to Christ. Her faith was strong and she believed God would give her and her family a second chance. Karl went to jail for six months. God took care of Catherine and the children. Catherine stuck by Karl. She believed in him. She knew they would never be the same after this trial. Her love for Karl grew leaps and bounds as she made the decision to remain by his side. Both of them gained a greater appreciation for the love of God and the love they had for each other. They took the limits off and made a decision to explore love in ways beyond their dreams. The love in marriage will be tested and tried. Real love can survive the greatest tests of time and tribulations and produce a desire for more time to express love in magnanimous ways.

## EXPLORING LOVE

Exploring includes becoming familiar with by testing.[1] We can explore love as it relates to our marriage relationship with the intent of making sure we are loving each other to the fullest extent. Exploring invites us to try different things with the desire to establish a pattern of love that produces the greatest result in our marriage. As we explore we learn more about each other. As we explore we find that our ingenuity sparks and we create a pattern of love we can call our own. It can be monotonous because we will continue exploring new ways to express ways for as long as we are here on earth together. I beseech you, friend, start exploring today.

## LOVE THAT SERVES

Agape love is divine love that comes from being directly connected to God through Jesus. The Holy Spirit operates in our lives through agape love. Agape love is the basis for divine love. It is the tangible expression of God's love. The divine love of God is the only way we can selflessly serve our spouse. Agape love sent Jesus to the cross. Agape love is what we use as a basis for following God's commands. Agape love is what Jesus has for us as He willingly gave His life for us.[2] Agape love is the type of love that Jesus is referring to when He says "Greater love hath no man that this, that a man lay down his life for his friends."[3]

He goes on to say in John chapter eighteen verse fourteen, "Ye are my friends if ye do whatsoever I command you." In researching love, I found an interesting point. When God commanded a husband to love his wife, He used agape love. He commanded husbands to love their wives as Christ loved the church. It takes agape love to love the unlovable. We know that Christ loved us while we were yet sinners. Romans chapter five verse eight reminds us that while we were yet in our sinful mess Christ climbed up on that cross and died for our sins. He did not wait for us to get it right. He loved us even though we were blind to righteousness. We have a chance to express that love to our spouse too. Agape love will cause you to die to what you want in order to serve your spouse. It takes agape love for a husband to wash his wife in the Word when she is coming against him in a negative manner. Yet, God requires us to love our spouse with Agape love. The wife must "agape" the husband and the husband must "agape" the wife. We find some of the truest expressions of agape love in First Corinthians chapter thirteen. God never approves of sin so we must be mindful of His holiness. He will never compromise His Holiness and we must learn to follow suit. In fact, to sin for the benefit of your spouse actually hurts them more than it helps them. When you sin for them, you diminish the light of God shinning through you. You ruin your witness of Christ before them. Saying no to sin helps our witness remain strong.

## WIVES EXPRESSING LOVE

I found in the Word that God wants the older women to teach the younger women about how to love their husbands.[4] The Bible shares in the same reference that wives have to learn how to be disciplined enough to love their husbands and their children. The fact that wives have to learn to do so is an indication that a wife does not naturally know how to love her husband God's way. There is nothing natural about sacrificing and serving someone else. Due to our sinful nature, we want someone else to serve us and sacrifice for us. God commanded wives to be submissive as an expression of love. The Holy Spirit will teach wives how to be submissive in all things. The Bible said in Titus chapter two verse four that wives need to learn how to love their husbands. The word used is philandros, which specifically pertains to a wife loving her husband. It means to be fond of, to be friendly towards and to be affectionate as a wife.[5] It actually means affectionate as a wife and the love a wife has for her husband. God created a special love that He wanted wives to learn to have for their husbands because it is not natural. Both philandros and agape love are supernatural.

Agape love is divine. It is derived from loving God. It is our nature to be selfish. God uses our love for Him and our spouses to teach us how to obey Him. As we seek to please Him, we will find that every area of our life will, slowly but surely, start lining up with His will. Instead of a wife using her powerful influence to lead her husband away from God, she will use it to draw him closer to God. A wife that is fond of her husband will seek the Lord about his purpose and pray until she gets a breakthrough. She will build him up and not tear him down. She will encourage him to be all that he can be in life. She will build her house with her words and her actions. This wife will be affectionate towards her husband. A wife that learns the oracles (heart) of God will be a godly powerful source of power that the enemy will not be able to reckon with. She will walk in a place in prayer. That way she can see the enemy's head and cut it off her family's life. She will be able to cut the enemy down each time with precision and clarity because she is in tune with God. It takes a wise wife to petition the Lord, "Father, clean me up so that I can truly represent You. Do what You have to do in me but please do not leave me like this. I want to be all that You created me to be today and every day." We ask God for what we believe we will receive according to our faith in His Word.

## LEARNING HOW TO LOVE

Loving our spouse the way God requires us to will always help us grow together spiritually. Agape love is a fruit of the Spirit. First Corinthians and other love scriptures show us how to allow the love of God to mold us spiritually. Learning to love our spouses God's way will always require Him. He has given us access to Him through the Word of God and Holy Spirit.

Agape is the Greek word for charity or love.[6] Charity is the greatest of all loves. Charity cares regardless of the circumstances. This love is a sacrificial and giving love. First Corinthians is our "Love Road Map". Love begins with God pouring His love into us. We then receive that love and learn how to love God back and love ourselves. When we learn how to love ourselves, we can then love others. We express agape love in deeds not just words. Agape love requires more sacrifice than friendship love or sexual love. Both friendship love and sexual love benefit us directly. However, Agape love benefits the person we love. We are the beneficiaries of God's love because through His expressions (or actions) of His love we were saved from a life of sin and now have eternal life.

Agape love is the fiber of any marriage because it says, "I will give my very best for you and I will die to my selfish will to show you with my actions that I do truly love you." Furthermore, "Love is not what cha say… Love is what cha do". Love is what love does. Love is an action verb. Love without works is dead. Love demands a motto like Missouri, "Show me". Agape love is the love of the Spirit that shines through our actions that we see expressed in the natural. Agape enables us to be a real friend to our spouses. As we allow God to work on us, in and through us we are then able to open up and attend selflessly to our spouses' needs. Agape love enables me to serve my spouse sexually, mentally, socially, emotionally and willfully. It is the expression of the Cross as I lay down my life for my spouse that I get to fully enjoy the benefits of being married successfully…God's way.

John chapter three verse sixteen is an amazing example of agape love. Let us look at it more closely. It says, "For God so loved the world that He gave His only begotten Son, that whosoever believes in Him should not perish but have everlasting life." Salvation is something we do every day. We live a saved life by the power of Holy Spirit. We do what God says to do in His Word. Salvation requires us to obey God and live Holy. It is not just going to church. We live the agape way daily. Now ask yourself, do I really believe? Salvation is not just a decision; it is a lifestyle. Salvation is a direct benefit of God's love.

## LOVE DEFINED

A definition of love according to the dictionary is "to hold dear or cherish; to have passion; to be devoted; to be tender; to take pleasure in; to thrive in."[7] We will look at each aspect in detail as it relates to marriage.

When we love our spouses, we should hold them dear and cherish them. In marriage, we have to learn to hold our spouses dear to us. We must treat them as if we cherish them. When we cherish something, we take good care of it. For example, if I cherish my car I will wash it and keep it clean. Ephesians chapter five calls for husbands to wash their wives in the Word of God. God commands husbands to love their wives. A husband who cherishes his wife wants to do all he can do to keep her in good standing. He wants to keep her looking good on the inside (by the Word of God) and on the outside (by trips to the mall).

Passion for our spouse is evident and expressed in our actions. Having passion for someone includes having a powerful appetite for that person. We express passion by the way we treat our spouse. If we are passionate about them then we will desire to be around them and make them happy. We will enjoy their company and sometimes miss them when they are away. Being devoted to your spouse includes being faithful to them and enabling them to trust you. A devoted spouse will go the extra mile to ensure that the needs of the spouse are met. The devoted spouse will make sure that his or her spouse knows how dedicated he or she is to the marriage. A devoted spouse is dedicated entirely to the success of the marriage by any holy means necessary.

A husband that loves his wife will grow to have the passion of Jesus Christ. That same passion drove Jesus to die a brutal death for us. We are sinful by nature and yet He died for us. As a result, God commands husbands to love their wives as Christ loves the Church.[8] A husband with passion for his wife will do his best to obey God's commands and his wife will follow suit. God comprehends the power of love so much that He commanded the husband to love his wife just as Jesus does the Church. The wife is more likely to submit when love is in the picture. The passion that God gives us for our spouse enables us to love them and continually learn how to love them more.

An expression of love is tenderness. Expressing tenderness is especially important during times of conflict and times where communication is challenging. Wives should be able to appreciate the delicate, sensitive, gentle, loving and fragile way their husbands handle them. Both the husband and the wife should appreciate the benefit of being able to take pleasure in one another. Taking pleasure in your spouse includes being satisfied in and enjoying being with them.

We have been given the opportunity to thrive in the presence of our spouse. We should be one another's biggest cheerleaders. We should encourage each other and foster an atmosphere of success by speaking life at all times. The word thrive means to grow in. A flower thrives in sunlight because without sunlight the flower will die. We must understand that our marriage thrives when we shed the sunlight of love. The more we shine our light, the more we grow. We must allow our spouse to experience the growth of love through our actions and words.

Expressing devotion and tenderness to our spouse is vital to the marriage being successful. Taking pleasure in our spouse is something we have to purpose in our hearts to do when they are not what we deem worthy. Love covers a multitude of sins.[9] We can take pleasure in knowing God is pleased with us for our sacrifice. He is pleased to accept our willingness to obey Him by giving up what we want to embrace what He wants. He desires that we selflessly love our spouses enough to whole-heartedly obey Him sacrificially. Devotion and tenderness are fruits of love. Love is not the feeling we get when we see the person, but it is our action towards that person. Love calls for action. To show how much He loves us, God gave His very best.

When we love our spouse, we are patient with them and we are kind to them. When we love our spouse we do not envy what God does in their lives, but we encourage and push them to go further in the Lord. When we love our spouses, we do not show off what God has given us to belittle them, we do not pump ourselves up to believe we are better than them, and we do not act ugly because they did something we did not agree with. When we love our spouses we are not selfish, easily irritated or easily provoked to anger. Love will enable us to think good thoughts about them even when they do something that appears suspect.

We should think no evil thoughts but believe the best in our spouses. For example, Susie can choose to think good thoughts about Johnny when he comes home late. She can think positive thoughts, instead of thinking negative thoughts. Thus, she must give him the benefit of the doubt. When we truly love our spouse, we do not rejoice when they sin. Iniquity refers to secret sins. Jesus was bruised for our iniquities.[10] Bruises are under the skin and are not always easy to see. We should never rejoice in sin whether it is blatant or secret. However, we should rejoice in the truth as we get to know the Truth. The Holy Spirit will lead and guide us into knowing the truth found in God's Word. We can always rejoice because He is willing and available to help us. True love bears all things and still treats the spouse kind. True love believes good in all things even when it looks bad. True love has hope in all things even when it looks hopeless. True love endures all things even as Jesus endured the cross for our sins. True love never fails. The love of God never fails.[11]

## CASE STUDY

I have a case study that applies to husbands loving their wives: Susan's abuse started when she was a little girl. Therefore, it is to no surprise that she deals with depression, suicidal thoughts and a very low self-esteem. Susan's mom was never married to her father, so he was not around much. In fact, it was her mom's best friend who sexually molested her. Susan's mom never did anything about the abuse even though she suspected something was wrong. Susan never addressed the abuse with her mom. They both act as if it never happened but it did happen. Susan blames herself for the abuse. Susan's mom also deals with strong bouts of depression. Susan accepted Christ as her personal Savior but she never took the time to develop a real relationship with Him. Susan's aunt took over her life and did everything for her.

When Susan got married, she felt like Alice in Wonderland because she did not know what to do. She never had to cook or clean when she lived between her mom and her aunt. The idea of rearing her son overwhelmed her. Susan's husband Jimmy had his own issues. One of his issues was that he had the tendency to blame others for his problems. Susan quickly became the source of his misery. Jimmy verbally and physically abused Susan. Susan felt hopeless and worthless. She wondered what was the point of living a life where the people who were supposed to love her kept hurting her. Jimmy could not love Susan because He did not know how to. Susan needed to allow God to teach her how to love herself and then she could learn how to love Jimmy. Love for God can be expressed by living as He instructs us, obeying His Word and hating sin. Love is more than saying the words "I love you". God gives us access to love. We experience true love only through Him.

## GOD IS LOVE

God is love and the power to love comes from God. "Behold, what manner of love the Father hath bestowed upon us, that we should be called the sons of God: therefore the world knoweth us not, because it knew him not."[12] God has lavished us with His love. His love purifies and cleanses us through the shed blood of His Son, Jesus. God really loves us. He loves us enough to saturate us with His love so that we look like we are His children. God loves us so much that He destroyed the hold sin had on us. Our marriages should look so much like God that the world does not understand it. The world will not understand our marriages because the world does not understand who God is. When the world sees our marriages, they should see the Word of God being lived out.

A husband's prayers may be hindered or not answered if he does not love his wife as the Bible commands.[13] We receive whatever we ask Him for because we keep His commandments. His commandments are to love Him and to love one another. The marriages that keep God's commandments can do so because they live in Him. We live because of Him and without Him; we cannot live as He designed. We find in God the peace and joy that marriages need to survive and thrive. Any marriage in God will prosper. Any marriage in God can have the Holy Spirit in the midst. The Holy Spirit will always lead us in the way of righteousness.

The Bible tells us a lot about love. We can find all we need to know about love in the Word of God. God calls us His beloved because He loves us in spite of our daily mistakes. We fall short daily, but God has chosen to love us anyway. He gives us the command to love one another but we have to obey Him. He lets us know that to love one another is of God. It is especially helpful to know that if we love others then we can rest assured that we are children of God. We must get to know God. That way, we can express His love to others. If we do not love then we do not know God. It is evident that we know God when we love others because God is the manifestation of love. God manifests His love towards us because God sent His only begotten Son into the world, that we might have a chance to live through Him. It is not that we loved God but it is that God first loved us when we were in sin. God sent His Son to be the propitiation (payment) for our sins because we needed it. We could not save ourselves. We should also love one another since God loves us. We have never seen God and we claim to love Him. It is when we love our brothers and sisters that we truly express our love for God. God dwells in us. As a result, He perfects His love in us as we read and meditate on His Word. We must spend time with God in order to be able to express love to His people.

God is love.[14] We do not come into the world knowing how to love. God teaches us how to love others and ourselves in a way that is pleasing to Him. To know God is to love God and His people. There is no way we can know the God of love and not love each other. Some Christians say they love God but their actions say something different. Christians do foolish things at times. Sometimes we act as if we do not know God at all. We act like that because we have not taken time to get to know Him. However, this is not the norm. As a part of the Body of Christ, we should reflect His behavior in our lives. Loving our spouse can be a confirmation that we have taken the time to get to learn how to love God.

To be a Christian and not love our neighbor is not Biblical. God's command is for us to love our neighbors as ourselves. We must serve in love because God teaches us how to love. Some people work hard to make other people happy and at the same time exhibit a strong disdain for their spouse. This type of behavior contradicts God's Word. We must first know and love God. Then He teaches us how to love ourselves. Next, He teaches us how to love our neighbor. Our closest neighbor is our spouse. God's love in us enables us to love others including our spouse. God loved us enough to sacrifice His best for us. We must love our spouses enough to sacrifice for them. If we do not know how to love God then, we must learn how to love Him. Our own righteousness is as a filthy rag.[15] Some people wonder how we can ever know how to love an all-righteous God. The same all righteous and holy God must place His Spirit in us and teach us how to be like Him. Holy Spirit living in us equips us with the ability to love our spouse. If your spouse is not saved, you must cover him or her in grace because he or she does not know how to love you, yet. Our main prayer must not be about our unsaved spouse's actions but about his or her salvation. The Bible commands, "You must be born again."[16] Both spouses being saved can create an atmosphere of harmony in the marriage. Being born again is required to be in God's family. God's love is so pure that it takes unholy people and makes them holy. His love takes unclean people and makes them clean. His love takes unrighteous people and makes them the righteousness of God in Christ Jesus.

Early in my marriage, I just wanted my husband to love me and make me have that gooey feeling of love. I wanted that fairy tale foolishness and it made me disgruntled and unappreciative of him. I found something wrong with everything he did. Some days he wanted to give up. One night the light went off in my mind and this time I got it. I could not believe I was acting like a little girl. I wanted what I wanted and it was not happening. I wanted him to make me whole. I wanted from him what I could only get from God. He was tired of me and I was tired of him, but we still tried to figure out a way to make our marriage work. He said he would try one final effort to make the marriage work. I told him that he might as well keep his last ditch effort because I was sure I was going to mess up again. We tried to talk for the millionth time but to no avail. We only managed to point out each other's faults. We were good at blaming one another without successfully assessing ourselves to see our contribution to the friction manifesting in our marriage. I was fed up because all I wanted was for him to love me my way. I wanted him to consider me. I thought I just wanted to be second to God. I thought I just wanted to have what God said I could have. *However, what I really wanted from him was something I could only get from God.* Only God could make me whole. Only God could meet every last one of my needs.

## LESSONS LEARNED ABOUT LOVE

I thought about giving up because it had gotten so hard but God would not let me. He told me that to give up on Tommy is to give up on Him. We had both really hurt one another. However, all I could remember was my hurt. I kept rehearsing how bad Tommy hurt me. While God had to keep reminding me that we had hurt one another and in doing so we had really hurt Him. I am sure it hurt God to see us acting as if we had no clue about how to make our marriage work when He had given us the Bible as a road map. I am sure it was especially saddening to Him to see how many marriage conferences, marriage books, marriage tapes, CDs and DVDs we had devoured to see no results because we forgot to deal with our personal issues first. How silly of us to try to fix our marriage and neglect to allow God to fix us. I wanted to love my husband unconditionally but I could not seem to get it right. I had a problem receiving God's unconditional love. I had not sowed unconditional love so I could not reap unconditional love. Once I received God's unconditional love, I was able to reciprocate that same love to my husband. I learned to appreciate what my husband did do in an attempt to please me. No, evidently it was not exactly as I wanted but at least he was trying.

The Holy Spirit spoke to me after a fellowship or argument between

Tommy and I. He said that by faith I had to love Tommy without any evidence of him loving me the way I wanted. He revealed to me that love says, "I will, even if you won't". My attitude at that moment was not good. I am sure I rolled my eyes a few times before I submitted. Faith includes loving someone in the hopes that despite not seeing the evidence of the love you desire at that time eventually they will love you the same. By faith we know that if we sow love that we will reap love because God's Word is true. We really do reap what we sow. I was reminded to watch the seeds I sow. When I see fruit manifesting that I do not want I must honestly look at the seeds I have sown. If I want to see peace, then I have to sow peace. Oh, how important this principle is. By faith, we sow what we want to see spring up in our marriage. I could not love my husband the way God designed without God. Only God could do it through me. I had to be willing to step back and allow God to be God through me in my marriage. I realized that no matter what my husband did to me it would never hold a card to what God had forgiven me for doing. Regardless of all I have done, God still loves me. I was not condemning myself but I was remembering how much I need God to forgive me for my mistakes. Sadly though, I kept falling short in my marriage. I said to God in distress, "I don't know what to do." I knew the outcome I wanted but I could not see how it could happen. My husband kept saying just tell me what to do and I will do it. Of course, we had been here before. I did not think his change or mine would last very long. This time he was saying, "I love you. Please help me express it in a way that is acceptable to you. All I want you to do is to be nice to me, to be my best friend again, to support me, to be my help meet and to have my back." He pleaded, "I can't find any peace in my house or with you because it looks like I will never be able to make you happy." Indeed, he was right because he will never give me what only God can give me. He could never make me whole. I did not get that revelation until the next day.

    I said to my hairdresser and very dear friend, "Kim, I just want him to love me". She responded with, "Baby, you want that man to love you like only God can. I have been there baby girl. It took a divorce for me to really see me." She went on to say, "You are looking to that man to love you like only God can. You are spoiled and selfish." Yeah, she put it to me just like that! She said, "I had a good man and you have one now". She went on to inform me that she had never had a song recorded on CD in a studio by her husband for her. My husband recorded a song in my brother's studio saying how proud he was of me for graduating with my Master Degree. I believe that song encouraged me to pursue and secure my Doctorate Degree. In the song he said, "Dr. McCall… Yeah! You can do that too!"

    She said, "YaQuanda, they mess up but they love us." All I wanted was a nice hairdo and I got the truth that cut me deep. It hurt because I love God too much to hurt Him by hurting my husband. In all actuality when we mistreat our spouses, we are really mistreating God. God made our spouses in His image. We should respect them as we do the Lord. I was going to have to do some soul searching. The Bible reminded me that it is the little foxes (things) that could really spoil my marriage.[17]

My mom, Vanessa Y. Williams, told me when I got married that I needed to take good care of my husband at home in every way. She kept telling me how I needed to cook for my husband and just be good to him. I did not want to hear that. I wanted him to take good care of me. The Lord reminded me via the Bible that to love Tommy is to love Him. I made a decision to love that wonderful husband of mine and get what I need from God to be whole. I stopped pulling on him to fill voids that only God could fill. I snatched up those little foxes that kept me from appreciating him. I cooked and was good to my husband. I loved him as God loved me… in spite of me. I thought all I needed was for husband to love me. However, all I really needed was to appreciate the way he did try to love me. As I look only to God to fulfill every need, I thank Him for all the needs my husband does meet as we both grow together in the Lord. Yes, we all desire for our spouse to love us "our way". We must accept that God's way is the best way. We must allow His way to be the only option. In all reality, His way is the only way that leads to true success.

God's love must be in our hearts for a marriage to be successful. "Hereby know we that we dwell in Him, and He in us, because He hath given us of His Spirit."[18] We live in God and He lives in us. We know this because He gave us His Spirit. Holy Spirit is the Spirit of God who lives in us. He is the power that works inside of us to help us love our spouse the way God intended. To expect a sinner to totally love his spouse is like expecting a leopard to change his spots to stripes. It is not possible. "Herein is our love made perfect, that we may have boldness …: because as he is, so are we in this world."[19] The only way our love for our spouses is perfected is through the love of God. God lavishes us with His love. Jesus died because of that love. The Holy Spirit manifests the power of that love inside of us. The reason we can have boldness is simple. It is simple because as Jesus is so are we in this world. We never have to be servants of sin. Jesus never sinned. He is perfect and He perfects Himself in us. He is sinless and holy. We do not have to sin against God by mistreating our spouses because we can be as Jesus is. Jesus is always our model. The world's standards are excessively low for us to deem anything it sets as righteousness. We are like Christ in this world and we do not have to habitually sin. Sin is temptation first. If we denounce the temptation, we reject the sin. We will strive towards perfection until we go to heaven to be with the Lord. If we keep doing our best then God will do the rest.

## FAITH TO LOVE WILL CONQUER FEAR

We love by faith. The Bible says, "There is no fear in love; but perfect love casts out fear: because fear has torment. He that fears is not made perfect in love."[20] This scripture hits home for me. I had such a hard time with fear because I suffered verbal and physical abuse in a previous relationship. I had my hair literally pulled out when a guy I barely knew tried to sexually assault me while I was in college. The fear associated with living in sin overtook me. I lived in fear. I listened to every thought the devil suggested to me. I had not realized the love of God. I walked in fear and not by faith. I had not learned how to love by faith. As I set my heart to learn more about God, His perfect love cast out the very fear that ruled in my heart and in my mind. I believe God's love casts out fear because He knows that fear torments us by what might happen. That fear saturated my marriage. I was so scared of the things that my husband might do that I almost went crazy. I jeopardized my relationship with God in order to keep my husband happy out of fear. I did things for him that I knew was not godly out of fear. I also put my trust in him over God out of fear. I was so afraid when my husband was not home that I could not sleep. I would keep all the lights on. I even slept with a knife by my bed. My fear was in my mind but it seemed so real. The Lord began to reveal to me that He would take care of me. It was still so hard not to be afraid when my husband was away. I did not trust God. I can remember saying, "But God is in heaven! What if somebody comes in to kill me? He is too far away to rescue me." It is funny now but it was not then. I learned through loving corrections from God that I could trust Him. I needed to trust Him above all. Slowly, but surely, I began to trust God to take care of me when my husband was away.

As I realized the perfect love of God and allowed that love of God to cast out fear, I became a new person for God. I walk in a boldness that enables me to believe that as long as I walk with God, I do not have to be concerned by what might happen. Even death has to bow down and obey the God I serve. Because of God's love, spouses can rest assured that fear does not have to have a place in their lives. God perfects us in His love. God is true love and the ability to love is a by-product of Him perfecting us in His love. Having the faith to love is essential to canceling the fear that robs us of true peace and joy in marriage. Faith in God will cause every other fear to disintegrate to the point that it does not negatively affect us in our marriages. Have faith to love, my friend.

## CASE STUDY

Let us consider the case study of Jimmy and Susan that I mentioned earlier. If Jimmy truly loved Susan, he would not beat her up with his fist or his words. Jimmy has veered off from the road that God developed for husbands. Jimmy evidentially does not understand the example that God set. God loved the world so much that He gave of Himself. When we look at Jimmy's heart, we can see that he does not understand how to love his wife. A good way to look at his heart is to look at his actions. His actions will show us what is in his heart. Jimmy is not sure if he is saved. Jimmy is not a part of a local fellowship so he has no real accountability. Jimmy has not allowed Jesus to be Lord of his life. Jimmy does not believe in giving to the poor. He scolds Susan if she uses his money to help others. Jimmy is not affectionate to his wife. He mistreats her and abuses her. Jimmy is a partner of a prestigious law firm. He follows every lust of his flesh including drugs and adultery. His professional career has exceeded his marriage and his life. Everything takes a back seat to Jimmy's career and lusts.

There is hope for Jimmy! He can be born again and filled with the Spirit of God. Jimmy must allow God to teach him through the scriptures. He can let God teach him how to love his wife. Jimmy likes to debate the scriptures and find loopholes. Susan has her own issues in that she has to allow God to make her perfect in His love. The rejection and sexual abuse she has suffered pushes her to seek acceptance from Jimmy and others. Susan does whatever Jimmy says hoping that he will accept her. Susan has often put her relationship with the Lord on the back burner for Jimmy. Susan must grip the fact that God accepts her in Christ Jesus. Susan has not allowed God to make her perfect in His love. Her fears sometimes cause her to lash out at Jimmy. Susan and Jimmy can have a successful marriage if they are both willing to look on the inside into their own hearts. When they look into their own hearts, they must not argue, blame or make excuses, but allow God to clean out the residue left there from sin and lies of the devil. Susan cannot love Jimmy until she learns how to love. God teaches us how to love others. Jimmy will continue to beat up on his wife and habitually sin until he accepts Jesus Christ. He must allow Jesus to show him the way. To love and be loved are blessings from God. Love comes by the working of Holy Spirit through Jesus Christ. We must comprehend that God gives us the power to love.

God is the originator of love. The Lord gives us the evidence of true love. God does not physically take us and give us a new body, a new spirit or a new soul. He saves our soul. He restores or rejuvenates our spirit but we still have our same body. God has not changed. However, since Adam sinned we have a new set of rules in relation to God. Every person alive has the breath of God. The atheist and the non-believer both have life because of God. They just deny that He is the reason they are alive. Consider this example: If I get a sex change, never acknowledge that I was a woman and live as a man, I will still be a woman. Whether or not I acknowledge that I had a sex change, I am still a woman. Whether we acknowledge it or not God's breath is the reason we have life. I went into that to impart into you that there is no true spiritual life without God. Jesus said, "I am the resurrection and the life."[21] Without God's grace there is no physical or spiritual life. He is the power behind all we see and do not see. I drove that point home to say that everything we need to love our spouses is in us via the Holy Spirit. The Word of God and a working relationship activate our gifts given to us by God. We have the components in us to love others. However, if we do not hook up to the Power Source, we can never love the way God intended for us to. God has given us what we need to survive but we cannot do it successfully the way He purposed without Him. We must have a direct link to God by Jesus through the Holy Spirit.

I make this point clear because of a conversation I had with young woman. We will call her Latisha to protect her privacy. Latisha was in her second marriage. Her complaint was that her husband did not love her. She said he could not love her because he does not love God. After I assessed their marriage, I found that he is saved and he has a working relationship with God. I found that Latisha wants from Harry what only God can give her. After talking with Harry, I found that he has the ability to love her but he has yet to do his part because it is uncomfortable for him. Salvation restores us back to God. We have gained access to everything God has once we accept Jesus Christ. As a result, Harry has access to the arsenal of weapons God has to combat not loving his wife God's way. We are naturally selfish and self-serving. God loves our spouses through us because we are not in a place to do it ourselves due to our selfish ways. God has placed a hunger for Him in us. We have a God sized hole in us that only He can fill. No matter how hard Harry tries to fill that hole in Latisha he will not succeed. That hunger she is searching to satisfy can only be found in God and Him alone.

    People spend countless years trying to fill their lives with people, places and things that will never fully satisfy them. They must get to God and get a real relationship with Him. Latisha will never be able to meet all Harry's needs and vice versa because we will always need God for certain things. God fills us and fulfills us. In marriage, there are spousal needs that we can meet. However, these needs are secondary to God meeting our needs. People have a tendency to deplete us. Nevertheless, God consistently restores us. Harry will mess up and so will Latisha, but God will not. He is perfect and so is His love. He is a loving God. God desires for us to love each other. God made us in His image and thus He made us in the image of love. God never took back His image after Adam sinned. I am still my Father's child even when I mess up. I was God's creation before I was saved. Whether you are His creation or His child through Jesus, you are still made in His image. I was created to love and so were you. Love is a big word because God is a Big God. Moreover, to be frank, if He is love then some of that stuff we call love is not really love. Harry must do his part and love Latisha the way he knows how to love her. We must start where we are to get where we want to go. Once he loves her by faith, he can then learn to love Latisha the way she wants and needs him to love her. God will love Latisha through Harry and vice versa. Yes, they will still have obstacles to overcome in life. However, they will no longer be obstacles or pitfalls for one another.

    When God is able to love our spouses through us, then and only then, can we experience the fullness that He intended for marriage. I have some personal experiences that relate to Harry and Latisha. I was saved when I got married but I was not sold out to the things of Christ. I was a carnal Christian. It was still all about me. I was stuck in the "me" syndrome. I wanted to love my husband but I was selfish. I just thought about what I wanted for myself. My focus for a while was, "How is this going to benefit me?" I never allowed YaQuanda to run out so God could step in. All I needed to do was love him the way I knew to love until I learned how to love him the way he wanted or needed me to. I needed to be willing and obedient to God's Word to see His fruit manifest in my marriage and life. I did all I knew to do to love God and my husband and eventually God activated Himself in me. As He was able to fully use me, my husband was able to experience the joy of having a wife the way God had intended.

Most wives have many responsibilities. I remember being too tired to really enjoy quiet time with my husband. I would ask God to give me a stronger sexual desire for my husband to meet his sexual needs as often as he desired. I knew I was not doing as well as I could in that area because I was always so tired by the end of the day. I started to prioritize and make sure I got sufficient rest at night. I realized that it was already in me to meet my husband's needs. After I started from where I was by faith then, I sought God to take me to the next level. Everything God wants to do is in us but it requires us to do something first. Once I submitted to making the sexual desire that God created me with a priority, then I was able to seek God about making it stronger so I could continuously please my husband in that area. Sexual expression is not love. However, healthy intimacy in a marriage is a bi-product of the benefit of marital love. God gave sex to married couples. He gave us sex to express our love and to multiply. It is up to us to work at it to make it pleasurable. Marriage requires effort on both parts. Once we do our part, God does the rest. Yes, we do our best and He does the rest. There is no failure in God because right when you think it is a failure, He takes it and works it out to your good.

## A MESSAGE TO WIVES

God spoke to the wife and commanded her to submit to her husband in His Word. When a husband loves his wife as Christ loves the church, he gets a chance to love that wife so good that she will do anything to please him. Jesus Christ is the best example there is of a good husband. After a husband grasps the fact that he must go all out to secure his wife then he can benefit from her willful submission. When we look at the word submit, we find many expressions of this word. Wives must admire their husbands. They must adore him. They must defer to him, which is yielding and submitting respectfully to him. She must esteem him higher than all else next to God. She must honor him in her actions, attitudes, words and thoughts. A wife must look up to her husband as the man of God he was called to be. A wife can look up to her husband in faith even when he is not yet walking in his God-given call. This wife is a wife worthy to be adored and appreciated. She is a woman of extreme faith. Wives must love their husbands too. God has called us to love our neighbor as ourselves, which includes our spouse. Wives must notice their husbands and compliment them on their strengths. Wives must obey their husbands in faith that no matter what happens God will work it out for their good. Wives must daily pray for their husbands because their blessings for the family are coming through the head. The head of every wife is the husband. God is a God of order. When that husband is in position with God, there is no good thing God will not give to that family.

Wives must commit to praying for their husbands. Wives must continuously praise their husbands and their efforts. Husbands are made in the image of God and they thrive off praise. I do not care if all he does is tie his shoe correctly. His wife had better throw him a "The Best Shoe Tying Man on Planet Earth" party to celebrate him. Praise is the avenue to a man's heart. When he knows he is pleasing his wife, he will keep doing what pleases her as she keeps praising him. A wise wife will see to it that she praises her husband. Wives must prefer their husbands to any other man. Wives must respect their husbands because this is one of his most important needs. A man needs to be respected and reverenced. God made him in His image. As a result, husbands enjoy being respected and reverenced. It helps them feel good about themselves in a positive manner. Wives must support their husbands. A real wife will put on her cheerleader uniform, get her pompoms and shout, "Jesse! Jesse! He's our man. If he can't do it no one can!" Husbands thrive in an atmosphere where they are respected and reverenced.

Wives must venerate their husbands, which includes letting him know by her words and actions that he is worthy of being respected and reverenced. Wives must worship their husbands as their little "l" lord. God is the capital "L" Lord that we all have to worship. However, a wife is wise to honor her husband as Sarah did Abraham in the Old Testament when she called him lord. Wives speak life as they call their husbands lord because that means he has authority. That authority includes calling things that are not as though they are and speaking things into existence. It also includes doing all that Jesus did when He walked the earth. Worship is the simple act of adoring your husband as the image of God that you "see" by faith. Wives worship the most High God by faith. We have never seen God. However, we still worship Him by faith. Sometimes wives may have to honor their husband by faith. God will always help us obey Him. God is faithful and He will bless and honor the wife who honors her husband for His Name sake.

Looking at the case study previously mentioned, we find that the way we are reared does play a part in how we act as married couples. Generally, if we do not make an asserted effort to be different we will be the same in our marriage as our parents (if they were married). Jimmy's mom is very controlling and he does not want to be transparent with Susan because of his fear of being controlled. His fear of being controlled causes him to withhold affection from his wife. Jimmy's dad beat up on his mom too. Jimmy agrees with that type of control, so he tries to control Susan. Out of fear, he does the opposite of what God desires him to do. The love of God can cast out the fears that Jimmy deals with. Susan's fears can be cast out too. Jimmy and Susan can both experience the freedom and peace in their marriage that God intended.

We must agree with what the Bible teaches us as truth to fully comprehend it and live by it. We know the truth of God's love for us by His actions. We may never fully understand how God can love a sinful world like He does. However, we must still grasp the truth that He does love us. Our lack of being able to comprehend how God could send His Son to save a wretched and sinful world does not negate that it is the truth. We must seek God daily to understand what

He has for our marriage and us. God is the foundation of love. He is the expression of love. He is the author of love. He is the editor of our actions. The world is looking to see if we look like Him. When God sees areas that fail to line up to His nature, He reveals those areas to us. He reveals them in an effort to get us to agree with Him and allow Him to change us. When we are married, we owe our spouses the benefit of allowing God to shape us according to His mold. Understanding love is a lifelong journey. We will start the process early in life. However, the Father will continue loving you until the day you meet Him face to face. We must always be aware that God leads us by example. Open your heart and mind and allow God to show you how to love…His way.

Fear cancels out faith. Without faith it is not possible to please the Lord.[22] Love is an act of faith. When we love our spouse, we are saying, "I trust God because He is love. He will guide me into all truth about how to love my spouse." We literally have to agree with God that if our spouse never learns how to love us, we will still love them. Love is a vulnerable place. We must be in God to be under His protection. He will help us see that in order to love others we must first love Him. Having the promise of God in your marriage is not like magic. It requires dedication and hard work. It requires a "by any holy means necessary" attitude. God will honor our obedience to His Word. As we are willing and obedient, we will be able to enjoy the benefits of Him here on earth. Abundant life starts now. God has some blessings for us as married couples that nobody else can access. He has stored up some blessings especially designed to enhance our marriages to His glory. Now that we have talked about love, it is time for you to explore and indulge!

# Chapter 6
## APPRECIATING LOVE AND FRIENDSHIP

"I wish she would just tell me how to love her," sighed Henry. "I have been trying so hard to show her that I can love her. I just don't understand how to love my wife." he interjected. Sitting there with Henry gave me an opportunity to ask a series of questions. I asked Henry, Do you know her love language? He replied quickly, "What is that?" I explained, "That is the way your wife receives love from you. Her love language could be receiving gifts, receiving compliments, non-sexual touches, having things done for her around the house or spending time together. Her love language is the way she feels loved by something you do or say." Henry looked sad for a moment. Then a light bulb went off in his head. "She likes for me to help her around the house and especially with the kids!" he said in a loud tone. From that day forward Henry did his best to serve his wife Diane the way she needed him to serve her. Knowing her love language gave him the upper hand in expressing love to his wife the way that she desired. Do you know your spouse's love language?

## KNOWING WHO GOD IS

As we get to know God, we really get to see a glimpse of who He really is. We can know God by what He does. The more we know Him, the more we can follow His example. We know God to be Elohim. That means He is the Eternal Creator. When we walk in love like Him. He will use us to establish opportunities to lead people to Christ, which creates an eternal place in heaven for them. God expresses His love to us by being Jehovah Jireh. That means He provides for us and meets our needs. In the marriage setting this is also relevant because there are needs that only our spouses can meet or satisfy. Let me come from another angle about how God expresses Himself as love in our marriages. He is Jehovah Nissi, which includes being our victory. God wants to be the victory in our marriages. As long as we are in Him then we are victorious. No matter what or who comes up against us, we can make it because God has guaranteed us victory in His will. He is our Healer because He heals our marriages with His loving presence. He is our peace so much that when the economy is going down the tubes, we can stand together in our marriages knowing that God is going to take very good care of us. We can truly see that God's love is evident by what He does in our lives. Others will see God revealed in our marriages. We too have to make sure that love is what we do and not just what we say.

God has designed many ways for a married couple to enjoy each other. Loving each other the way God has revealed will help keep the marriage flourishing like trees planted by living waters. We can find living water in the Word of God. He is faithful to teach us how to love each other completely. He teaches us how to love one another in spirit, soul and body. To experience God's love through our spouse is a great benefit and pleasure.

A working definition of revelation is God uncovering a truth we could not see beforehand. The root word in revelation is reveal. Revelation is simply the Holy Spirit revealing or unveiling something that we could not originally see. We can read the Word and look at a scripture we have read several times and the Holy Spirit reveals something that we did not see the previous times we read it. Anytime we seek Him for revelation we must be open to Him showing us things that we have not seen before. We must allow God to reveal His heart concerning our spouse to us. The wondrousness of God is that He can take a flawed person and present them faultless before the presence of His glory![1] He tells us that if we cry out to Him and seek Him, then He will show us wonderful things that we had never seen before.[2] These things can include His wonderful plans for our marriage. God has unveiled a way for us to get a clear understanding about loving our spouses completely. We can learn how to love the way He intended through His Word.

## LOVE AND WAR

Jesus Christ is at the right hand of God interceding for your marriage.[3] He knows what you need to be made whole. He is ever before the Father talking to Him about your purpose and destiny. Jesus wants your marriage to work out to the glory of God. Moreover, since God is for your marriage, He is more than the whole world stacked up against it.[4] God reminds us; as long as we are His children, we can win against the world. You can stand strong in your marriage, as long you believe God's Word by faith. There is a place in God where marriages stand that prevents the gates of hell from prevailing against them. The strength behind our power is love. Nothing we do is acceptable to God if love is not our motive. No matter what we accomplish, if love is not the foundation, then we are like rats on a mini treadmill; we are moving but we are not going anywhere. Love empowers us to do the work of God. Love is the fuel behind our power. Worldly agendas can destroy godly marriages if we fail to guard our marriages.

We have to stay mindful that we are at war. The enemy is mad at us for obeying God and getting in the flow of God via holy matrimony. We have to stay fully equipped in order to stay in the flow of the Father. We have to keep our hearts saturated with truth so that we do not believe the lies of the enemy. We have to keep on the breastplate of righteousness so that we do not habitually commit sin nor operate outside the boundaries that God sets for marriage. We walk in peace and not in contention or confusion when we have our feet shod with the preparation of the gospel of peace. We do not get beat up by the wiles and tricks of the devil when we have the shield of faith. We have to cover our marriages with faith. We must believe that no weapon formed against our marriages will be able to prosper.[5] We do not have to worry about people who have spoken negatively about us. Who we are in Christ protects our minds when we have on the helmet of salvation. We do not fall into the traps set against our minds when we know who we are in Christ. We must know who God created us to be. We must also walk after Christ in our marriages. We have to understand that what we do does not take away from or add to who we are in Christ. However, our actions will always reveal what we really believe. Salvation is a gift from God. We do not base salvation on our works. We work the works of righteousness out of relationship with God and as a response to His goodness. This should be the same in our marriages. We do the right things for our spouses because we love them and want to please them. Marriage should change our minds so it is no longer all about us anymore. We have to decide to serve our spouses in response to the goodness of our God. We have to renew our minds daily. We must believe that all things including a successful marriage are possible with God. Prayer is the key to success. Prayer is simply two-way communication, which involves God talking to me and me talking to God. We must learn to seek God for a life that reflects prayer. A praying person will grow to being a calm person who trusts that God will do just what He said. His Word is full of promises for our marriages.

A praying spouse understands we must walk in the fruit of the Spirit. The first fruit of the Spirit is love. We must walk in love as it unlocks the other eight fruit. Love is evident in our marriages by what we do. I believe that love opens us up to the fullness of the expressions of the fruit of the Spirit. It is by having the love of God ruling in our hearts that we can have joy in the midst of a trial. It is having the love of God that enables us to have peace in the midst of the storms and waves of life. Yes, it is love that gives us the strength to suffer long and still be kind. It is love in operation when we can be good to our spouses when they are not being so nice to us. Love pushes us to be faithful to God when we do not see what He is doing in our lives. The power of love makes it possible for us to be gentle. When someone is treating us unfairly or someone is taking us for granted, love empowers us to be kind. It is the love of God in our hearts that permits us to walk in self-control when we are being provoked beyond our natural limitations. Yes, love is necessary for us to see the manifestation of the fruit of the Spirit in our marriages.

We know that there are three parts of man. We are a spirit, we have a soul, and we live in a body. The spirit of man is the very breath of God as described in Genesis chapter two, verse seven. The body includes our hands, feet, head and the other parts we can physically see and touch. The soul of man includes emotions, feelings, passions, intellect desires and the mind. The mind expresses our thoughts and our thoughts become actions expressed through our body. The mind is a powerful entity. God's Word is the standard for our actions. It is by His Word that we know if we are operating in good or evil. The more positive actions we sow, the more positive fruit we will see manifested in our marriages. Our actions based on God's standards of behavior will affect our spirit man in a positive manner. When we obey God, we get the benefit of His Spirit leading us and guiding us into His will for our lives. God is so awesome that He has given us an expression of love that ministers to every part of us. There are several Greek and Hebrew words used to describe love. We have learned about agape and will look at a few more. We find that agape love is what ministers to the spirit man. We find that phileo love is what ministers to the soul.

## NAKED AND NOT ASHAMED

Even today, we can still see the results of Adam and Eve's sin of disobedience. Adam and Eve became ashamed of their nakedness. They were aware of their filthiness outside of God. As a result, they began to try to cover themselves. Couples today are ashamed of who they were in sin. They are ashamed of who they are based on man's standards. Sadly, we are still trying to cover ourselves with fig leaves. From the pulpit to the bar, we see men and women trying to cover themselves. They use scriptures without the power of holiness. They use alcohol, drugs, sex and a plethora of things to attempt to cover themselves instead of allowing the sacrifice of Jesus to do so. As spouses attempt to cover themselves, they in turn alienate one another. They begin to hide behind the fig leaves of cheap imitations of God's glory. When Adam and Eve disobeyed God, they saw that they were naked. They had been naked all along, but they were clothed in the glory of God. When they sinned against God, they saw their shame. They went and sewed some fig leaves together to attempt to cover themselves. We have to get to the point where we are real with our spouses and ourselves about our issues. The couples that attempt to cover themselves are unknowingly resisting the power of God released through Jesus Christ to heal them instead of covering their issues up. Adam and Eve tried to cover themselves with fig leaves but God took an innocent lamb and sacrificed it for their sins against Him. It is the same way now. God has called husbands and wives to sacrifice for their spouses and serve them in true holiness. Selfishness has set in and these couples forget or just do not know about the healing balm found in Jesus Christ. It is a sad scene when a married couple neglects to get in position so that God can present them as one before the presence of His glory. We have to stay in the flow of God through obedience in order to reap the full benefits of walking with Him.

When a couple allows sin to set in and never allows God to cleanse them fully through Christ, they miss a chance to represent God in the bedroom, boardroom and every room that life has afforded them. God have chosen wives and husbands in Christ to represent Him. God knows that people need to see Him in us so that they will believe in Him. We should show our spouses what God looks like by expressing His attributes. God is love. That means we should show them what love looks like. A husband is a wife's representative of God. Her husband should be the next best thing to God. He should be good to her because he loves her. He should get to know her. A good husband will dwell with his wife according to knowledge. He will find out what she likes and what she dislikes. He will make sure she knows that he cares and adores here. The husband that follows the heart of God for his wife will have a special place in her heart. The wife that can represent God when ministering to her husband's needs will also reap the benefits of having his heart fully devoted to her.

We find in the Word of God that the LORD God called unto Adam, and said unto him, "Where are you Adam?" [6] We know by this passage that there was a problem. We can tell sin had set in and tried to hide Adam from the glory of God. It was not that God did not know because He is all knowing. When God asks us a question it is for us to determine where we are. He is usually calling us to assess how far we have drifted from Him.

And Adam said, "I heard Thy voice in the garden, and I was afraid, because I was naked; and I hid myself." [7] Do you see the scriptural correlation of the point mentioned before? Adam had sinned and he tried to cover himself. We cannot fall into this trap. The sacrifice of Jesus Christ is the only covering we will ever need. As husbands appropriate the Word of God they are in fact extending the sacrifice of Christ in their marriages.

And God said, "Who told you that thou were naked?"[8] There were things that Adam did not know or need to know because the glory of God was present. When we get to the point that we want to know more than God does, we have set ourselves in a place of fear. Fear says I do not trust God so I need to know what is going to happen in my life. Faith says I do not know what is going to happen tomorrow but I know Who holds tomorrow! Then God asked Adam, "Have you eaten of the tree that I commanded you not eat of?"[9] Here again is God revealing Adam's sin to him by asking him another question. Adam had directly disobeyed God.

And the Adam said,"The woman that You gave me, she gave me of the tree, and I did eat." [10] It is still the same now as it was when God asked Adam what is this thing that he had done in disobeying Him. Sadly, we are still using Adam's famous response today. Just as Adam blamed Eve and Eve blamed the serpent, so do spouses blame each other for their actions. Men say, "How can I be attracted to her when she does not do this or she will not do that?"They say, "how can I be the head when she will not let me lead or she will not follow me." Let me interject right here that nobody can stop you but you from being what God designed you to be. If God said you are the head of your family then that settles it! No matter who comes against it, it is still so because God said it and that makes it so. We have to stop blaming each other for what we fail to do in response to what God spoke to us.

I hear wives saying, "How can I be attracted to him when he does such and such?" God has given us a way that enables us to minister to one another in His glory. We all have to get in a place in God where we tell our flesh no and shut up! It is by evil design that as soon as you get married, you begin to see your spouse as all they are not. It is at that time that the enemy tries to get you to break your vows because your spouse is not who you thought they were. People change and we have to accept people for who they are outside of sin. We cannot change a person's will but we can stay in the flow of God's will. Prayer gives spouses the power to endure the process of taking two people and making them one in God. We must allow God to show us how special our spouse is. Our flesh will begin to desire everything our spouse is not to lure us into sin. If we are not careful, we will magnify their faults instead of their strengths. God will show us the good in our spouse if we allow Him.

There are many expressions of love. We have discussed agape love in much detail. We will discuss friendship love now and sexual love in the subsequent chapter. Allow God to show you how to love your spouse in the way He intended.

## UNDERSTANDING FRIENDSHIP LOVE

We describe friendship as a shared bond between two people. Friendship is a choice. We choose our friends. Friendships are valuable to human life. Having a friend in your spouse can be amazing. Losing the art of friendship in any marriage can be detrimental. Friendship creates a bond that inhabits some of the happiest times in our lives. Having someone around that chooses to be your friend can help us see the beauty of our individuality.

Friendship can include talking on a regular basis. Friendship within marriage includes thinking good thoughts about your spouse, which inspires you to appreciate them and want to be around them more. Friends are trustworthy. Honesty and truth are the foundation for having a valuable friendship within your marriage with your spouse. Lies will destroy any relationship. Friendship includes believing in each other. Having a spouse that is my best friend is especially helpful when I am struggling with believing in myself. Again, friendship is a choice. We must choose to be friends with our spouse. Friendship includes respecting each other's differences. A friend will love you for you. They may try to help you when you have areas you fall short. However, at the end of the day, a true friend loves you with your flaws and all. Married couples who are best friends must learn to prioritize their friendship. Being available and being there as a friend can really push the closeness we desire in our marriage.

The type of love that ministers to the soul is phileo. This type of love speaks to the mind, emotions and will. This type of love ministers to who we are on earth. Again, we are a spirit that lives in a body and we have a soul. Although Jesus in our Friend, it is not likely that He is going to come down to earth to have a cup of coffee with us when we are having a bad morning. God knows we need a friend so He gives us a few good ones. Our two very best friends should be the Holy Spirit and our spouse. The Holy Spirit befriends us and shows us truth. Our spouses befriend us by being there for us when we need them. The Greek word phileo means to befriend denoting personal attachment, common interest and to be fond of.[11] God knows how important it is for us to have friends and companionship. He made this a part of our intricate make up. God gave us a host of brothers and sisters to love but not all of our church sisters and brothers will be our close friends. He gave us our spouse to be the fondest of us and vice versa.

Our spouse knows us and desires to be with us. There is a personal attachment between spouses. We express this personal attachment in many different ways throughout our marriage. There should be a special bond between a husband and a wife. We define a friend as a person you know, like and trust.[12] God has given us a special expression of love in a friend. This love speaks to our mind or intellect and helps us to make intelligent decisions. This love speaks to our mind and reminds us that we now have the mind of Christ and do not have to entertain every evil thought that comes our way. Oh yes, we need a friend in our spouse. This love speaks loudly to our emotions by caring about our feelings. Our spouse should be able to pick up when we are going through something in our emotional state and speak life to us to bring us back into the flow of God's Word. We do not have to let our heart be troubled. We can trust that Jesus cares for us. That fact alone indicates that we choose to allow things to trouble us. We all can use a friend to help us remember to obey the Word as it relates to our mind, will and emotions.

God gave us our spouses to be close to us. I wrote a song titled, "You don't know me". This song reminds us that only Jesus can know all about us and still love us. He knows our every thought. He knows the fullness of our good, our bad and our ugly but He still loves us. No, He does not love our sinful ways but He loves us. Our spouses should be the next best thing to Jesus. Our spouses should know us and in spite of our faults still love us. They must love us enough to share the truth about us in love. Oh how we need a friend to help us stay on track. We should be able to be transparent with our spouse. This is where sin can come in and destroy our marriages if we are not careful. We are supposed to be naked in how we feel and what we need. However, due to sin sometimes we cannot share our inner thoughts or feelings with our spouses because we are ashamed. We have to embrace the freedom in Christ to be free of all guilt and shame. Once we confess to God and repent which means we changed our mind, we can walk in the forgiveness of God. Sometimes, people will bring up what happened in that past but we have to get to the point where we say, "Look, that happened in the past. I am a new creature in Christ now and I am free to be me in Him!" There are times that we go running to God and He leads us to share our hearts with our spouses but fear of rejection keeps us from obeying Him. There are times that I say Father I need a hug. The Holy Spirit reminds me that He desires to hug me and hold me through my husband but I have to let Him. I have to trust Him to be God enough to protect me at all times.

Fear can interfere with the benefits of love. God has given us phileo love to minister to our soul and our need for a friend. Fear is simply a lie that appears to be real or truth. We find truth in God's Word. The Holy Spirit is the power behind the Word. He gives us the revelation that we receive. He gives us access to the truth of God's Word. Fear robs us of our joy and peace in God. As long as we neglect to trust God and His love for us, we will never be able to appreciate our spouse. We will sleep with one eye open wondering if they are going to betray us.

While there is no guarantee that they will not, there is a guarantee in God that He will never leave us nor forsake us. He will be our very best Friend no matter what. We have to learn to press into God and give our spouse room for error. People make mistakes but love says I love you in spite of your mistakes. I love you as Christ loves me, in spite of me. The expression of phileo love encourages me when I am down. Phileo love ministers the truth of God's Word to my mind when I am tempted to believe the enemy's lies. Phileo will minister to my emotions and give me kind words when I am angry and upset. A friend will be able to remind us that emotions are good supporters but horrible leaders. We must never follow our emotions but follow the Word of God. We may not feel like God is with us but the fact of the matter is that He is with us and He loves us very much.

Phileo love will minister to my will. This is important because God gave us free will to make choices. While we cannot change a person's will we can pray that the Lord's will be done in their lives. When our will is set to disobey God, we need the friend in our spouse to speak the truth to us in love. We need someone to care enough to help us because we evidently cannot see the destructive path of our choice to disobey God. We must learn to build our friendships with our spouses by spending time together and getting to know each other. We just need to have fun with our best friend and enjoy our spouse's company. Our spouses should be our "go to guy" or "go to gal". They should be the person that we run to next to God about our life. We run to God about our spouses as needed. Then we run to our spouses about everybody else. God has given us a piece of Himself in our spouses. We must learn to embrace them as the representative of God. God will not come down to earth just to rub your back in the time of need. However, He has given you the next best thing in your spouse. He has given you a person to hold you and tend to your needs in every way.

We have to embrace our spouse in faith that they will represent God in a manner pleasing to us. God has given us a friend to depend on and we too must be dependable. We must always remember to sow into our marriages what we want to see in our marriages. If we want to see more hugging and kissing in our marriage, then we need to kiss and hug our spouses in faith. We have to live by faith because we are all individuals with a free will. We must respect each other's differences and love each other for who we are. We must never try to change our spouses to fit our mold but encourage our spouse to be all that God created them to be. God has given us a friend in our spouses. Someone to care, to share, to hold, to talk to, to spend time with, to like, to know, to enjoy, and to embrace as a gift from God. God has given us a friend to hold our hands and to speak words of life to our broken feelings. I admonish you to embrace your friend in your spouse and cultivate that relationship to the utmost. You have a true friend in your spouse if your spouse is in Christ. However, sometimes by faith you have to embrace them as that friend until we see the fruit. Allow phileo love to manifest in your marriage through your spouse. Choose your spouse to be your best friend today and enjoy what God has given to you to His glory!

# Chapter 7
# ENJOYING SEXUAL LOVE

Michael sat there feeling very uncomfortable sitting in Dr. Traveler's office. Yarina was equally as uncomfortable but she knew they needed to have this session with Dr. Traveler. Dr. Traveler is a Christian counselor that specializes in helping married couples over come sexual dilemmas that hinder them from having the level of sexual satisfaction they desire. Michael and Yarina both shared their predicament from their standpoint. Dr. Traveler assured them that they could have the sexual fulfillment that they desired. We all experience problems in our marriages but sexual frustrations can be hard to overcome. God was not slack in helping us understand how to enjoy expressing sexual love to our spouse. The Bible has an answer for every issue.

## EXPRESSING LOVE SEXUALLY

God has given us a way to love our spouse naturally and sexually. This type of love is described by the Hebrew word Aheb. Aheb has many different expressions. It is used to depict having affection for one another.[1] Aheb love is applicable in marriage. A husband and a wife can express aheb in the form of kissing, hugging, sexual intimacy, etc. Aheb is also used to describe sex outside of the way that God intended. That lets us know that what God created for good, the enemy can take and use it to destroy us if we fail to adhere to the guidelines set by God. Aheb includes sexual affection. This type of affection is natural. People who do not know God can have sexual affection towards each other. God created us with what we need to be fulfilled His way in our marriage. However, please do not get it twisted; it is possible to misconstrue what God meant to be beautiful by giving into our sinful desires. God designed the body of the man and the woman. We are naturally wired to desire one another. It is perversion when a man desires another man sexually and when a woman desires another woman sexually. It does not take a rocket scientist to look at the makeup of our bodies to see that we are not physically designed to be sexually active with the same sex. God hates the sin but never forget that He loves the sinner. Sexual perversion including fornication and homosexuality are sinful. God isn't glorified when we sin. He gets the glory when we submit to His ways.

God designed us to come together and know one another intimately for our pleasure and His. It is His delight to give us good things. Sexual intimacy in the confines of marriage is awesomely good! Can I get an "Amen" on that? If I cannot get an "Amen", then you need to go back and ask God to help you and your spouse to have the best sexual intimacy you have ever experienced! The enemy deceives couples all the time. He leads them to believe the lie that sex is better when it is sinful. Making love the way God created is definitely a good thing. God in His awesomeness gave married couples a way to express love in the natural. It is one of the aspects of love we can take pleasure in. God gave us aheb so that we could minister to one another in that area.

It must be the joy of heaven when married couples take pleasure in one another as gifts from God. God desires to pour His joy into our hearts about our spouse. God wants us to be satisfied sexually in our marriages. God was very specific when he told us through Apostle Paul not to defraud each other or hold back sexual intimacy from one another.[2] God knows that sex is an expression of love when it is expressed in the marriage bed. I have learned that when I counsel couples I can tell a lot from asking a few questions about their sex life. The details are theirs to keep but I can begin to tell where they are in their marriage by their expression of love in the form of making love. If a woman does not desire her husband then there is a problem that needs to be addressed. If a man does not have a sexual connection with his wife consistently or at least desire to do so, then there is a big problem. Sex is a major need for a man. God designed the man to need a release in that area. I believe it is to make sure that men and women stay grounded together and produce life. Only a man and a woman together can produce life. Men need to have sex and that is why it is vital to any marriage that couples express sexual pleasure on a consistent and frequent basis.

God gave us the power of knowledge by informing us that Satan will try to destroy us if we do not have sex and have it often. God designed the man to release and the woman to receive. If either spouse is not releasing or receiving what they need at home, they could be tempted to fulfill their needs somewhere else in some form or fashion. I am not saying that every time a person does not want to have sex with their spouse that they are indulging in adultery. However, I am saying that God designed men to release. There are single men and special circumstances where as, God can help men keep that area under wraps as needed. Nevertheless, if there are no Biblical reasons for the couple not to enjoy sex then that is a vital area that needs remain healthy. A woman needs to be loved according to her design. If she does not get it at home from her husband, then she could be tempted. Again, I am not saying she will have a natural affair but in her mind she may begin to fantasize about getting her needs met or something of that nature. God designed the marriage bed and the union of marriage to meet needs. He is a Spirit and He is holy. Aheb love is an expression of how good He is to us to meet every need and give us pleasure in the process.

## LESSONS FROM AHEB

We find Aheb used in Hosea chapter two verse five when Gomer decided to leave her husband and go back to her lovers. These men brought her sexual pleasure and gave her things. They took sinful pleasure in her body that was on reserve for her husband only. She violated the temple of joy that God created for her husband. Her body was only for her husband to indulge and enjoy. She committed adultery. Gomer took something God gave her and perverted it for her own sinful desires. Naturally, we can be just like Gomer sometimes. We take the blessings of God and use them to our shame instead of His glory. Gomer was not satisfied with her husband. Therefore, she went out and was humiliated by the men she chose over her husband. Sadly, we find ourselves indulging in similar activities. Husbands and wives that commit adultery will find themselves in a mess of humiliating shame. They find that after they have indulged in the sinful pleasures of their flesh outside of the will of God, they have nothing to show for it. Satan always takes what God created for good and uses it in a way that God never intended. In Hosea chapter two verse seven, Gomer realized that she had nothing but thorns. After she had run into many walls of despair and chased down lovers who meant her no good, she realized that she was better off with her husband. It happens like that much more than it should. After spouses go out and see that the grass is not "greener" on the other side, they come running back home to mama or papa. Sometimes there is nothing left for them to run back home to. Oh! How we do God the same way. We do our own thing and enjoy our own way and when we hit a brick wall, we go running back to Him. He is so faithful to forgive us and take us back but that is not always the case in marriages.

  Biblically, divorce is granted because of adultery and hard hearts. Many times we believe the lie that the grass is more green elsewhere. Passionately, we chase behind a false picture of happiness. We would do much better to realize that our grass can be just as green on this side as it is on the other side of the fence. We just have to follow directions and take care of our own grass. Taking care of our own marriage is the key here. When I think of Hosea and how he had to love Gomer after she had rejected him and embarrassed him, I think of how much I appreciate God for loving me in spite of me. I am so thankful that He saved me from my life of shame in sin. I have found that God still requires some spouses to remain faithful to unfaithful spouses. It is relational and based on what God is doing in that marriage. I say to my brothers or sisters that have had to deal with the hurting effects of adultery: "Press in to the Father and allow Him to give you a heart like His". God is a forgiving God and we too must forgive. As I said when adultery has taken place, it is an individual decision based on a couple's relationship and walk with God as to whether they should stay together. God has used many husbands and wives as bait to save their spouse. No matter what or who, follow the heart of God!

  We use aheb love to express sexual love and the overall love between two people. The fact that it includes affection is what we must understand. God designed aheb to minister love from the husband to the wife as well as in other relationships. We express it between family members too. Each manner of affection is different based on the relationship rules that God set. For instance, Charles has affection for his mom that he does not have for his wife Taylor and vice versa. While aheb is the term used for affection in marriage, it includes affection shown in many types of relationship. The expression we are referring to is as it relates to marriage. I show my husband a different expression of aheb than I do my earthly father. You can minister aheb to your spouse by being tender towards them when they are going through. You can minister aheb by stimulating them with your actions. Sexual expression should be fulfilling to each spouse. We must learn to love our spouses the way they desire sexually and physically. God's design for married couples is for us to have affection for one another and express that affection through sex and other ways like passionately kissing and hugging. God reserves this type of affection to be expressed sexually between married couples only. God does not dwell in sin.

In the Bible, aheb is used to describe the love Isaac had for Rebecca.[3] Isaac was Abraham's son. Abraham is called the Father of Faith. When the Israelites would speak of God, they would call Him the God of Abraham, Isaac and Jacob. Who Isaac married was very important because he and his wife would be very instrumental in what God planned to do in the lives of His people. It was very important that he loved his wife and in a way that we can relate to. He could not love her with the agape love of God because the Holy Spirit had not come yet. He had to love her with aheb love. This was the essence of love in the Old Testament. It engulfed all that love was at that time. We have so much more now because of Jesus Christ and the Holy Spirit. Oh, bless the name of the Lord! Aheb is the love Jacob had for Rachel.[4] Aheb is the love Leah yearned for from Jacob.[5] The power of sexual desire is so strong that Jacob was willing to work for fourteen years for the woman he wanted! The fact that Jacob had sex continuously with Leah but did not love her as Rachel shows us that sex happens all the time without the connection and affection that God originally intended. We can pay attention to life now to see that fact as well. Even though Jacob married Leah, he could not love her the way she wanted him to because her father tricked him. Jacob's uncle tricked him into marrying the sister of the woman he wanted.

For many years, Jacob had tricked other people. However, the day came for him and will come for all when we reap the very things we have sown. Many of you cannot make it in your marriage because Satan has tricked you. The devil has been lying to you about your marriage. He is telling you that you married the wrong person. The enemy is telling you to throw in the towel and go get another one. However, let me tell you this, if you leave as you are and get married again, you will still have the same problem because the problem is you. If you will stick it out in your marriage and believe God, then He will blow your mind with restoration power! I stopped by to tell you that with God, you can take your troubled marriage and He can give you the marriage you desire. All you have to do is pray and obey.

## BUILDING SEXUAL INTIMACY

In marriage we have to remember that our body is not our own. We honor God by allowing our spouse have access to our body. Yes, we are busy people but making sure that we are properly connected is important. Marriage requires us to make sacrifices of other things to make sure our spouse is satisfied. Love-making should be good for both of us. If there are any issues, we need to communicate to one another.

Some sexual pointers are: build each other up sexually; serve each other sexually; make each other priority; stay faithful to building a friendship and encourage one another for marital and sexual growth. Eve and the temptation of the tree give us an example of how Satan tries to trick us. She never tasted the tree but believed it was good. Satan tried to get us to believe that what we cannot have is good. I have found that one of the tricks of the enemy is to remind us of all the faults, mishaps and mistakes that our spouse has made. If we find that we are being bombarded with negativity we need to assess our atmosphere. We need to start speaking the Word of God more in our marriage. We have to keep excitement and expectation going for one another emotionally and sexually. The enemy cannot win if we speak words of life over our spouse. We can combat the negativity that comes to our mind with thoughts of peace and good things about our marriage. We all have issues and that's why marriage is designed to be a safe place. A place where we can learn from our mistakes. Marriage is to be a safe place where we can find encouragement and comfort when we need it the most.

Remember wives, men are sight stimulated. They like to see you looking good. Find out what your man likes and do it. Do not forget to keep dating alive in the marriage. Even if you have to do it at home, do not forget to date. Keep up the pursuit in faith and fun. Keep learning more about your spouse and the things they like to do. Look for ways to pursue them. Show them that you are still madly in love with them. Do not become bitter and barren like Micah. Micah was bitter because of her father and her husband. She chose to be bitter. We do not have to be barren. We can produce anything we desire. We simply have to work together and see our goals happen. Forgiving one another will keep the atmosphere of the marriage free from unnecessary weight. It is hard to make love while trying to carry a lot of unforgiveness and bitterness. Deal with it and let it go. Do not let bitterness hold up the blessing God has for your marriage and especially in your bedroom. Sex is bigger than physical enjoyment but it is a spiritual reservoir of power, agreement and unity. Build up in your mind how much you want your spouse before you see them. Think about him and think about her. Put it out there for your spouse so your spouse knows you are thinking of them sexually. Keep marriage and sex fun! Do not let the monotony of life rob you of fresh ideas and fun in your marriage and in your sex life.

My husband and I teach marriage classes. We have been to countless seminars and conferences. We had to take what we learned and apply it to our lives. It was easy to learn and take notes, but it wasn't so easy changing our minds from what we had established a pattern of doing prior to learning new ways. Whenever we teach about sex, we have fun and make sure we touch on the hard issues that can be problematic in marriages. We like to us the acronym *S.E.X.* to talk about sexual success in marriage.

S - "Serve" Serving each other will make our times of sexual connection more intimate. As we serve each other during the day, we can build a reservoir of good emotions that help in the bedroom during the night. Of course, preferences and schedules play a large role in sexual intimacy. We have to learn how to serve one another cheerfully. As God loves a cheerful giver, so spouses love a cheerful server. Making love to your best friend is easier than making love to your worst enemy. Sometimes I think we forget our spouse is our friend. As friends, we seek to encourage one another. As friends, we know how to serve each other. Of course, sex does start in the kitchen. Husbands can initiate some good loving by helping wash a few dishes. Wives can jump start some good sex by dressing up the way their husband loves them to. Learning to focus on our spouse will make our marriages and our beds more fulfilling. Serving each other during sexual intimacy helps us to focus on our spouses being pleased. This is a key to sexual fulfillment for both the husband and the wife. Exploring different avenues can equal a pleasurable fun time together.

*E* - "Explore" Asking questions is vital to understanding what makes anyone happy. We especially need to ask our spouse what makes them feel good. We should inquire about things they like. "If you don't ask then you won't know" is a true statement. Exploring different options is good too. Many good Christian books can assist us in finding fresh new ways to enjoy our sexual time together as husband and wife.

*X* - "X! Marks the spot" Knowing your spouse's hot spot can come in handy during your time together. Being knowledgeable about what makes your spouse tick shows them that you are interested in making them happy. Knowing this can help them get in the mood when it is time for coming together. Let your spouse know you are interested in making sure that your sexual time together is good for both of you. Serving is the key that unlocks the gates of ecstasy in the marriage bed. Asking questions keeps the gates open. Here are some sample questions:

    1. How can we improve our sex life?
    2. Do I please you?
    3. What are some ways I can please you better?
    4. Do I serve you when we make love?
    5. How can I serve you better?
    6. What are some things we can explore together?
    7. What is that "X" spot for you?

Asking these questions communicates to your spouse, "I'm willing to listen and learn honey, so I can please you as I serve you..." This is a very important part of marriage.

Teaching the kids to respect the Sanctuary is very important. The marriage bedroom should be a sacred place. It is essential that parents teach their children to respect the boundaries of the bedroom. Teaching the kids something as simple as knocking before they enter will teach them to respect your privacy.

You may consider putting a sign on the door that says, "Do Not Knock Unless It Is an Emergency." Of course, you will have to clarify your definition of emergency. Changing the bedroom into a sacred place for coming together is important. Adding some flowers here or there or naming your room 'The Garden of Eden' can go a long way in setting the mood of the room. The marriage bed is undefiled and we have to keep the devil out by not allowing him to ride in on us through wrong thinking and sin. As we protect our marriage and our marriage bed, we can see the victory that God has for couples who love and obey Him. The benefits of following Christ are worth being serious about applying the Word of God to every area of our lives. You may consider keeping the intimacy schedule up for you and your spouse to look forward to indulging. Making the days of the week "speak life" could be fun and beneficial. You could consider, More of You Monday, Terrific Times Tuesday, Wedding Night Reloaded Wednesday, Talk to Me Thursday, Free Fun Friday, Sexy Saturday and Sacred Sunday and add flavor to the weeks ahead.

## LESSONS FROM YADA

Let me mention one other Hebrew word that is relevant to our study. We express Yada, which in English means to know or to experience. It is the most intimate relationship between a man and a woman that we express sexually. We see in Genesis chapter four verse one, Adam knew Eve and they produced children. This word was used throughout the Old Testament. This word was used to represent sex. It is amazing to me that the word they used literally means to know or experience. It is good to know and experience your spouse. When you know them, you get to experience a place that was created and reserved for you. It is true that in these days many people are stealing out of the temple of God. Every time a person has sex outside of marriage, they are stealing out of the temple. Our bodies are temples for the Holy Spirit and every time we have premarital sex or commit adultery, we are robbing God. We are stealing out of His temple.

In order to enjoy the full benefits of sexual intimacy within our marriage, we must seek to know God. Once I realize how much God loves me in spite of me, then I can really serve my spouse the way he deserves. We deserve the best because God gave His Son for us to enjoy His blessings to His glory! We should be in a place in our marriage where we can enjoy our experience of sexual expression with our spouse. My goodness, it takes a lot to stay saved and do right. As a believer, I should be able to enjoy my time with my spouse. For goodness sake, we have to learn to spend less time bickering and more time loving. We fight the devil but we love our spouse. We can get the purest blessing of marriage as we experience our spouse the way that God intended, which is in the fullness of His glory. I admonish you to experience your spouse tonight like never before. Set the stage and enjoy one another in the beauty of holiness. Make it a night truly to remember.

# MORE ON SEXUAL INTIMACY

Let me touch on a very important subject, "sex versus romance". After a lot of research, we have found that sex is physical for most men and emotional for most women. When a man has sex, it is generally external and produces the desired effect. However, when a woman has sex it is tied to her emotional state. I believe that sex starts before we get in the bed. I say that because women usually respond better to husbands who are in touch with their emotional needs. When a man helps out around the house, he is saying I want to serve you. A woman has to give her all to her husband when she has sex with him. She is a receiver so she has to take what he is releasing. This is not just sexual but in every area, women are receivers. We take a seed and produce a baby. Women take many things and produce a larger portion. That is why men must be very careful to treat their wives with respect and honor. If you reach out to her in the kitchen and tell her how beautiful she is and how wonderful she makes you feel, then you can reap the benefits from that in the bedroom. I will refrain from going too deep, but I do hope you get the picture. Sex is one of the four top issues that cause problems in marriages to the point that a counselor is needed. Sexual fulfillment is important.

Sexual intimacy is more than what we do. It is not a tool to be used in negotiations. It is a gift from God. In order for us to enjoy sexual intimacy, we must work on the quality of our sexual encounters with our spouse. Most couples complain about the frequency but if you beef up the quality, then you will see the quantity increase. The increase will be based on our desire for one another. Most men can have sex at anytime. He can do it faithfully after an argument, during an argument or with an argument brewing. He is wired for sex and has no problem most days getting in position for some loving. The problem we encounter is that his wife does not feel loved by him, so she is not interested in having sex with him. I am just going to be real for a few minutes. Husbands have to romance their wives to get the full benefit of her body. Participation is the best part of sexual encounters.

Romancing includes sharing your personal feelings. Romance your wife with flowers, notes, candy, fun trips to the mall, email, encouraging words, and any way you can think of that she likes. If a husband does not set the stage for sexual intimacy with expressions of complements, adoration, appreciation, exhortation and every other "ation" that it takes, then he will miss the full benefit of her accessibility sexually. His wife must know that he cares about her and not just her ability to satisfy him sexually. Just listening to her can sometimes put her in a place that both of you can enjoy the rumble in the hay. Sexual intimacy is set up all day long. Husbands must learn to follow the Spirit and make that call to their wife just to say I love you and adore you. When a wife's heart is set on her husband, she will set the stage consistently for her husband in ways that he still cannot get out of his head. Women have a great sense of creativity. Women can set up an experience of sexual pleasure that causes a husband to think on her all day long. This is a gift from God.

Sex within marriage can be a key to long-term success. The way we connect sexually says a lot about our personalities, commitment and desire. When we connect sexually, there is a lot of communication taking place. We can ruin intimacy when obligation becomes the reason why we have sex. Having a desire to connect sexually is important in marriage. It is important because our desires depict what we want and whom we want to be with. If we continually neglect our spouse sexually, then we are saying I do not want to be with you. This rejection can send a message that we desire to be with someone else. Men are hard wired by God to need a release sexually. Ladies, having a mindset of "just get it over with" may meet his physical need but it may not minister to the whole man. Most people want to be with someone who wants to be with them. We have the responsibilities as wives to make sure that we do our part to make sex creative and fun. Husbands, I will say this to you, the song goes like this, "And we know how the story ends." We know how the sexual connection is going to end. Husband, your wife needs you to make sure that she gets to the finish line before you do.

We have to ask ourselves what we like about having sexual intimacy with our spouse. If we really want to make the sexual connection pleasurable for both of us, then we need to communicate about it. If I like to have long foreplay with my spouse and he does not know it, then we are going to have an issue. I must communicate to my husband in a loving way what I like. If he likes being with me and I like being with him, then we will make sure we spend time together. If I like having sex with my husband then it will be priority for me. For example, I like a cinnamon flavored candy called Hot Tamales. Hot Tamales are a priority for me every time I go in the store. I actually go looking for them. If I cannot find them I will go ask an associate where they may be located. Surely, my spouse should be more important than candy! Nevertheless, intimacy in marriages suffers because we do not communicate what we like for fear of rejection or ridicule. Learn to expect a good time with your spouse. Eventually, your expectations will become your reality.

A woman likes to spend intimate time with her husband. Romance is not necessarily sex for women. Spending intimate time together that does not end up in sex is a key to wives enjoying time with their husband. Again, communication is the key and we have to be bold in marriage. We have to ask our spouse sometimes whether they enjoyed our time together. Men may fear this but it is important. Ladies may fear it as well. Nobody likes to be rejected. However, communication is the key to a solution. Asking your spouse, "How can I please you?" is a sign of maturity and selflessness. Sexual expression in marriage is like a box of chocolates. The variety is all the fun. God has given us the green light on enjoying each other's body. We just have to do our part. We need to want to be with our spouse opposed to feeling obligated. We have to share with them ways to make things better. We need to make intimate time with our spouse a priority. We need to be willing to ask how we can please them.

Here are some pointers that can help you spice up your intimate times together. Remember to add variety and keep it fresh. Come up with new ideas and have fun. Change it up sometimes and be creative. Communicate and express what you like and do not like. Make it a point to stimulate yourself by thinking on your spouse in stimulating ways. The mind is one of the greatest sexual organs. Set the scene in your mind but be open to enjoy the flow of the moment. We have to be careful not be locked on a certain way because that can blow the moment of sexual creativity. Take the time and address whether there are problems in your communication and your ability to be frank with your spouse about sexual issues. Remember that sexual intimacy is about you pleasing your spouse. You must be careful not to be caught up in your own satisfaction over your spouse's opportunity to enjoy you. As you serve your spouse sexually and your spouse serves you, then you can enjoy each other more. The wrong place for being complacent is in the bedroom. Do not let your bedroom be a room of boredom. Keep the spice alive to the glory of God! Always expect each time you come together to be exciting and invigorating!

Husbands caress your wives and talk to her. Wives put on something sexy and prance around your man. Men are sight stimulated and they like to see you looking sexy. Husbands, wives are words stimulated. If you talk to her then you can enjoy her. All the serpent did was take time to talk to Eve and she gave up her spot in the Garden of Eden. Husbands must learn to communicate openly and freely with their wives. She is hard-wired to talk and she has been talking for a long time. It is in our best interest to set up times to just talk and get to know each other's heart. We must be open to touching one another at anytime. Taking time to touch during prayer and touch while talking or watching T.V is a proper way to set up wonderful sexual expressions. Just be open to hear your spouse and do what they want you to do. If the Holy Spirit is not checking you about it, then go forth in the power of Christ and enjoy each other to the glory of God. Husbands must romance their wives. Wives must not resist their husbands. God has given us the benefit of sexual intimacy, but it is up to us to make sure that we enjoy it. We must learn to be sensitive to the oracles of God governing the pleasure of marriage reflected from the heart of God as it relates to us being sexually intimate. As we stay within the bounds of holiness, we will truly experience the fullness of representing God in the expression of sexual intimacy. God is concerned about every aspect of your marriage. He has ordained sexual intimacy to be as pure and satisfying as food to the body. Let us enjoy every blessing afforded to us by the Most High God. Let us enjoy our spouse to the glory of God!

## VESSELS OF HONOR

God wants us to make love within the confines of the marriage union. This is evident because He spoke about it in His Word. He created male and female to be married and make love to one another. God then is able to get the glory when we make love with our spouse. God's glory shines through us spiritually as we partake of the holy communion of sexual pleasure expressed between a husband and a wife. Pay attention because this really helped me and as God began to give me the revelation, I tuned in. Wives this is for you especially. God showed me that when I am making love to my husband I am a vessel of honor for Him. I didn't really understand it at first. But I comprehend it much better now. When God created Adam He made sure that Adam's every need was met. God was Adam's friend and they communed together in the cool of the day. He could meet Adam's spiritual needs because He is God. However, there was one need that God could not meet because He is a Spirit. God could not meet Adam's physical needs, mainly his need for sexual expression. So, what did God do? I am so glad you asked and I am glad that you are still reading this book. God put Adam to sleep and performed the first open body surgery and pulled a piece of "Himself" out of Adam and created Eve. God gave Adam "Himself" wrapped up in flesh (Eve). Remember that God breathed "Himself" into Adam after He formed him from the dust of the earth. God was the life on the inside of Adam. God pulled Eve out of Adam to do a work for Him. God was the power behind Eve's very existence. She was to do a work that God, "Himself" could not do. Eve would be able to make love to Adam and fulfill his physical needs. Eve was Adam's wife. God created Eve to be his helpmeet. That included making love to Adam to fulfill his physical need. Initially, that was all she had to do until they sinned. All she had to do was keep Adam satisfied and focused on what God had created him to do. However, she entertained a talking snake and got Adam off course. Unfortunately, some wives are still following in Eve's erroneous footsteps by talking to snakes and getting off course.

Ladies, do not roll your eyes at me just yet. God created Eve to be a helpmeet for Adam. She was to assist him in his endeavors to obey God. Let us just look at what the Bible tells us. Adam was formed by God to do a work. Adam did not have a helper suitable for him so God created Eve to assist him.[6] Eve had a job to do when she was presented to Adam. It was not about Eve getting what she wanted but about her taking care of the man that God had created her to be with. If more wives would take the time to seek God about their husband's purpose and help him fulfill it, we would have less friction in our marriages. We would definitely have less competition. Eve was taken from Adam. Therefore, she was there to complete him. She was his rib and if a man finds a wife, then he finds a good thing because she is his missing rib. She completes him in ways he cannot even explain. She knows him and she pushes him to do what God called him to do.

One day the devil comes to Eve about this forbidden tree. Let us please be aware of the corrupt flesh we live in. The flesh loves to sin. The flesh loves to disobey God because the flesh hates God.[7] When God says no, your flesh says yes. The enemy will try to plant seeds of doubt in our minds. He does that to make us doubt what God said. We have to know without any doubt that He has spoken to us about our marriages. By faith, we must fight to see that what God said has the platform to manifest in our lives for His glory. We have a part to play in the things that God does in our marriages.

Temptation is set to destroy us by luring us one sin at a time away from the holiness of God. The devil tempted Eve and she bit the fruit. He set the trap and instead of adhering to God, she listened to a voice that was not God. Wives, you must be careful not to listen to any voice that is not of God. Whenever the Lord speaks, His words will line up with the Bible! What Adam did was far worse than Eve. Adam had a direct relationship with God. It was God and Adam alone at first. Eve was deceived but Adam made a conscious decision to disobey God. Adam should have known better than to listen to his wife and disobey God. You see when Adam sinned, he introduced sin to the seed that would come after him. The seed of man is why the enemy fights men who love God. The devil knows if he can get men to sin and walk in disobedience to God, then he can corrupt their seed. One thing is for sure, Eve was successful in one area God gave her as a wife. She had made such good love to Adam that he was willing to forsake all to keep her happy. Wives, if you can walk in a piece of the influence that Eve had on Adam for the glory of God then you can see the true fruit of God in your marriages. Making love to your husband is a gift from God that gives you an influence in his life like none other. That is why fidelity is so important! I admonish you to stay faithful to one another and to God.

Seriously, God has given each wife an opportunity to make love to her husband for His Glory. It is a need He wants met in man. It is amazing to me that God used His image to form a woman and gave her to Adam to have as his own. If we could simply get this revelation, our sex lives would be off the Richter Scale. There would be real fireworks in the bedroom because God would be included in the plan. If every wife could look at sexual connection with her husband as a chance to make love to the glory of God, then we would see less dissatisfied husbands and more satisfied wives. God took out of Adam what he needed and put it in Eve. Eve was not formed from dirt as Adam was. She was designed to meet his needs. She was hand made by God for Adam. Eve was made with the breath of God already breathed into her because there is no mention of God having to breathe life into her like Adam. God hand-designed Eve and gave her to Adam to represent Him. Wives, how are you representing God in your marriage? When God presented Eve to Adam, it was all eyes on Eve! Adam's response was, "Wow! This woman looks good and she is all mine." I can hear Adam saying, "I cannot wait to minister to her over there by the waterfall!" Actually, he said, "This is now bone of my bone and flesh of my flesh."[8] Adam took immediate ownership of Eve. She must really have been representing the Lord. We know Eve was top of the line because when it was time for Adam to choose to obey God or follow her, he followed her. She was a bad girl, a brick house, a foxy lady and Sunshine! She was all that and a bag of chips. It is only God the Most High that can bless you so good that you even consider picking the blessing over the Bless-er! Adam recognized that Eve was his personal gift from God and he was ready to meet her every need. The problem set in when pleasing her became more important than pleasing God. Do not fall for that trap, man of God. Always obey God in the fullness of His Word no matter what, who or where. God is your Source of life. Obey Him at all costs!

## ENJOYING EACH OTHER

Adam did not have parents so when God told him to leave his parents and cleave to his wife He was talking to us. Adam had already forsaken God and got out of position to indulge in the famous scene where he bit the forbidden fruit. Now, here was God letting us know that in order to be successful in our marriages, we have to let go of our parents and cleave to our spouses in a way that enables God to make us one. We become one flesh in the physical when we have sex with our spouses. When we grasp the fact that we are now bone of our spouse's bone and flesh of our spouse's flesh, then and only then can we truly be naked. I am referring to being physically naked now. Adam and Eve were physically naked but they were covered in the glory of God. That is how marriages should be now. We should be naked before one another physically and not even give it a second thought.

Sin is the reason we encounter wives who are not able to be naked physically before their husbands. The shame that sin created in women is what makes her want to cut the lights off while making love instead of allowing her husband to feast his eyes upon every part of her glorious body. Hear me out because this is serious. Men are sight stimulated and that is why Adam went berserk when God presented this fine, foxy and very naked woman to him. He was like Whoa mama mia! If he were here now he would give God a shout out and a high five because baby must have had major back, front and side-to-side. Adam was well pleased with his helpmeet. She would help God meet his every need in a major way. Now let us get back to being naked wives and not ashamed. Men have to cover their wives as God did Eve so that wives can be free indeed. Whenever, I encounter a wife in counseling that is not able to be naked physically with her husband I find one or several of these scenarios to be true: 1. She is still carrying some shame or guilt from her past and has not allowed God to set her free. 2. Her husband has neglected to cover her past. 3. Her husband has covered her and she has failed to receive it.

Getting the root of why a wife struggles to give herself totally to her husband is important to the health of the marriage. As wives leave being little girls and mature they get to enjoy the responsibility of being a great helpmeet for their husbands. Husbands have to be mindful not to run away from the hard issues of finding out why their wives are struggling because together a couple in Christ can conquer anything.

The enemy comes into our marriages to destroy every aspect of them. The enemy knows that if he can keep us from expressing the type of love that ministers to each aspect of the man and the woman, then we will never fully reap the benefits of a God-directed marriage. God performed the first marriage ceremony and presented Eve to Adam as his wife. Sin set in and made ugly what God made beautiful. God made the body of a woman so intricately beautiful and desirable for man that it is a shame for him not to be able to enjoy her. God made the breasts round and the body shapely. God created the love box of the wife that hides the love cable of the husband. I pray that we will one day allow God to put us back in the protection of His glory. His glory covers us and allows us to enjoy one another. The marriage bed is undefiled.[9] The word used to represent undefiled is the same word used to describe Christ after He rose from the dead. You cannot be in God and defile the marriage bed. The Holy Spirit will tug on you if you even remotely attempt to be led away from the holiness of God. Let us learn to enjoy loving one another is spirit, soul and especially body!

## THE WARNING

Proverbs chapter five is a serious passage of scripture. While it is clearly written to a man, we can apply it to women as well. Being sexually pure has no gender bias. We have to protect our marriages from the evil that seeks to tear our marriages apart via sexual immortality.

> *Drink water from your own well—share your love only with your wife. Why spill the water of your springs in the streets, having sex with just anyone? You should reserve it for yourselves. Never share it with strangers. Let your wife be a fountain of blessing for you. Rejoice in the wife of your youth. She is a loving deer, a graceful doe. Let her breasts satisfy you always. May you always be captivated by her love. Why be captivated, my son, by an immoral woman, or fondle the breasts of a promiscuous woman? For the Lord sees clearly what a man does, examining every path he takes. An evil man is held captive by his own sins; they are ropes that catch and hold him. He will die for lack of self-control; he will be lost because of his great foolishness.*[10]

The wisdom found in this passage of scripture is enough of a warning for every marriage to have a strong sexual love bond. Ladies, we may look at this verse as applicable to the men but we must also beware of temptations that lure us away from sexual purity in our marriages. Let us build and strengthen our sexual love bond on purpose to the Glory of God!

# Chapter 8
# MEETING YOUR SPOUSE'S NEEDS

"You never meet my needs! You are selfish and all you think about is what you need. I'm sick of this marriage and frankly, I am sick of you!" screamed Alana. Of course, Oliver was outside and too far away to hear her words of frustration. He had already stormed down the driveway to walk the dog. Alana and Oliver were arguing again about meeting each other's needs. Alana wants Oliver to be more affectionate. Sadly, Oliver does not know how and he is not willing to learn. Oliver believes the wife should do all the house chores. He believes he should be able to have sex anytime he feels like it. As I counseled this couple, I shared with Oliver that if he assisted his wife emotionally, she would be more willing to meet his needs sexually. He was reluctant to allow me to counsel them because he feared his wife and I would "double-team" him with women stuff. He could not have been more wrong. I am on the side of the marriage. I want the marriage to work so I looked for ways they could both meet each other's needs so the marriage could flourish. Unmet needs can be a constant source of conflict.

## THE IMPORTANCE OF MEETING NEEDS

We can trace our actions back to what we understood to be truth or fact. We express whatever we grasp as truth in the things we say and do. We can trace our actions back to what we think. What we think reflects the principles that we have grasped as truth. The sad thing is that marriage is one of the most important decisions we will ever make. Yet, it is one of the least explored and least researched areas of our lives. We go to school for years to learn how to do a job. However, when it comes to understanding the truths and principles behind a successful marriage we do not necessarily have a school to attend.

Only God can meet all of our needs. Philippians chapter four verse nineteen reminds us, "But my God shall supply all your need according to His riches in glory by Christ Jesus." Our spouse cannot meet all of our needs. One of the erroneous beliefs we bring into marriage includes believing that our spouse will meet all of our needs. Setting our expectations too high will cause unnecessary frustration. We are setting ourselves up for disappointment when we do not place our expectations on God. Of course, there will be needs met by your spouse. However, we will experience greater joy and appreciate the efforts of our spouse if we remember that God will ultimately make sure He meets our needs. He will impress upon the husband to do his part. He will impress upon the wife to do her part. We cannot make our spouses do their part. However, if we intentionally meet the needs of our spouse and sow that seed, then we will reap the harvest of having our needs met.

The Bible will teach us what we need to know and understand about marriage. We are wise to seek God's Word for counsel on all things. Our marriage should reflect the truth of God's Word and be an example of God's special love. Marriage in itself is supposed to be unselfish. Spouses are supposed to serve one another. Nevertheless, men sometimes have the wrong attitude while they are in the process of looking for a wife. Women also have the wrong attitude while waiting for a husband to find them. We say things like, "I'm going to find me a good man." or we say, "I'm going to get me a good, saved wife that can cook". We have failed to consider what we need to bring to the table in terms of being a blessing for our future spouse as well. What we should say is, "I can't wait to get married because I have studied, prayed, and I have all my bills paid so I can be an asset to my future spouse." We have to change our attitude to one of gratitude to the Lord for blessing us with a spouse. As we remember to be thankful, we will not neglect to take care of our spouses. It is when we stay in a place of me, me, me that we neglect to take care of the needs of our spouse. Sometimes, we are so busy looking to get our own needs met that we neglect to do our best for our spouses. Meeting the needs of our spouses must be a priority in our lives because they are our ministry. Before I could serve my Pastor as I so desired, I had to make sure I was serving my family at home. Before I was able to serve others in God's house I had to make sure I had committed to serve my spouse to the best of my ability.

    We can find clues to the state of a marriage by the way a spouse responds to praise of his or her spouse. If you get a look like they just tasted some sour lemons, then you wonder if something is not going well in the marriage. If they light up in total agreement, then we know that their spouse is taking care of them to their satisfaction. No, we cannot live our lives in the shadow of what our spouses think. However, they spend the most time with us and usually know us the best. Therefore, beyond their issues they would be good at attesting to at least the facts about our behavior patterns. We have to do our part to make sure we meet our spouse's marital needs. We have to make sure we are not living a "Dr. Smeckle" and "Mr. Jive" life that does not line up with the Bible. We have to get serious about our ministry to our spouses because if God cannot trust us to serve the needs of our spouses, why would He lead us to serve anyone else? Serving is selfless and we must learn to do all that we can do to serve our spouses effectively.

    Our spouses are gifts from God. Even if Jody does not do everything right, then the least Suzie can do is serve him in faith that he will eventually adhere to the plan of God. If she sows service, then she will eventually reap a harvest. Faith without actions does not work. If I believe that God is going to teach my husband how to love me according to my needs then by faith I need to love him according to his needs. There is another choice, we don't have to fall into the trap of the enemy and give up on our marriage. We should consider serving our spouse by faith. We should trust God to make our marriages work with the help of the Holy Spirit.

    There are essentials that the body needs to live. When we do not meet our physical needs, the body slowly begins to die. The same principle applies to marriage. When we neglect the needs of the each other in marriage, the marriage begins to die. There are two people in a marriage with individual needs. We must have these needs met. If the body does not get water, then the person will suffer from dehydration and eventually die. If the body does not get food, then the body will starve and eventually die. Let us look at how this applies to marriage. We must give our marriage the water of love, peace, joy, kindness, gentleness, affection, affirmation, support, truth and patience in order for it to live. We experience dehydration when we are deprived of water. Water is a required element for life. I will use the analogy of dehydration in the body as it relates to neglected needs in a marriage. Neglected needs in a marriage cause a disturbance in the marriages flow just as dehydration does in the human body. When needs are not met it causes harm to the integrity of the marriage just as it does to the human body. Increased stress and negative effects are also included when dehydration begins to set in a marriage.

    Couples that respond in negative ways to one another will decrease the character of the marriage. Let us look at this process closely. A disturbance in the marriage's flow stops the marriage from growing. When trash is in the sinkhole, the trash stops the water up and the water gets dirty. Marriages that are not growing are dying. Every effort must be put forth to continue the flow that enables growth. God's plan for each marriage is unique. It is tailor made for each couple. The trust level plummets when harm is done to the integrity of the marriage. When a wife all of the sudden starts lying, she risks not being trusted to tell the truth. When the wife opens the door to being a liar, the next door may be adultery. Now she has caused a rip in the trust of the husband. The wife has now made a place for the devil in her marriage. The enemy now can kill the marriage, steal the joy and destroy the integrity of the marriage. We must guard the marriage from dehydration with God's help. Jesus is the living water. He wants to help marriages be successful in the way God intended.

    Increased stress on any marriage begins the process of demise. Stress in the human body causes all sorts of problems like high or low blood pressure. Couples must take care of their marriages as they would their own bodies. Two individuals come together to compose the organism called marriage. Negative effects on the marriage include arguing, cursing, fighting, not trusting, not communicating and a host of other things. Simply giving the marriage the attention it deserves and meeting the needs of each spouse in the marriage can offset these negative effects. Paying attention to each spouse's needs is the way to ensure that no needs go unmet or ignored.

    Signs of unmet needs are similar to signs of dehydration. Signs of dehydration include dry mouth, nausea, and headaches. Instead of dry mouth, couples speak to each other in a dry manner. Instead of nausea, couples may claim the marriage makes them sick. When couples badmouth one another, they say things that can destroy the marriage. Couples sometimes hold back affection and sex from one another. Instead of headaches, the spouses claim they did not use their head when they got married. We must hydrate the marriage regardless of what symptoms are present and stop the marriage from drying out. Marriages need the hydration of the Living Water. Jesus is the Living Water and He wants to help marriages stay wet with purpose. He wants marriages to stay wet with compassion and affection. Jesus wants marriages to live. God intended for marriages to grow and flourish like trees planted by rivers. When we plant a tree by a river, the tree gets the nutrients it needs to live because it is connected to the Source. God is like the river and we need to plant our marriages in Him to keep them growing the way He intended.

Sometimes couples get wants mixed up with needs. We do need food but it does not have to be a steak in order for us to meet the need of hunger. Eating some oatmeal could have the same effect. Couples must be very mindful not to call what they want a need. Being verbal and communicating what we need is wise. Most needs of men and women are very different from one another. The Bible says that God will give us the desires of our hearts.[1] He did not say that our spouses are responsible for giving us the desires of our hearts. In order to get what our heart desires in our marriage, we must be delighted about what God wants to do in our marriage. We must trust God and we must direct our expectations toward God, because He is the only one who can fulfill them all. God is the only one who knows the true desires of our hearts. He is all knowing so He knows what we desire and what we need. He is all-powerful so He can do it.

God can give us what we need and want if we dedicate our lives, children and marriages in Him. Dedicating our lives to God includes living for His pleasure. Dedicating our children to God means to raise them to His glory and for His purpose. Dedicating our marriages to God includes loving one another and respecting the Spirit of God that lives in our spouse. God had to rebuke me one day. When God rebukes us, it is to correct us. Oftentimes wives rebuke their husbands the wrong way. The best way to rebuke anyone is to do it in love, humility, meekness and with the Word of God. Rebuke means to correct. It does not mean cut down or beat down. God had to rebuke me because I called my husband names and I used to attempt to fight him physically if he made me mad. God let me know that it was "Him" that I called a name and it was "Him" that I tried to fight. I have repented and I have been very careful of what I say. Many times, we are not whole so we respond negatively in our marriages. God wants us to be successful in our marriages. When we allow our hearts to get hard, we make room for divorce.[2] God gives us soft hearts and He saturates them with plenty of forgiveness, grace and mercy. God wants us to live in the freedom that Christ died for in our marriages.

## THE NEEDS OF THE HUSBAND

Meeting the needs of each spouse is equally important. Husbands have different needs than wives. Some expressed needs of the husband are Sexual Fulfillment, Respect, Recreational Time, Physical Attractiveness, Domestic Support and Admiration. I will describe each one below.

*Husbands need proper sexual fulfillment.* God created men with a strong sex drive. It is physical for them. God has made provision for the wife to meet the sexual needs of the husband. A wife is wise to recognize the negative effects of withholding sex from her husband. Not meeting a husband's sexual need gives place to the devil. If God established that sex is an important component of marriage, then so should wives. Understanding that sex is a need for a husband should help wives be more available to their husbands. Marriage is for adults. When I am counseling married couples, I let them know from the onset that marriage is not for children. We have to be mature and make it work.

*Husbands need respect.* I have consistently found that husbands need respect and they want respect. Respect is a need and as the wife realizes how essential it is to her husband, she will treat it like water and make sure there is an abundance of it. Respect is a deep admiration that can build up a man's confidence in his abilities, value, and achievements. A man can tap into his greatest creativity and power when he gets respect. A wife is wise to esteem her husband in the highest. She can respect her husband by giving him the attention he deserves. Husbands do not like the idea of splitting the attention they need with cell phones and children. Wives should respond positively to their husbands. Most husbands do not like their wives comparing them to other men. They desire respect and honor for the man they are. A wise wife will celebrate her husband's intelligence by honoring his choice to be married to such a great woman. As wives celebrate their husband they are giving themselves props because they chose to be his wife. When a wife loves her husband for who he is, then and only then will she begin to really appreciate and respect the greatness that God had hidden in him. Respect is the key to any marriage being successful.

*Husbands need recreation time* and to have some fun that takes their minds off their responsibilities and pressures. They need to be able to do something that takes their minds off their everyday lives. Going out to eat or just a few hours without the children can ease a husband's mind. Husbands enjoy their wife's sense of humor. Life is very demanding for a man and he needs to be able to steal away with his wife and get a good laugh. Husbands like to have fun with their wives and they like to hang out with the boys. Watching sports or playing golf with the guys gives the husband some relief. Some wives do not like their husbands to do anything without them. A wise wife finds out what makes her husband happy and complies. Sometimes a woman will get married hoping she can change her husband. The chances of that happening are slim to none. A wife must accept a husband for who he is. A wife makes place for the enemy when she tears her husband down with criticism hoping she will change him. A husband needs praise for who God made him to be. A wife praises her husband for the good things he does, accepts him for who God created him to be and prays about the issues that she knows he needs help with.

*Husbands need their wives to look beautiful.* Men are sight stimulated. God wired men to like to gaze upon women. It is not a sin when men are stimulated in the proper confounds of marriage. A husband needs his wife to look beautiful. He wants to gaze upon her beauty. A husband needs a wife that believes in her own inner beauty. She must know that God made her special and especially for her husband. It really throws a husband off when his wife is always putting herself down or comparing herself to other women. Husbands want their wives to be intelligent. This only means that he desires her to be willing to learn and apply what she learns. A husband needs a wife who understands her God-worth. Her God-worth is in the fact that God loves her so much that if she were the only sinner on earth, He would have sent Christ to die for only her. Yes, husband's need a confident, secure woman. They desire that the wives do their best to look and be their best.

*Husbands need a dedicated wife that makes sure she takes care of her house.* A wise wife may have to stay up late or get up early but she will not neglect her responsibilities in the home. Husbands need a comfortable and well-kept home. In other words, he needs the house to be clean. A wife who is also a mother has to make special adjustments to her schedule to ensure that the house is clean. The husband may understand sometimes but he needs his castle to be clean. Stepping over dirty diapers after a long day at work will rub him the wrong way. My mother-n-law, Ladonna Fennell, shared a nugget with me early in my marriage. She instructed me to make an announcement when my husband came home. If I were on the phone, I would say loudly, "Girl! I have got to go my King is home!" I would say it with emphasis on King. He loved it then and still loves it now.

Wives have to be persistent. Husbands who work all day in stressful jobs do not want to come home to a stressful house. Husbands need tranquility and a place where peace welcomes them at the door. Again, a wise wife will put the children to bed on time or put them in their room when daddy gets home so he can have some time to unwind. Bombarding him before he can even get in the door can rob him of his desire to look forward to coming home. Stress kills intimacy and causes husbands to have physical problems as well. Wise wives understand that husbands do not need to be boggled down with stressful environment all day at work and then at night when they get home. A wise wife know whether the kids screaming "Daddy! Daddy!" is plus or minus for her husband. Some fathers enjoy that type of welcome, while other fathers prefer a different quieter welcome home. Neither preference diminishes the father's love for his children. A wise wife is well aware of that. We understand that wives work outside the house as well. This can be stressful. Wives cannot use that as a reason not to meet their husband's needs. This is the time that we have to come up with creative ways to meet our husband's needs. Working outside the home and handling the needs of the home is not an easy task. We celebrate wives who successfully manage their jobs, households and marriages. Husbands and wives have to learn how to be effective in their marriages.

*Husbands need admiration.* God made husbands in His image and likeness. God loves praise and so do husbands. God loves praise so much that

He created everything for His glory. Husbands are just like that, and they want their wives to build them up and lift their spirits when they are down. Nobody likes being torn down with criticism and negative comments. Wise wives give their husbands permission to fail and they let their husbands know that they are for him. Both spouses will make mistakes but that should not diminish the praise-worthy attitude the wife has toward her husband. Giving husbands the permission to fail can be a prelude to one of the greatest successes in his life. Praising him will increase his creativity and cancel his fear. Wise wives know to encourage and praise the behavior they want to see repeated by their husbands. Praising the husband is included in the call for submission.

The Bible calls for wives to submit to their husbands just as they submit to the Lord. No one wants their spouse to just tolerate them. We tend to gravitate to people who celebrate us. Word to the wise: Celebrate your husband and you will see the greatness in him explode for the good. Husbands like admiration for the things they accomplish. Admiration is regarding your husband with sincere wonder and approval with the highest esteem. An admiral is the second highest rank in the Navy. A husband needs to be the Admiral in your life, which is second rank highest to God. You must admire him and hold him in high esteem. Strong admiration will open up the creativity in the husband. When a husband gets admiration from his wife, he feels good about himself.

A wise wife understands the power of admiration. A husband needs to be first priority next to God in his wife's life. He must know that when his wife loves God that God comes first. Nevertheless, he wants to be next. Wives who are mothers and have a job have to juggle a lot. A husband wants his wife's attention. He needs to know that regardless of what is going on that if he needs her then she is there. Wives who are mothers have to use wisdom. They may have to put the children to bed early so they have time with their man. A wise wife knows that even if she has a lot of juggling, she needs to make sure her husband knows that he is first priority outside of God. I have witnessed husbands that do not know God become jealous and enraged about their wives relationship with God. Wives must stand their ground about the Lord and use wisdom along with caution when dealing with a husband who does not understand the love she has for God. A husband needs to know that his wife is dedicated to him. He needs to know that she will be around regardless of what is going on in her life.

## THE NEEDS OF THE WIFE

The needs of the wife are equally important as the needs of the husband. Here is a list of the needs of the wife that I found by researching and surveying wives: Wives need their husbands to Love them Entirely, Affection (Non-Sexual Touches), Conversation, Honesty, Financial Support and Family Commitment.

*A wife needs her husband to love her entirely (romantically, emotionally and spiritually).* This is the hope and desire of every young girl. We train young girls from an early age to anticipate the day that they will have a storybook wedding and a husband that will love them with passion and romance. A wife can rest when she knows that her husband loves her. Loving her completely entails striving to love your wife via her body, soul and spirit. When we get to know our spouses, we can meet their needs and love them the way they need and desire love. A husband must strive to be more passionate about his wife. He must be intentional about the way he expresses his love to her. It is upsetting sometimes to see how some husbands pour more passion in watching a football game then showing their wives how much they care about them. I have sadly witnessed husbands take more joy out of taking out the trash than showing affection to their wives. Generally, this is an indication that the wife has disrespected the husband in some manner or he has not learned how to show affection.

Husbands need to woo their wives. They also need to seek after their wives in a romantic manner. She may enjoy candlelight dinners (even if they are at home), a back rub, a massage, a large portion of your check or whatever it takes to make sure that she knows without a shadow of a doubt that you love her. Love is what love does and wives need a husband that will do what love does in every manner of the word. Now, we understand that some wives are selfish. A selfish wife chooses not to be satisfied with what their husband does. It is at that time a wise husband will sow love and pray. He is wise because he understands that prayer will change him as God works on his wife. Nobody likes rejection in a marriage. A good husband will do all he knows to do to love his wife the way that God has commanded him to.

Wives need their husbands to love them emotionally. They need touching, caressing, hugging, kissing and romancing. They need to be touched in a manner that is pleasing to them and their husband. They need to have nice things said about them. They need to be hugged and for no reason at all besides the fact that they are loved by their husbands. Wives need kisses that do not always lead to sex. Again, they need romance. A husband has to seek after his wife in a manner that lets her know that she is still the apple of his eye. She needs a husband to love her spiritually. Praying together is a great form of spiritual intimacy. Even having personal devotions and Bible Study at home is good spiritual intimacy. Husbands are encouraged to have special time to spend with his God and his wife.

*Wives need to be touched for reasons other than sex.* Wives are emotional beings and God created them that way. Generally, based on the research, sex is not a top priority for women but non-sexual touches help them feel good about themselves. The husband who hugs his wife has a better chance at making love than the husband that demands sex. Women need to be touched outside of sex. A wise husband will dwell with his wife according to the knowledge by adhering to her need for plenty of non-sexual touches.

*A wife needs open communication in her marriage.* Women love to talk and they talk a lot more than men do. Husbands have to learn to indulge in conversations with their wives. A wife needs to be free to talk about anything with her husband. A wise husband makes time to spend talking with his wife.

*A wife needs honesty in her marriage.* Having a husband of integrity is very important to the woman of integrity. The wife who longs to please God should long to please her husband as well. Integrity includes the husband being incorruptible. The only way to be incorruptible is to be in Christ Jesus. The blood of Jesus gives us our righteousness and integrity. Integrity involves trust and a wise husband will ask God to teach him how to be a man of integrity. Wives need a faithful husband. Faithfulness is a fruit of the Spirit. A wife wants to know that her husband is walking with God. It gives a wife comfort when she knows that her husband's walk with God is real. A wise husband will ask God for faithfulness if he does not think he has it. Faithfulness is not always automatic. Some couples have to learn how to be faithful. Faithfulness sustains the fibers of a marriage's purity. Sin destroys marriages and being faithful is the first step to denouncing sin's access to destroying the marriage.

*Wives need their husbands to be committed to the marriage and the family.* A successful marriage requires commitment. A wife needs to know that when the going gets tough the husband will not leave the marriage. Wives whose fathers abandoned them really need to know that their husbands are in the marriage for the long haul. Being committed may mean that the husband may have to give up a few wants to take care of his family. Nevertheless, a wise husband will communicate commitment to his wife in his actions and with his words. Wives need to know their husbands are committed fathers. Parenting can be tough, and it is wise to share the responsibilities of parenting with her. A wife needs a family oriented man. A wife who is also a mother has to know that her husband is committed to the wellbeing of the family as a whole. Since husbands are single until they get married, they have to learn to be family men. A family man includes the children in his life. A family man commits his children to God because he knows the power of God's love. In order for a man to be a true family man, he must be in the family of God. God teaches His sons how to be fathers. A wise husband will seek God and ask Him to teach him how to be a family man.

*Wives need to know that their husbands are going to secure them with what they need (Financial Support).* God made Adam first and gave him a job before Eve came on the scene. Security includes knowing he will not leave because he is fully committed. Security also includes the husband doing his part to insure that he takes care of his family. I am a stay-at-home mom. As a result, I know what it means to depend on my husband for everything. I realized that God is my Source but He uses many resources. My husband's businesses (we owned several pharmacies) are the resources that God uses to make sure we have enough money. God will never contradict His Word. His Word says that He will meet all of our needs.[3] We will never have to worry because God will take care of us. A wise husband will make sure his wife knows that he will take care of his part at any cost. I have learned to appreciate my husband maintaining things that need to be fixed around the house and keeping up the yard. I usually help him fix things but

I need him to do the things that I cannot do. A wise husband will maintain the things around the house that fall under his responsibility. Designating responsibilities is a wise decision in marriage. This small act can cut down on disagreements about who does what in the marriage. Just because Henry mows his yard and takes out his trash does not mean that James has to. James' wife may not have a problem at all taking out the trash because she knows James travels a lot. We have to be careful not to try to make our marriage fit in some imaginary mold. Communication is the key in all things that are successful.

## COUNSELING EXAMPLES

What we need must be verbally expressed to our spouses so that they know what we need them to do. We have to be specific. For example, I would say, "Honey, I need you to accept me. I hate rejection. Please figure out a tactful way to correct me in love. I need your acceptance. I know I need to be corrected and rebuked at times but please help me walk out of this issue I have with rejection". I could also say, "Dear, I need your approval. I need to know that our relationship is important to you. Please help me by prioritizing us and our time together." I have said to my husband "Baby, I need your attention. I like it when you pay attention to me. I need you to think of me. I need you to be concerned about me. I just need you to call me sometimes." We have to express these needs to our spouses the way that they like us to. For instance, we can eat out together, run one another baths or take a shower together. We can go for a walks around the neighborhood, send an email or text just to say I love you or help with house and yard. We can also give each other back rubs. Saying with your actions that we love being around our spouse can do wonders in our marriage.

While, we do not have to attempt to be God and meet all our spouse's needs, we should do our best to be there for them in ways they need us to be. Again, there is a difference between needs and wants. We all have to be careful not to put our spouse in the prison of meeting our needs all the time without us considering their needs. God is the only one who will meet all of our expectations according to His Will, Word and Way. We must learn to give our spouses our very best and a lot of grace. Grace says you may not deserve this, but I will give it to you because I love you. We all need a lot of grace when it comes to being there for our spouses. We all make mistakes but we should also learn from them. When we fail to meet our spouse's needs that are well within our ability, we cause a rip in our marriage. We cause our spouses to look at us as though we do not care about them. They may respond negatively to our lack of doing our part. We must do our best and follow the Spirit.

Here is an example; Paul is struggling to meet Vanessa's need for acceptance because he deals with anger. In his anger, he tears her down with his words and he is never home. She feels she is never good enough for him. She also feels that he just is not interested in being with her. He spends more time at work than with her. He hardly has anything good to say about her. He always does things his way and never considers her. They went to Dr. Jones for marriage counseling. Dr. Jones first addressed the immaturity of Vanessa. She said "always" and "never" too many times which lead Dr. Jones to believe that she was over exaggerating. We have to be careful of using always and never because usually we are over exaggerating a point we want to get across. After she dealt with Vanessa, Dr. Jones found out that Paul does pay Vanessa some attention but he does not pay it to her the way she would like him to. Vanessa was mad, upset and ready to take it to the next level. However, Dr. Jones helped them sort through things. The doctor explained to Vanessa that she needed to grow up and get in a position to serve her husband. Paul worked 10-14 hour shifts so that she could stay home with her four children. Then Dr. Jones asked Paul why he thought it was necessary to make negative comments about his wife when he was called to cover her and assist her in fulfilling her destiny. After consistently coming to their sessions, because both parties were willing to change they saw drastic change for the good and a more harmonized relationship. They were both willing to meet each other's needs. When we willingly neglect to meet each other's needs, we set our marriages up to fail in that area.

When people have needs that are not met they do crazy things. They become very controlling, they can become depressed, hooked on drugs and/or have affairs. They have low sex drive (that alone is enough for husbands to meet the needs of their wives) and they become very short and downright critical. They develop health and weight problems because they either eat too much or do not eat enough They overdo things, exaggerate, do things to get attention, get mad quick and express anger in unhealthy ways. They oppress others and do many other crazy things we do not have room to list. Unfortunately, when needs go unmet the issue of conflict arises. This conflict can be avoided or at least minimized if spouses would simply do their very best to meet their spouse's needs.

In order to meet their needs, they must go to their spouse and ask them how they can meet their needs the way they need them met and be willing to comply. Marriage is for mature adults. Children want their way and refuse to compromise. As married adults, we must grow up and be mature. Things will not always go our way but we should be mature enough to recognize when our spouse is trying to comply and compromise. Some things do not come natural and the supernatural power of the Holy Spirit has to help mold us into the person our spouse needs us to be. Our spouse at that time needs to have wisdom enough to pray and stay out of God's way. Marriage is a sweet, wonderful, invigorating experience when we do it God's way. Let us do our very best to meet our spouse's needs, be quick to apologize and be willing to comply with changing our ways to meet their needs according to the leading of the Holy Spirit. In addition, for your information and revelation, He is calling you and leading you to comply as long as it does not cause you to sin.

There will have to be some personality checks. You must be careful not to fall into the trap of your spouse's attempts to change you in a way that God never intended you to be. If I am bubbly and cheerful then I can find a way to meet my spouse's needs without becoming melancholy and gloomy. We have to be mature enough to recognize that we can meet our spouse's needs without becoming someone that God never intended for us to become.

## CASE STUDIES

Justin likes Latasha to show him a lot of attention. Latasha is an ordained minister that travels all around the world preaching the Gospel. Justin demanded that Latasha stop preaching, stop all that faith talk and be a quiet little lady that lives in a shoe. Latasha was confident in herself and knew she could not stop preaching. She knew that she was a woman of faith. She was not the little quiet lady that lived in the shoe with all them darn kids she didn't know what to do. Latasha did know what to do. She set up a candlelight dinner with her husband and explained her call to him. She expressed concern for his feelings and she compromised by offering to cut down some of her volunteer work to make sure they had a date night every week. Justin was not being insensitive but he was angry and felt neglected. Latasha realized that she has not done all she could do to make him feel less neglected. She had not done her best to meet his needs. Latasha complies without drastically changing who God called her to be and does her very best to meet Justin's needs.

Tawanda would like Jesse to support her school aspirations by being there to help with the kids as she studied for school. Jesse traveled a lot. His job required him to travel at least two weeks out of the month. Tawanda, Jesse's wife, demonstrated an ungrateful and unthankful attitude towards him. She wanted Jesse to find a job that enabled him to be home with her more often. She was not considering that she was a student and had not contributed to the finances of the marriage in over three years. She was also not considering that if he did get another job then he would possibly make less money. If he makes less money she would have to work and they would spend even less time together. Jesse went to Tawanda and explained everything to her. He acknowledged that he needed to do a better job of helping her when he was in town. Jesse said he would set up a baby sitter to help on the weeks when he was out of town. Jesse could not attempt to meet his wife's need for support by quitting his job just to appease her. However, there were many things that he could do to make sure her need for support was met.

Charlie is saved but he was dealing with some issues. He liked pornography. He wanted his wife to indulge in pornography and dress in inappropriate manners. He liked her to be "hot" when they went out. Taylor was struggling because she did not want to be a temptation to the other men they encountered. She also felt sleazy when she dressed up the way Charlie wanted her to. Charlie told his wife that he needed her to show him the type of affection that included doing things that she knew were ungodly. Taylor is Charlie's godly wife, she loves the Lord and she follows the Spirit of God. She does her best to live holy. She wants to meet her husband's need for affection. However, Taylor cannot and will not compromise her walk with the Lord to meet her husband's sinful requests. Taylor set up a dinner with her husband and she explained to him that she could be all he needs her to be in the bedroom but she would represent God in every aspect of her life. She found comfort in knowing that the marriage bed is undefiled and they could have fun together sexually. She explained to him that because of her convictions, she could not indulge in pornography. She also shared her desire to dress in a manner that was also appropriate for her daughters. After Taylor talked with Charlie, he realized that he was being insensitive. He appreciated that he had a wife that was not sleazy or sleeping around on him. He appreciated that she took good care of the house and he appreciated that she took great care of the kids. At this point, he began to appreciate the jewel that God had given him in his wife. He no longer competed with her. He did not tear her down anymore, but he embraced the woman of God that she was. This is a classic, "Charlie got over himself". We all have to get to the place where we "get over ourselves." God is faithful. We have to be faithful to His Word. We have to be faithful to being who He created us to be. Let us do our very best to meet our spouses needs to the glory of God.

God has given us some eternal truths about what He desires for our lives. He desires for us to get in a place of knowledge and come out from that place of ignorance. Ignorance is simply not knowing or being unaware of something. Until I came to know Christ, I was ignorant about Him. However, the more time I spent seeking to know Him the more intimate we became. With knowledge also comes responsibility. The Lord wants His people to walk in a level of knowledge and understanding so that we can be responsible and accountable in all areas of life. Once we come to a place of knowing God's Word as truth, we need to be able to live it. As we live in His truth, we are able to draw others to Him. The things that we did in ignorance were under grace. However, once we come to the knowledge of truth we are accountable for the truth we know. For example, I gave my two-year-old son grace when he took the scissors and cut my favorite leather sectional sofa worth thousands of dollars. However, the next time I held him responsible for knowing that cutting mommy's sofa was not acceptable. I held him accountable and disciplined him appropriately. We have to understand that when we cut or fashion our lives like the world while walking in ignorance, we are under grace. However, once we know better, we are expected to do better. Let us take all the revelation of how to have a successful marriages the way that God intended and be accountable and responsible for living it out to His glory.

## SOME WANTS OF THE HUSBAND

*A husband wants to know that his wife values his opinions.* The wife may know more about the children's schedule, but she should still entertain her husband's ideas. Shooting down the husband's suggestions will cause him to retreat. Rejection can be the demise of a good marriage. A wife who rejects her husband may find that he is looking elsewhere for praise. He may not commit adultery, but he may unconsciously attempt to fill the void. Men like their wives to celebrate them. A wise wife will use her words to speak life to her husband. She may not agree with everything he says, but she must learn how to communicate with her husband her feelings without devaluing his choices. There will be times when the wife has to submit to the Word of God. The Word prompts us to submit to our husbands in all things. For example, if a couple cannot agree on what color to paint the garage, then the wife should allow her husband to make the decision. Generally, the husband will be more apt to comply to the wife's request if he knows she respects and values him. The wife must remember her issues and how God accepts her in spite of them. She can appreciate her husband for who he is when she understands her own flaws. No man wants rejection in his marriage. Every man wants to be accepted. A wise wife will encourage her husband to express his opinions and respect them just as she would her own.

*A husband wants a wife that builds his self-esteem.* His wife understands she must build his self-esteem on purpose. Building his self-esteem includes praying for him and encouraging him. The wife has all the tools she needs in the Word of God to help her husband know who he is in Christ Jesus. Husbands want their wife to encourage them. Encouraging good behavior is better than discouraging bad behavior. A wise wife knows the power of being positive and encourages her husband instead of discouraging him.

*A husband wants appreciation when he goes out and works hard for his family.* Appreciation is highly valuing your husband and being thankful for him. A wise wife knows the power of expressing appreciation.

A husband wants his wife to be woman of moral character who is trustworthy. No man wants a wife that he cannot trust. He has to know he can trust her with his innermost secrets. A wise wife keeps her husband's business to herself. She is letting him know he can trust her when she respects his privacy and refrains from allowing his issues to be a topic amongst her girlfriends.

*A husband wants his wife to be honest.* She is not deceptive but she is genuine and sincere. Women can be manipulative by nature. Women know how to use what they have to get what they want. A husband does not want this quality in his wife in a negative manner. However, he can appreciate it in a positive manner. An honest wife knows that what she has to offer is enough and she does not need to deceive anyone. She is a truth-telling woman. She will not garnish her integrity to get anything. She knows that all she cannot get honestly she does not need. When a husband knows the Lord, he can appreciate that God has given him a good thing in his honest wife.

## SOME WANTS OF THE WIFE

*A wife wants her husband to walk in the leadership that God called him.* Husbands who are saved and have a personal relationship with Jesus have less of a problem being spiritual leaders. He should pray with and instill biblical values in his children. The husband who puts God first learns how to love his wife. He learns because the Holy Spirit is teaching him. Christ is the head of the church and the husband is the head of the family. A husband that is following Christ can lead spiritually because he is following the Head. Christ is the Head. Christ gives life. He is the only way to God the Father. However, the Bible is clear in that wives are to submit to their husbands whether they are saved or not. In fact, the wife's submission and tenderness is what God uses to draw her husband to God. The husband is the head and he has the final say so for his family. He is wise to consider his wife an equal when making decisions. He is wise to value her and her input. Nevertheless, God is clear in that as long as he is not asking his wife to sin, she is Biblically required to submit to him as unto the Lord.[4] This is not a bad thing when husbands love their wives as Christ loves us. A wise wife will whole-heartedly submit to her husband when she knows the Word requires her to. She will submit because she will soon learn that God will honor all those who submit and obey His Word. Promises always come with obedience. God is faithful to bless us as we obey Him.

*Wives want their husbands to help with decisions making.* Wives who are also moms make many decisions. They make decisions about the house, the bills, the cars, the children and the church. A wise husband will offer to help with making the family's decisions.

*Wives want to have their opinions valued.* We can link having our opinions valued to acceptance. A wise husband will make sure his wife knows that he values her opinion. A husband honoring and cherishing his wife is a God given gift. God commanded that husbands honor and cherish their wives as they would their own bodies.[5] God made women emotional and a wife still has her emotions after she accepted her marriage vows. She needs to feel honored. Husbands of honor treat wives with respect. Cherishing a wife includes nurturing, cultivating and showing affection. Wives are like flowers; they are all different, yet, they all need the water of respect, the sunlight of being cherished and the love that pulls the weeds of lies out of their garden. A wise husband will search his heart and tend to his wife as his own body. He will nourish and cherish the best gift that God ever gave him in his wife.

*Wives want tenderness from their husbands.* A woman is the softer side of a man. I do believe that when God made woman, he took the softer side of Adam and made woman. God is such a loving and tender God, that His children should be an extension of that love. A wise husband understands the power of love and happiness. He knows how to tenderly express that love to his wife.

*Wives want mutual submission from their husband.* The Bible says that we are to submit to one another. A husband who submits to God's authority can appreciate his wife submitting to him. Submission is not an open door for the husband to walk all over his wife. In fact, submission is God's way of having order in the marriage. A wise husband knows who he is in Christ and will submit himself to his wife. Just like we see in Galatians chapter five verse twenty-one,

"Submitting yourselves one to another in the fear of God". Mutual submission requires each spouse to surrender. We can surrender and submit to one another in love. To surrender to one another is very important. Spouses must be very careful not to abuse this God given surrender. We must allow Holy Spirit to lead us in order for us to see life in our marriages. There should be no one more important than our spouse except God.

    We should not assume we know what our spouse is thinking. We do not know for sure because we are not them. If there is a break down in met needs, we simply need to communicate. We also need to make sure we are serving our spouse the way they need to served. Serving one another includes making sure that the needs we can meet are met on a consistent basis. As our marriage receives the proper nourishment, we will reflect the marriage that God desires us to enjoy.

# Chapter 9
## CONQUERING NEGATIVE CONFLICT

"I wish I never would have married that girl!" screamed William as he drove off from the house. As the tires skidded in response to him pressing the gas, so did his anger in response to he and Katie's argument. He ranted on and on as he drove down the street. He complained about how Katie cooked. He spoke negatively about the way she cleaned the house and managed the kids. He just rattled off everything that came to his mind. He felt like there was no harm in venting being he was in the car alone. The only problem was that as he raced out of the house his cell phone pocket dialed Katie. She assumed he was calling to apologize but got an ear full of complaints. She was hurt, angry and confused. She left the phone off the hook hoping he would look and see that he had called her by mistake. As he reached into his pocket, he realized that he had called his beautiful wife and smeared tar all over her white dress with his malicious and venomous words. He had hurt her immensely. He could not even remember everything he said. "Uhh hello…" he stammered. "Katie…" was all he could slowly push out of his vocal cords. All he heard was sobbing on the other end of the phone. William felt as low as the belly of an earthworm. He began to cry himself. He knew he had hurt his wife. He knew this would not be an easy conflict to resolve. Fear and doubt crept in as blame started rising up. William knew he needed help to clean this one up. He put the phone down on the seat and began to pray. He cried, "Lord, please help me fix this mess I made!"

## COMPREHENDING CONFLICT

We are encouraged to "Let nothing be done through strife or vainglory; but in lowliness of mind let each esteem other better than themselves".[1] We have to learn how to show each other respect even when we disagree with one another. Conflict is simply a disagreement. We define it as a clash, contention, or sharp disagreement over interest or ideas.[2] We are all very different. No two people are alike so conflict is inevitable. The inevitability of conflict is not the issue. The issue is how we handle conflict when it arises. God has called us to treat our spouses in a Christ like manner. The issue remains sometimes that we have not allowed Holy Spirit to teach us how to handle conflict in a peaceful manner. The best way to assess how to handle conflict is to know yourself. If you know that you blow off the handle at the drop of a dime, then you need to retreat and pull back when you see conflict is brewing. Pulling back is good but you must still deal with the issue at hand. Leaving issues unresolved will do more damage than good. There will be times that we have to confront the issues. Confronting in love will ensure peace. We cannot conquer what we refuse to confront. We must learn to follow peace. If you sense that peace is lifting then you must get up and follow peace until a later time. There will be times that we have to let it go. The process of letting it go includes forgiving the person in question and releasing them from punishment. You will know you have not truly let something go when you bring it up again or attempt to punish someone for something he or she has done to you.

We must understand that we need to handle conflict in a Christ-like manner. A major problem occurs in marriage when a spouse does not behave like Christ. The question of what would Jesus do is always relevant in times of conflict. There will be many opportunities to disagree. One of the major quirks in marriage is the failure to understand that we cannot walk together unless we agree. There will be times we have to agree to disagree. A big problem arises when we attempt to get our spouses to be just like us. It will destroy your marriage because no one wants anyone to change him or her into someone else. There are no two people who are exactly alike. We must learn to embrace the differences of our spouses. We are communicating to our spouse that we are superior when we attempt to make them like us. God is the model and we should look more like Him. We should remember that God respects our choices.

Wives deal with unnecessary hardship when the husband neglects to embrace and fulfill his role in the family unit. Conflict is inevitable when spouses fail to do what God called them to do. While there is always going to be role sharing, it should be understood that a man will handle the responsibilities of the husband while his wife assists him. We understand also that a woman will handle the responsibilities of the wife while her husband assists her. Whatever the two of you decide should be what you stick to with a lot of grace applied. While there are natural things both parties can do like washing dishes, it is the husband's responsibility to wash his wife in the Word. A wife should be able to draw from the rivers of God in her husband. There should be enough Bread of life and rivers of living waters in him for her to be satisfied. Conflict is inevitable when a wife has to draw from a well outside of her husband. A husband must stay in His Word and develop his relationship with God. If there is no Word in him then his wife will have nothing to draw from. Having needs that cannot be met can lead to major conflict in any marriage.

Insecure spouses are not able to release one another into their God given destiny. God has chosen the family unit to do major work for the kingdom of God. Husbands must be secure enough in their calls to be able to release their wives to do what God has called them to do and vice versa. Spouses should assist each other in fulfilling their God given destiny. A wife will happily choose to submit to her husband who shows her the love of God in words and deeds. Lack of submission stimulates conflict in marriages.

Husbands and wives must check themselves against the Word of God to see if they are where they need to be in Him. Conflict can happen when a husband and wife are not growing spiritually. This is not referring to salvation. The saved spouse must cover the unsaved spouse by loving them and showing forth the love of God in the marriage. However, when a couple is not growing spiritually there is the potential for conflict. The conflict stems when one spouse is very serious about their walk with Christ and the other spouse does not take his/hers seriously. The non-committed spouse can eventually become a hindrance to the committed spouse. The committed spouse must take it serious and pray for the non-committed spouse to get serious about his or her walk with God. Our walk with God is the most important relationship that we will pursue. Husbands and wives both need to be in a right relationship with God. There must be a common agreement to seek God's kingdom as our primary desire. The husband and wife should grow together as they share some of the same goals in their walk with God. They both should be growing individually spiritually. They should be able to discern what God is saying to them about the direction of their family.

## THE ANSWERS TO CONFLICT

Communication is an answer to conflict. A breakdown in communication is generally the root of conflict. Effective communication can and will diminish negative conflict. Just talking is not always efficient communication. Couples must work hard on changing themselves and not their spouse. That is why it is important to know who we are marrying. Pre-marital counseling opens the door to deal with issues that cause conflict before the marriage starts. Communicating effectively is also a requirement for successful marriage. Communication problems cause conflict and conflicts challenge commitment.

There are some vital keys in communication. Showing our spouses we care breaks conflict. Listening to our spouses and praising them for what they do destroys conflict. Speaking the truth and being open enables couples to enjoy one another in love. The way we handle our conflict is indicative of whether our marriages will last. When conflict arises and we simply criticize and complain, we are setting ourselves up for failure. When we are immediately defensive, we put our spouse in the place of not coming to us. The marriage begins to die when communication stops. We must not allow contempt to arise in our marriage after we have had a conflict. Contempt has the potential to destroy any marriage. Contempt is a fruit of unforgiveness and bitterness. A marriage that has unforgiveness and bitterness seeping out of it will eventually die. When we put up a wall against our spouse, we begin the process of pushing them away from us. When a spouse can no longer go to their spouse, they may turn to someone else. In the best scenario, they turn to God. Intimacy in marriage is essential. Intimacy diminishes when conflict is not resolved in a godly manner. God built marriages to have victory in life's battles. He created marriage to survive conflict.

## DESTINY FULFILLER OR DESTINY KILLER

Conflict will come in our lives. However, there will be times we have to stop and assess our role in the situation. Here are some roles we can play in our spouse's life. I can stop and ask myself if I am being a Destiny Fulfiller or a Destiny Killer? Destiny Fulfillers helps their spouse fulfill their destiny and purpose set by God. Peter wholeheartedly wanted to help Jesus fulfill His destiny. His original intentions were to be there for Jesus. Sadly, Peter showed signs of a Destiny Killer too. Destiny Killers help Satan hinder the process of destiny in others. In Matthew chapter sixteen verses twenty-two to twenty-three, Jesus shared that He had to go to the Cross. Peter in his ignorance said he would not allow Jesus to go to the cross. Jesus rebuked Satan. Jesus knew it was Satan using Peter in that heated moment. We can apply this to our marriage. We can help our spouse fulfill their destiny or we can get in the way. Either way it is our choice. There will be many opportunities for spouses to make mistakes. A Destiny Fulfiller recognizes he or she has made a bad move and corrects it.

## DESTINY ENHANCER OR DESTINY CANCER

As a spouse, I can assess whether I am being a Destiny Enhancer or a Destiny Cancer. To be a Destiny Enhancer includes increasing the value of others by helping others see their own value and glory. The Bible admonishes us to be kind to each other. Helping one another find and fulfill their purpose is kindness in action. Destiny Cancer eats away at the value and significance of others. Sadly, we can act like a cancer in our marriage. Upon realizing our struggles to encourage our spouse, we can seek God and He will help us. King Saul in the Old Testament is an example of a person being a Destiny Cancer. He ate away at the life of David. He tried to kill him. He rejected what God said and valued his own desires more. In marriage, we have to be careful not to allow the enemy to use us against our spouse.

God is good. He will always help us. Sadly again, some people are looking for a reason to give up on their marriage so they neglect to fight for their marriage. Even if I was a destiny cancer, God is still well able to heal me. In fact, I was a Destiny Cancer for a little while in my marriage. My husband was following the dictates of God and working to establish a business. I had issues. I was jealous and did not want him to succeed. I began to eat away at him daily with my nagging and my negative words. The poor man would work fourteen-hour days, drive three to five hours a day and come home to a Destiny Cancer. I give thanks to God that my husband loved me enough to stay married to me. God dealt with me about my heart issues. I confessed my jealousy to Him and my husband. I turned from that behavior. I became my husband's greatest Destiny Enhancer next to Jesus. There is always hope. We need to concentrate on being a Destiny Enhancer instead of looking at our spouse. Today friend, let this be a time of personal reflection. Allowing God to heal your spouse includes you praying but allowing God to heal you requires some soul searching and a willingness to allow Him to intervene.

## MARRIAGE KEEPER OF MARRIAGE KILLER

We should be mindful in marriage of two other options. I have to consider if I am being my Marriage's Keeper or my Marriage's killer. We have to personally assess this in our marriages. Of course, I am not seriously suggesting we are literally our marriage's killer. I am however, referring to times we can speak either words of life to our spouse or words of death. This is especially relevant in marriage because we all make mistakes. If I make a mistake, I need to know my spouse is not going to kill me with words that speak death. For example, I had a decision to make when my husband's business did not work out as we had planned. I could beat him up with my words or I could build him up with my words. This time I chose to build him up. I had already indulged in my share of tearing him down. I chose to speak life to him this time.

Let us look at a Marriage Keeper. Ephesians chapter six verse one says, "Brethren, if a man be overtaken in a fault, ye which are spiritual, restore such an one in the spirit of meekness; considering thyself, lest thou also be tempted." While this scripture refers to a dear brother in Christ that has fallen into a negative situation, we can apply it to marriage. It would read like this, Wife, if your husband has made a major mistake and cannot get out of it, you, wife, are required now to be spiritual and restore your husband with works of kindness and meekness; considering yourself because you might be the one making a major mistake the next time. This is applicable to husbands as well. This application of this verse hits home for me. I have made many mistakes. Each time I made a mistake, I hungered for my husband to speak life to me and restore my peace of mind. This is a benefit of being married to a godly spouse.

When I was my Marriage's Killer, I acted a lot like Cain in the Bible. Genesis chapter four verse eight says, "… Cain rose up against Abel his brother and slew him." I would look for reasons to slay him with my words. I had a real heart issue. We can test our heart by analyzing how we respond to other people getting a blessing for which we were praying. I wanted to be in business with him. It was not possible because I was home with our young sons at the time. I became the wicked witch of the east. Each time something went wrong I would harp on how this was such a bad idea. I was speaking death to his destiny and our marriage. I do not know for sure if things would have worked out better with his business if I had prayed more. I do know our marriage would have been better if I had not have been "hating" on the man for being successful. At that brief moment, I did not realize that any victory he got was our victory together. Marriage is a place where both positions mutually respect one another. Let us learn from my mistakes. Let us grow together and support one another.

## RESPECTING DIFFERENCES

Respecting differences is very important to success in marriage. God was intentional when He created heaven, earth and the entire universe. We limit ourselves sometimes by our minuscule view of life. We often see things through our experiences. God created Adam. However, He made Eve. I believe God had Eve in mind as He created Adam. God created Adam as a male. He did things the way males do things. God never expected Adam to be Eve. Eve was a woman. God never expected her to do things like a man. In marriage, we have to learn to respect our God-given differences. We will not see eye to eye on everything. We will disagree and that is okay. We just have to be very careful not to allow our disagreements to go unresolved. Unsolved conflict can fester and grow worse. Learning how to deal with conflict helps us to keep intimacy strong in our marriage.

## INTIMACY IN MARRIAGE

A working definition of intimacy is to be close to someone; to be familiar to someone; to be up close, private and personal with someone.[3] There are three aspects of intimacy. We express each aspect in a way that meets the needs of the spirit, soul and body. Those three aspects of intimacy are spiritual, emotional and physical. The spiritual aspect includes praying together; reading the Word together; attending marriage seminars together; attending church services together; encouraging each other in the things of God, supporting each other and helping each other pursue the purpose that God has set. Emotional intimacy ministers to the soul of your spouse. The soul includes the mind, the emotions (or feelings), the thoughts, the intellect and decision making process. This aspect includes spending time reading together, talking to one another, encouraging one another, respecting one another, speaking life to one another, building each other up, and simply being a help to the point of meeting the emotional needs of your spouse.

The physical aspect of intimacy includes meeting the sexual needs of your spouse and sharing non-sexual touches. My husband and I have come to realize that this includes initiating sex, foreplay, setting up the scene throughout the day so that the experience can be enjoyable to both of us. Intimacy is vital to all marriages. Understanding that conflict disturbs intimacy is essential in establishing a firm foundation of intimacy. We must understand that to communicate and be committed to the success of the marriage will increase intimacy. The number one intimacy killer is conflict. Intimacy enhancers are communication and commitment. We have to pursue both of them on purpose.

## THE POWER OF INTIMACY

The power of intimacy in marriage is life changing. God made provisions to ensure that the husband and wife could be strong in the area of intimacy. He made the necessary provisions to ensure success in the marriage. Neglecting to follow God's commands is homicide to any marriage. There is no way for the marriage to be as God intended without obeying Him. The marriage may appear to be fine but under the surface is emptiness and disappointment. Disobedient couples cannot experience marriage the way God intended for it to be experienced. When the required parts of a remote control car are not all there the car does not work properly. Marriage is not a toy but it does work in the same manner. We must put marriage together correctly. God knows what needs to happen to ensure success. To try to have a marriage without God is comparable to groping around in the dark. The idea of not going to the Creator about His creation is not wise. God is not slack in His love for His children. His love is abundant. Jesus came to earth and died so that marriages can live in God. God intends for marriages to live in the abundance of all that He has.

When God took the woman out of the man, He took out everything that the man needed to be complete and placed it in the woman. The soft side of man is in the woman. The womb of man is in the woman. The nurturing heart of man is in the woman. Everything that a husband needs in marriage is in his wife. A husband is wise to understand that his wife is everything that he is not. She is all he needs outside of God to be complete. Together a husband and wife can conquer the world. God commands the husband to leave his father and mother. A child's mother and father are the direct authority in that child's life. When the husband leaves his mother and his father, he now has to submit directly to the authority of Christ. Whereas his parents were responsible for him; now he is responsible for his wife. He must embrace all that she is and all that she is not. Intimacy is a necessary component for a successful marriage.

## NO MORE SHAME

We must understand that intimacy is a vital part of marriage. Adam and Eve were naked in all aspects of the word. Yet they were not ashamed. Sin had not yet entered into the world. As a result, Adam and Eve were able to enjoy the beauty of each other without feeling guilty. Sin introduced shame to humankind. Couples are wise to look toward having complete nakedness in God and being naked before their spouse. Spouses should not be ashamed of who they were before they were married. We must denounce shame. Holding on to shame causes problems in marriages. It is so sweet to be transparent and know that complete acceptance is available with God. As believers, God never deserts us or disowns us. A similar acceptance should be found in marriage. Spouses should be able to accept one another. Constant rejection destroys intimacy. Being naked and not ashamed is being intimate.

In most marriages, couples fail to realize how much damage not being intimate does to the growth of the marriage. We kill the intimacy that comes with mutual submission when we try to dominate the marriage. We miss spending intimate or close time together when we allow ourselves to be over committed to other things. Couples experiencing consistent conflict about money minimize chances of intimacy. Sometimes those negative feelings linger in the air. Selfishness closes the door to chances of putting our spouse first and tending to their needs and wants. When in-laws put their noses in a marriage, the couple can experience a breakdown in cohesiveness. God specifically said to leave mom and pop and cleave to one another. Some people come into marriage with television dreams and storybook ideas about what they want in their marriage. These unrealistic expectations destroy intimacy. They destroy intimacy because the other person will never meet those expectations. For instance, the wife may come into the marriage expecting the husband to buy her a mansion. However, if the husband works at Burger King and does not intend to leave that job, then the wife will never be happy in that marriage. The sad thing is that she knew all of this before she said, "I do". We must learn to respect the choices of our spouses. We cannot change them into our little robots and even if we could we would still never be satisfied as God designed.

## EXPOSING INTIMACY KILLERS

A jealous spouse will kill the intimacy in a marriage with false accusations. Gambling, drug and alcohol abuse destroy intimacy because the gambler and the drug addict is incapable of thinking of anything outside that habit. The alcoholic is drunk all the time and who wants to be intimate with a drunken person. Loneliness drives a wedge between husbands and wives. When a spouse feels lonely and neglected, the last thing he or she wants is to be intimate with the person that is causing them to feel the pain they feel. Sexual frustrations can be resolved as couples work together to please one another. Sexual dissatisfaction may cause them to pull away from each other. When needs are not met, spouses may look elsewhere to satisfy the void. They may not commit adultery but they may begin to start working too hard or drinking heavily. They may get involved in pornography, which is a sin that has destroyed many marriages. The lust that takes place as two people watch two other people have sex can become a stronghold that destroys marriages and personal relationships with Christ. Pornography introduces lust for another person into the marriage. It can cause deep trauma for any marriage. It is difficult for any spouse to compete with pornography. Air brushed pictures are not real. Wives that have had children may not look like Playboy bunnies. It can lead to unrealistic expectations. Pornography is a noted cause of sexual dissatisfaction in marriages. Again, sex is reserved for married couples and it should be private. We cannot minimize the perversion of pornography. Sin always destroys marriages.

A person with low self worth feels unworthy and generally does not allow intimacy to be a part of their lives as a result. There is help for us. We have to be real with each other. We have to show each other in loving ways the areas we need to work on. We have to share with our spouses how we like to be treated. We need to sow intimacy into our marriage, realizing that we do reap what we sow.

I know we say the mind is the battlefield. However, sometimes I feel like marriage is a battlefield. From the onset, we see our enemy fighting us in the area of marriage. Of course, the mind is the place where battles are fought, lost and won. Nevertheless, couples find themselves at war with one another at some point in the marriage. It is a bit naive for us to think that we will never have conflict. No doubt we will have conflict, but communication is the key while commitment is the door. Let me explain that analogy a little more. Husbands and wives are two different people with different backgrounds, upbringings, opinions, and make up. We will disagree at some point in our marriages no matter how hard we try. Learning how to agree to disagree is the key. Learning how to communicate is a key. Learning how to show forth commitment to the marriage is the door to success. Marriage is not for the immature or the faint of heart. The faint at heart cannot withstand the heat it takes to remain joyfully married.

## REASONS FOR CONSTANT UNRESOLVED CONFLICT

| Money | Power & Control | Pride | Insecurities |
|---|---|---|---|
| Value-differences | Work schedule | Selfishness | Dishonesty |
| Misunderstood-feelings | Unmet-needs | Parenting | Sex |
| Lack of quality time | Friends | Habits | Family |
| Expectations | Communication issues | Hurting-each-other | Disrespect |
| Personal-differences | Responsibilities | Disregard | Always-right |
| Ungrateful | Blame | Ignoring | Lack of trust |
| Not-satisfied | Mistrust | Prejudice | Parents (In laws) |
| Low-self-esteem | Annoying-behavior | Alcohol abuse | Salary-challenges |
| No-conflict-resolution-skills | Anger-issues | Constant anger outbursts | Drug use & Addiction |
| Church-schedule | Upbringing | Competitiveness | Immaturity |
| Inconsiderate | Argumentative | Impatient | Demanding |

## RULES FOR HANDLING CONFLICT PROPERLY

1. Find out what the actual conflict is really about. (Listening to understand is the key.)
2. Stick to the current issue. (Resist the urge to pull up old stuff.)
3. Listen with the intent to respond with actions to what your spouse is communicating.
    a. (I.e. When my spouse says I hurt them when I call him a certain name, I will have to listen to him with the intent of doing something and not trying to defend myself. In this case, I would simply refrain from calling my spouse that name.)
4. Act like friends, look at each other, hold hands and do not walk away.
5. Keeping control of the first five minutes of the discussion can help dictate the rest of it.
6. Deal with hurt feeling first.
    a. We cannot effectively handle conflict if one of us is hurting.
    b. This is the proper time to apologize. (i.e. I am sorry. Please forgive me.)
7. Be accountable for your own actions. Refrain from blaming your spouse.
8. Use words like "I feel" or "I think".
    a. Stay away from starting sentences with, "You this" or "You

that".

9. Don't speak negatively over your future with, "You always will" or "You never will".

    a. Refrain from saying, "This will never work".

10. Don't exaggerate with "You always this" or "You never that".
11. Don't be sarcastic or matter of fact. No one likes their spouse to patronize them.
12. Don't hit below the belt with unnecessary comments that you know will hurt.
13. Don't yell and do not call names.

    a. If the discussion blows up do not continue.
    b. Stop now before it goes too far.
    c. Agree now to resume the discussion later.

14. Don't threaten the fibers of your marriage with crazy statements.

    a. Statements to avoid include, "I quit." "I'm done." "I hate you." "This marriage is doomed." "This marriage will never work."

15. Do not shut down or give the silent treatment.

    a. Shutting down can sometimes feel like being shut out.
    b. Neither one of them is good for handling conflict properly in marriage.

16. Use the Drive-Through or Drive-Up method when arguing.

    a. Repeat back what you heard your spouse say.
    b. Then give them a chance to clarify that is what they were saying.

17. Arguments should be private.

    a. Arguments do not have to resort to yelling or name-calling.
    b. We can disagree like two sensible adults with efforts of a solution.

18. Win-Win solutions are easier to agree upon.

    a. Consider both sides for a proper solution.

## PREVENTIVE MEASURES TO MINIMIZE CONFLICT

1. Prioritize your spouse. Make pleasing them a priority.
2. Consider each other when making decisions.
3. Commit to work together to eradicate conflict over money.
4. Discuss beforehand how you will raise your children.
5. Communicate to resolve sexual conflict.
6. Get help for any addictions.

Remember, friend, conflicts are simply differences. Disagreeing is normal and there is nothing abnormal about having healthy disagreements within marriage. Conflicts are not problems. Problems are unresolved conflicts. We definitely need to talk about our concerns. When handling conflict properly, we need to focus on facts, feelings, opinions, intentions, expectations and actions. Facts include what actually happened. Feelings require being vulnerable but can shed light on why things transpired the way they did. Sharing how something made you feel can be a gateway to a new level of intimacy and oneness. Spouses have to learn how to let their spouse in to their world. You have to help them see things through your eyes sometimes.

Sharing our opinions can be helpful if our spouse desires to hear them. We should be apprehensive about spewing out our opinions all the time when they have not been sought after. An opinion is simply what we believe. Sometimes what we believe is relevant and sometimes it is not. Learning the difference will save us from unnecessary conflict. Intentions are the things we plan to do in response to the conversation. Sharing our intentions gives our spouse a chance to see that we desire to diffuse any negative residue from the conflict.

Expectations are what we expect our spouse to do. This is not always easily shared because it can sound selfish. However, we should share our expectations with our spouse so that they can agree or disagree to comply at that time. That way we are not disgruntled when they do not meet that expectation. Actions help us to commit to work together. We are human and we are prone to make mistakes but together we can capitalize on every situation we encounter.

## HANDLING FINANCES IN MARRIAGE

Learning how to properly handle conflicts about finances is imperative because finances are the number one source of conflict in marriage. Budgeting is a valuable part of marital success. The Bible says in Ecclesiastes chapter ten verse nineteen, "… but money answers all things." We find in Matthew chapter six verse thirty-three, "But seek ye first the kingdom of God, and his righteousness; and all these things shall be added unto you." As we seek God, His kingdom and His righteousness, we see that He provides us with the money we need for things. Things include clothes, shelter, food and water. Of course, we have to know what we need culturally for the success of life offered in that culture. We have to be careful not to get needs and wants mixed up. We may think we need something but God may have already supplied that need in another manner. We have to remain in consistent communication with Him to know how He is providing for us. A budget can include a balance between monthly income and monthly bills. We need to ask questions like: How is our credit? How can we clean up our credit? Who will pay the bills? Who will work outside of the home? When will we have children? How many children do we want? When will we buy a house? When will we buy a vehicle? Where are we going to tithe? Are we going to give to charity? Where will we go to Church? We must make decisions together. These questions can help us in our budgeting process and minimize conflict.

Money concerns in marriage can include necessities like food and clothes, transportation, student loans and other loans, raising kids, giving to charities and how to handle it when our income is not enough to pay the bills. Money concerns are medical and dental expenses or insurance, shelter, good or bad investments, credit cards, travel and business ventures.[4] Learning how to compromise is the key to success in correctly handling conflict about finances. The Bible does give us instructions on how to handle conflict. The Bible shares with us that the husband is the one to make the final decision. It more accurately says that wives are to submit to their husband in all things.[5] Things reflect earthly things. Order is necessary for success. Someone has to make the final decision and in this case, it is the husband. As a result, if there is a disagreement about buying a new car then the husband is supposed to have the final say. It may not be as easy for a wife to submit to this truth but it is necessary. If a wife desires something, she can always pray and ask God to speak with her husband about it if he is not heeding her request. At the end of the day, the husband has the final word and his wife should respect that.

The Bible gives us some specifics about the order of "things" in marriage. As previously mentioned, money is the answer for buying or securing things.[6] Money cannot buy the fruit of the Spirit but it can buy some natural fruit like apples and oranges. We are spiritual beings living in a body and we have a soul. We have to understand that God supplies according to our needs within the system where we live. We are in a system that requires money to buy things. Money is a means of exchange. God will make sure we have the money we need to buy the things we need. Matthew chapter six verse thirty-one through thirty-two says, "Therefore do not worry, saying, 'What shall we eat?' or 'What shall we drink?' or 'What shall we wear?' For after all these things the Gentiles seek. For your heavenly Father knows that you need all these things." We do not have to worry because God will take care of us as we seek the spiritual things that matter the most.

Money is a major source of conflict because of fear. Fear can set in and rob us of our peace. God said He would meet our needs. Focusing on God's Word can help us in times of uncertainty. Surely, in challenging times we should draw closer to God and closer to each other. God is all-wise and He knows we need order in our marriages. He set the husband as the head of the family. He did not set the husband as the head of the family for nothing. He did it for a divine purpose. He gave the husband the authority that comes with the position. We find this truth in Ephesians chapter five verses twenty-three through twenty-five. The verse says, "For the husband is the head of the wife, even as Christ is the head of the church: and he is the saviour of the body. Therefore as the church is subject unto Christ, so let the wives be to their own husbands in everything. Husbands, love your wives, even as Christ also loved the church, and gave himself for it;" Husbands are to take care of the wife as Christ takes care of the church. As husbands take care of the house then there can be minimized conflict. This is a time where both spouses are working equally as hard from day to day on a job. However, God has given us the formula for success in finances and other decisions in marriage. He has instructed the husband to be like Christ and be as a savior to the family. He is responsible for taking care of his family just as Christ takes care of the Church. Because of a husband's God given authority, the wife is required to submit to him in all things. There has to be order in the family unit. God is not the author of confusion.[7] We are wise to respect His Word. The family unit only needs one head. God has chosen that to be the husband. Anything with two heads is a monster. Let us remember that as we maximize the Word of God in our marriage, we will minimize negative conflict.

## IN-LAWS ARE NOT OUTLAWS

It would be an injustice not to deal with the controversial topic of in-laws. Let me first start out with the first commandment with promise. The one that says children honor your parents so that your days will be long. This promise may seem irrelevant these days, but it can be detrimental to our days being long. Our spouse's parents become our parents when we marry. We need to be wise and heed the Word of God that commands us to honor our mother and father in-laws so that our days will be long. Yes, they may be trying us in every way but the Word of God is still true. We must honor them because God said it is right. God was very specific when it came to the place that our parents would have in our lives once we got married. He instructed us to leave our parents and cleave to our spouse. This instruction is essential to the building of our own families. While our parents should not directly run our lives, they have contributed greatly by what they have done for us.

Generally, we find that there is a negative vibe associated with mother in laws. This is stereotypical and not always true. Perception is everything and how we perceive a thing will determine how we receive it. How we receive it determines how we handle it. Believers must override the negative vibe associated with mother- and father-in-laws and allow God to give them a fresh view of them. Each couple must personally assess how to deal with each other's parents as it relates to their involvement in the marriage. I remember a story about a man, his wife to be and his mother. A man took his fiancé' home to meet his mother. When his mom met her, she said, "I do not like her." The son said, "Mom, she is just like you". The mom said, "That is my point. You only need one of me in your life." While that seems comical, it carries a singe of truth to it because we do marry what we liked in our parents. We tend to shy away from the things we see in people that we did not like in our parents. It is very important that we work together to make sure that our in-laws do not become outlaws. It is up to each individual couple to decide how they will handle the family that they have married into. It is essential that couples while dating establish rules that they must adhere to as it relates to the in-laws.

A man noticed that his mom was mistreating his wife so he spoke to his mom about it. She was very hurt but she established a respect for her son's wife and his marriage. As the Lord expressed His love and kindness to us, we have to express that same love and kindness to our extended family. Believers must always take the humble road. We must never allow our unsaved or almost saved in-laws to persuade us to act unkind or vindictive. We must embrace them with the love of God. The love of God will cover a multitude of sins and give us a chance to live as Christ did. We must aim to win our in-laws to Christ or they will persuade us to act in ways that are unpleasing to God. I remember a teaching that helped me to understand the power of persuasion. Either I am going to "persuade or be persuaded". I have chosen to be the commander in chief of my atmosphere. My in-laws will not be outlaws.

## 8-STEPS TO RESTORATION AFTER CONFLICT

The atmosphere can be very sticky after an argument. We speak hurtful things in frustration and anger. In most relationships, there is generally one spouse who is quicker to seek restoration. In marriage, there should not always be the one spouse that apologizes first. Both spouses must be mature and learn how to approach each other after an argument. In a perfect world, there is always a race to see which spouse will apologize first. However, in real life sometimes restoration after an argument takes a while. Stalling one another is not healthy. Storming out of the house in a rage is not the best way to handle conflict either. After the dust settles and the guns stop smoking we have to reconcile. The number eight signifies a new beginning. I am going to share eight steps with you that can help restore your relationship to a peaceful state. Both parties should familiarize themselves with these steps. Reports show that both of you will need them at some point in your marriage.

## STEP 1: STOP
Stop going over the argument in your head. One thought can revisit all the emotions from the argument after it is over.

## STEP 2: LOOK
Look to the hills (God) for help. And know this is the time to pray. As you pray for your spouse and pray for yourself, you can begin to see things from a different perspective.

## STEP 3: LISTEN
Listen to Holy Spirit speak to you about your contribution to the argument. Conflict happens mostly because spouses are not meeting needs. Allow God to show you His heart.

## STEP 4: SEEK
Go to your spouse and apologize for your contribution to the argument. This is not the time to bring up what they did or said. This is the time you ask for

forgiveness for what you said, did, or neglected to do. Seek peace and resist more confrontation.

## STEP 5: HEAR
Hear your spouse's heart by listening with your heart. Respect their feelings even if it does not necessarily line up with the facts as you see them. Do not get defensive or shift blame. This is the time to listen to your spouse with sympathy and empathy. You must listen to understand and not listen to rebuttal.

## STEP 6: CONFESS
Confession is simply agreeing. Agree with your spouse that they did feel that way… even if that was not your intention. You cannot argue with the way someone feels or felt about a situation. Saying, "I am sorry you felt that way. That was not my intention" is a good response.

## STEP 7: SOLUTION
Seek a solution that benefits both parties involved. Focusing on solutions is the key at this point. Learning to separate the person from the problem is important to restoration and reconciliation. Seasoning our words with love and kindness will benefit us greatly.

## STEP 8: ENJOY
Enjoy your new opportunity to live in peace. Learning from our mistakes is a vital part of life. Being humble is a key to having a successful marriage. Cooperating with one another will ensure that we have harmony in our marriage. There may be other issues but today we resolve to restore our relationship to a place of peace. Scheduling a time to deal with other issues is also an option at this time.

# Chapter 10
## COMPREHENDING COMMUNICATION AND COMMITMENT

"I don't want to go to the movies!" screamed Sharon. She was fed up with Patrick continually telling her what they were going to do for date night. For the last four months, he had chosen the restaurants, the movies and all the places they went each night. By now, Sharon was fuming. In all actuality, Sharon was upset because she neglected to communicate how she really felt with Patrick. She chose not to share her true feelings in an effort to keep the peace and now she was exploding. Patrick was flabbergasted! He could not believe what was happening. He thought he was doing the right thing by choosing the activities for date night. Sharon had not shown any interest in deciding where they would go each night. Shaking his head in disbelief, Patrick said to Sharon, "We need to talk".

Understanding Communication

Communication is equally about our tone and the nonverbal expressions than the content of what we are saying. The tone of our voice is expressing our thoughts more than we know sometimes. We have to realize that we communicate through many expressions including our eye contact, body posture, hand gestures, facial expressions and actions. We learn in life that what we do will generally override what we say. Communication is more than words or simply talking. Communication is the exchange of thoughts, feelings, hopes, dreams and desires. Communication is to fellowship with one another and it includes sharing during that time of fellowship.

Communication involves spouses being aware of each other's personality types. We must understand our own personality type as we allow the Holy Ghost to assist us in our communication efforts. We refer to Jesus as a Lamb.[1] He is also referred to as a Lion.[2] The lamb and the lion are applicable to personality types as it relates to communication. Lion personality types are strong, dominant and usually have a proclivity to take control of situation. Sometimes, lion personality types need to pray about less aggressive ways to communicate. The spouse with the lion personality type may need to pull back at times and listen to what his or her spouse is saying. Lamb personality types are extremely relaxed, calm and prone to take the back seat opposed to leading. The lamb personality type may need to step up to the plate and share his or her heart about situations that arise. Lamb personality types need to articulate their feelings so they are properly considered. Generally we find ourselves somewhere in the middle of the lamb and the lion. Finding a healthy balance is the key to effective communication. For example, the lion personality type generally comes on the scene and commands everything to be as he has said. The lamb personality type usually will just go with the flow. An issue with that is the person with the lamb personality type may start to resent the fact that they are not considered. Learning how to share with each other how we feel is important. Understanding your personality type and your spouse's type is essential to effective communication.

We are experiencing real communication when we can commit to listening to what our spouse is saying to us. This is evident when we listen with our whole heart. This is evident when we respond only to what they have said. We must focus on understanding what our spouses are saying without jumping to conclusions. Good communication includes having a mindset to hear what your spouse is saying to you and making every effort to comprehend. Many times, a spouse will minimize or belittle what the other spouse is saying. This diminishes proper communication in the marriage. Each spouse must commit to grasping the reality of what the other person is saying. For instance, if a wife is afraid of ants and shares her fear with her husband, if he laughs at her, he is communicating that he doesn't take her fears seriously. Her husband should make sure that he offers her his understanding with compassion and empathy even if it seems silly to him. Wives must also resist the urge to express nonverbal actions that cause her husband to believe that she does not really care about what he is saying. We communicate through our facial expressions and body posture.

We should be in a mode of listening to our spouse when they come to us to communicate their ideas or feelings. We must make sure that we take the time to let our spouses know that we understand them and validate them before we express our opinions. Good communication involves balancing what our spouses say and what we heard them say. We should not be defensive or accusatory when they come to communicate with us. Even if our spouse's posture is screaming, "argument" we must stand firm and not be swayed into that argument. We must remember to leave the past in the past. Whenever there is a heated conversation, we must resist the urge to throw the past in our spouse's face. We must always be open to learn things about ourselves that we need to change. We must be willing to search our lives and see where we can stand improvement in areas of communication.

## EFFECTIVE COMMUNICATION

We can defuse negative conflict with communication. Effective communication is vital to a marriage's survival. Listening with your heart will help foster an atmosphere of trust. Coming up with solutions is better than arguing over the problem. Learning to be your spouse's safe place will help foster an atmosphere of open communication. When we know we are each other's safe place, we can share everything with each other. We can be real without fear of ridicule or rejection. We can share silly stuff and not feel ashamed about it. We can laugh together. Learning to laugh at yourself will help making mistakes easier. We all make mistakes. Learning when to laugh and when to cry is a key to personal growth. Speaking highly of one another, helps open the lines of communication. Realizing that how we say something to our spouse is just as important as what we say can make our communication more fruitful. Sometimes we do not get the results we were seeking in communication because we have not learned how to speak kindly to one another. Paying attention to the time we say certain things is essential as well. If your spouse is tired then that is not a good time to criticize him or her. Having pillow talk is a good idea too. Enjoying pillow talk after having an intimate time together increases the connection between good sexual intimacy and good communication.

Having pillow talk with no intentions of having sex makes it more genuine. Sharing and communicating with one another increases our ability to connect with each other at a greater level. Speaking life is another key to good communication. Most people do not enjoy negative communication on a consistent basis. Encouraging one another is good. As we encourage one another, we communicate to our spouses that we believe in them. A study has shown that when women touch men and encourage them, they make them feel like they can do anything. Wives have the power of touch and encouraging word. Wives have to purpose in their hearts to be positive and speak life to their husbands. Husbands and wives can build the confidence of each other simply by speaking words of life to one another.

## TWO FORMS OF COMMUNICATION

Men need sex and women need to talk. Both are forms of communication. Men need to exchange physically. Women need to exchange emotionally. Both forms of communication are a priority in marriage. Let us apply a few principles of communication to sex and talking. Mutual concern during sex creates a good experience for both parties. Mutual concern during talking allows a woman to feel more of a connection to her husband. Husbands get to learn new ways to express love to their wives by listening with concern when she is talking. Mutual concern includes eye contact, body language, voice tone and frequency. These four factors can make sexual intimacy and pillow talk exciting.

Listening while your spouse is talking is a necessary component of a real conversation. A conversation is a form of two-way communication. Listening does not just mean hearing what your spouse is communicating but listening includes hearing with the intent to respond appropriately. Listening well help you to processes what your spouse is saying. Wives have to learn to give their husbands a chance to communicate in a way that is comfortable for him. Men usually do not offer a multiplicity of words in a conversation. Wives have to learn to appreciate the differences. Listening during sexual intimacy allows each party to be attentive to whether their spouse is pleased.

Everyone likes to be encouraged. Praise is a form of encouragement that is beneficial to marriages. Verbal affirmation is a type of praise. Praising a man can unlock his heart. There is a power in knowing your spouse believes in you to the point of verbalizing it. Couples have to learn how to focus on each other's positives. While dating, that is the time to call out all the negatives before you make the decision to get married. However, after the vows we have to learn to seek out the positives and pray about the negatives. Praising one another after sexually intimacy is healthy. Praising each other for listening or communicating better is good incentive to keep doing it.

Speaking the truth in love is learned behavior. We are selfish by nature and selfishness causes us to speak on terms of how things affect us. Leaning to season our words with grace requires us to focus on our spouse. If there is something difficult that I must communicate to my spouse, then I need to make sure my words are drenched in grace. There are times when people say, "Well I just told him" or "I just told her the truth". If either of those communications produced a hurtful response then we need to add more grace. Grace is the most appreciated when it has been received. We are more eager to give grace when we realize how much grace we have received.

Sex can be difficult to discuss sometimes. Communicating that we are not being satisfied is not always easy. However, it is necessary and sharing a solution with the issue is the key to properly communicating sexual concerns. For example, if a wife does not get to "reach the finish line" before her husband during sexual intimacy, she can communicate to her husband in a way that does not crush him. Most men take pride in pleasing their wives. As a result, wives must season their words with grace for the continued benefit of their husband continuing to aim at pleasing her.

Openness includes intimate discussions. Openness is at its best in that safe place. Learning to talk about difficult topics takes time and effort. Checking how we respond is important. Openness in sex gives each spouse a chance to communicate sexually a way that he or she likes. Openness in communication helps both spouses feel free to share anything with each other. Shutting down is a communication barrier. Always be careful not to shut down on your spouse. This can feel too much like being shut out, which can cause a breakdown in communication.

## TECHNIQUES FOR GOOD COMMUNICATION PART 1

1. Use the Drive through method:
    a. Spouse-1 has a chance to share about something.
    b. Spouse-2 repeats what they heard them say.
        i. Start with: "So, what I hear you saying is…?"
    c. Spouse-2 confirms or corrects them.
2. Use Sandwich Method:
    a. Ask your spouse if it is a good time for a critique.
    b. Give your spouse one compliment or encouragement
    c. Share in love the area you desire to critique.
    d. Remember to stay solution oriented in your communication
    e. Share the second compliment with your spouse.
3. Learn to schedule arguments.

4. Learn to keep The WAVE (Warmth Acceptance Victory Encouragement) going in your marriage.
5. Remember there may not always be an instant breakthrough but patience is the key.
6. Choose to build the integrity and validity of your marriage.
7. Speak life based on God's promises for your life and marriage.

## TECHNIQUES FOR GOOD COMMUNICATION PART 2

1. Clarify what you think they said. "What I hear you saying is…"
2. Share what you thought they meant. "What I thought you meant was…"
3. Clarify what you think they want you to do. "What I believe you want me to do is…"
4. Ask for clarity if you do not understand. "I don't understand what you mean when you say… Please help me understand." (Please bear with your spouse, as they may get frustrated about having to explain what they meant.)
5. Do not ask too many questions.
6. Refrain from asking questions that blatantly have nothing to do with the current conversation.
7. Discern when to talk and when to be quiet and listen.
8. Do your best not to get defensive and defend yourself.
9. Listen and then share your feelings after you have conveyed your earnest listening skills.
10. Be solution oriented after your spouse feels understood.
11. Do not be your spouse's counselor.
12. Do not assume that what is petty to you is petty to your spouse.
13. Actively and attentively listen, even if the situation seems trivial or petty to you.
14. Learn to hear your spouse's heart by listening with your heart.
15. Train your mind to listen with the intent to understand.

## UNDERSTANDING COMMITMENT

Commitment is required for any marriage to be successful. Commitment is "the state or an instance [like marriage] of being obligated."[3] Our word is binding before God so we must be careful what we agree to. When a couple says "I do" then God expects them to do it because they said they would. Marriage is a covenantal agreement we make with God. Although we treat it like a contract, it is not. Marriage is a life-long commitment. The Bible shows us that God was committed to us. He loved us enough to allow His Son to be sacrificed for us even when we did not deserve it.[4] Husbands and wives are smart to understand that the battle and the war are with the devil and not each other. The Bible tells us that we are not fighting our spouses. We are fighting spiritual wickedness.[5] As believers we have authority over evil spirits and they must flee in Jesus' name. We may experience conflict. However, when we said we do, we accepted the responsibility of being committed and working it out. Be wise and handle conflict about finances immediately. Money issues can destroy a marriage if the conflicts are not resolved quickly and through the Word of God.

A husband's faithfulness to God shows he is trustworthy with God and his family. Once a husband has developed that trust then God and his wife will release more of them to him. Consistency breeds trust and being consistent can foster an environment of trust in any marriage. Being able to depend on someone to keep his word is very important. Faithfulness in marriage will be tested. The enemy knows if a husband is not faithful and trustworthy, then his family will not trust him. They will not trust him to yield to the Holy Ghost and lead them into purpose. It is important for husbands to have mentors. God mentored Adam and in turn, Adam mentored his sons. Mentoring is a vital part of growth because if a man does not have a model, then he is likely to build the wrong mold. A husband receives mentoring so he can learn how to:

1. Identify his wife's purpose
2. Release his wife to the purpose
3. Understand her needs and provide them
4. Understand her fears and protect her
5. Understand her desires
6. Speak life into her
7. Understand her makeup
8. Believe in her

A mentor must teach a husband to have integrity, valor and character because they are all learned behaviors. A husband must be a man of his word. A man that keeps and honors his word is a precious jewel in his family. God honors His Word and we must be more like Him. Wives need mentors too. Wives need mentors to teach them how to:

1. Help her husband fulfill his purpose
2. Pray for him daily
3. Encourage him
4. Support him
5. Understand him
6. Have his back when he falls short
7. Be a safe place for him
8. Believe in him

# COMMITMENT TO PROSPER

Commitment is essential to prospering. The principle of no pain then no gain is a key to prosperity. If we are not willing to work at our goals, they will never happen. Prosperity of life includes spiritually, mentally, financially, physically and relationally. God wants us to prosper in every area of our lives including our marriage. As we suffer through the necessary pains of life, we are able to appreciate the prosperity found in Christ. Suffering together will draw couples who are grounded in God closer to one another as we commit to our marriages. Suffering can also be a wedge driven through marriages. It becomes a wedge when we do not know how to work together. Working together can secure victory in most areas.

Husbands and wives must stay close to God so they can stay close to the vision and purpose for their family. Husbands must be men of prayer. They must have consistent communication with God to hear what He has to say about the direction of the family. A husband can make sure that demons and people respect his wife and her calling. As her covering, he can take a stand and protect her from being disrespected or abused. He must be able to discern what is brewing in the spirit realm against him and his family. A wife can make sure that her husband walks in the favor of God by being there for him. A wife makes her husband look good when she honors and respects him and his vision. A committed wife can be measured by her ability to birth her husband through prayer into his God-designed potential and purpose. A wife must be a woman that prays continuously for her family. Prayer changes everything. Wives can release their family into destiny via prayer. Prayer is the key. I know we say Pray Until Something Happens. However, I am strongly persuaded that we need to learn to pray until we see what God said happening in our lives. Husbands and wives must be committed to prayer. Commitment is what ushers in prosperity in the fullness of God's design. Prosperity will manifest in a marriage when the husband and wife both commit to honor God and invest all in Him to His glory.

The ultimate and greatest example of commitment is God. In Romans chapter five verse eight, we see that while we were still sinners, God allowed His Son to die for us. While we were so undeserving, He died for us. God is committed to us, and He never gives up on us. While we were still in our mess, He sent His Son to die a horrific death on the cross. Before the prostitute was delivered, God was still committed. Before the homosexual became straight, Christ died. Before the liar started telling the truth, Christ suffered. God never gives up on His people. God looks at us and sees us in Him. We must take heed to His example and look at our spouses in Christ. We need to learn to speak life and not death. We need to call our spouse what they are in Christ and not what they are in the flesh. God showed us His love while we were sinning. The least we can do is give that same love to our spouses.

# CASE STUDY

Following God's example always leads to life. God is able to do more than we can ask or think.[6] There is nothing that God cannot do. If we are willing to commit to our marriages, then we will see victory. I have a case study in which a wife never gave up on her husband through the strength of God. Amy loved Sam. Amy went through a terrible divorce that devastated her. Sam loved Amy when she struggled to love herself. She had a son from her previous marriage. Sam treated Amy like a queen. Sam asked Amy to marry him. She said yes. They had a daughter together. Sam and Amy had a worldly marriage. Both of them had confessed Christ as children but neither knew Jesus intimately. They never read the Bible, they never prayed and they rarely went to church. As a result, Sam was surprised when Amy accepted Christ as her Savior and Lord over her life. Sam wanted to party but Amy had been changed. Sam began to resent and insult Amy. Every time he looked at her, it reminded him of how messed up he was. He hated her peace and that ridiculous smile. He hated what those church folk had done to her. He wanted the sinful woman he had married back. He wanted the old Amy.

The verbal abuse started small and later grew to be an everyday thing. Amy could not do anything right. Amy was having a hard time adjusting to her new way of life. Sam acted as though he hated her but she could not bring herself to give up on her relationship with Jesus. Sam did not realize it but he was trying to break Amy. He wanted her to be like him. Sam began to threaten to harm Amy physically. He never hit her in front of the children, but he called her names in front of them. The children loved going to church but knew how much their dad hated it and that caused conflicting feelings. Sam began to drink heavily and experiment with drugs. He became obsessed with using drugs and he had multiple affairs. He spent all their money. He lost his job. He began to steal things from the house and sell them. His verbal abuse continued and he started physically abusing Amy. He started pushing her in front of the children. Sam went to jail but that did not stop him.

Amy had a mentor that was an older Christian woman who encouraged her to never give up because God never gave up on her. Her mentor reminded her that just as Sam had hurt her, she had hurt God. She reminded Amy of just how much Sam needed to be saved. He needed Jesus to help him. She told Amy that if she needed to get away for safety that she and the kids could come stay with her until Sam came to know Christ. God is a good God. It is hard for me to grasp that He would want anyone to stay in an abusive situation. I know God is the Great Restorer. There will be times when we have to remove ourselves temporarily from abusive situations. Marriage being our source of pain is not God's best. Amy prayed and went on a fast. She allowed the lights to be disconnected to shake Sam. He just left and went somewhere else. She let his car be repossessed but he just got a ride with random people. Finally, Amy said to Sam "God never gave up on me and I will never give up on you". Sam broke down and cried. Her persistent love drew him to God. He apologized to Amy and their children. Sam rededicated his life back to Christ and joined a local Church fellowship. Sam went to a drug rehabilitation center and is now drug free. Amy and Sam went to marriage counseling and they renewed their vows. They now live in a prestigious neighborhood and drive a fancy car. Amy does not want for anything. Sam was honest with his children about his addiction. To his surprise, Amy never said anything bad about Sam to the children. If the love of a woman can draw a man, then how much more should we allow God to use us to draw His people back to Him? God never gives up on our spouses or us. While we were lost, Christ died for us. While your spouse has issues, you should not give up on them. Giving up is not an option.

## COMMITTED TO THE MARRIAGE

Marriage is two people coming together as one before God. The wife may be the right side while the husband is the left side. In this time and age, we do not consider the application of the scripture that relays that God takes two people and makes them one. Husbands and wives should share their entire lives together. It may seem old fashioned but God said for married couples to be one. The Bible says, ""Haven't you read the Scriptures?" Jesus replied. "They record that from the beginning 'God made them male and female.'" And he said, "'This explains why a man leaves his father and mother and is joined to his wife, and the two are united into one.'"[7] Jesus shared with the people that God wanted married couples joined together as one. "Since they are no longer two but one, let no one split apart what God has joined together."[8] Believers have to be careful not to split apart what God has joined together for His glory. God has a plan for each marriage.

The enemy knows the power of oneness. There is power in the prayers of agreement between a husband and wife. When they agree with God about what He wants to do and pray about it, God moves. The power of agreement is one of the reasons why the enemy tries to so hard to destroy marriages. He works hard to kill the marriages that are living for God. The enemy hates the idea of marriage so much that he even kills the marriages of sinners. I have noticed that as long as the couple is living in sin, the enemy will not mess with them as much. However, the minute they get married, he works even harder to destroy the marriage.

When two believers come together in marriage, they come as individuals. They must have individual relationships with God. The husband has a personal relationship with God and so does the wife. I have summed up the idea of marriage with a triangle. (See Diagram below) One side signifies the husband's relationship with God and the other side signifies the wife's relationship with God. The bottom line of the triangle signifies the relationship between the wife and the husband. Having an individual relationship with God is essential to marriage.

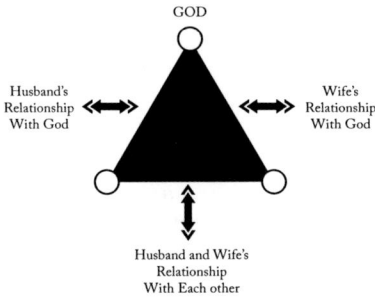

The two people come together and form a triangle with God, which keeps the marriage together. God is the connector. God is at the top of the triangle. He is on both sides of the marriage triangle. He is the power working to keep the marriage together. God created marriages to stand forever. A successful marriage will stand the test of time and trials. The marriage is successful because of God's grace and mercy. God will keep couples connected. He will help us stay together even when we want to give up.

*Consider the diagrams below:*
God is the Connector in Marriages.

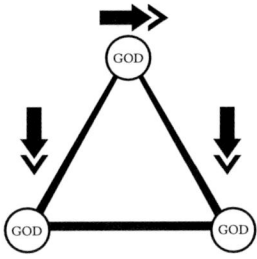

God keeps couples connected. His presence is essential to having the marriage He designed.

God is the Great Connector in marriage. He has given us life. He supplies us with what we need to be successful His way. Without God in our marriages, there are holes or doors for the devil to come in to kill, steal and destroy. If we do not have an individual relationship with God then when trouble comes, we have no hope. God gives us hope. Hope is essential during trying times. The enemy seeks to pull us away from God. We must make up our minds, hearts, and souls to fight for our relationship with God and our spouses. We do not fight with our fists anymore because we fight a spiritual fight now. Our prayer life and discipline are among our weapons of warfare. Our dedication to God is a weapon. Our obedience to God's Word is a major weapon. We do not ever have to suffer defeat in our marriages. God has given us access to Total Victory.

146 | *A Successful Marriage: God's Way*

When God is missing from our marriage, we have dangerous gaps in our connection that gives the enemy access into the marriage to try to steal, kill & destroy our marriage.

# COMMITMENT CAN CANCEL DIVORCE

Divorce is the direct result of lack of commitment. Divorce happens when "she won't" and "he won't". Success in marriage requires equal submission to God first and then to one another. The Bible clearly states that we must submit to one another.[9] This is a command to every Christian and it includes our spouses. The Bible commanded wives to submit to their own husbands.[10] The Bible also commands the husband and the wife to submit to God.[11] When spouses neglect to adhere to the Word of God on submission, they cause the fibers of the marriage to be torn. When God created Adam and Eve, His original intent was for them to live sin-free lives together forever. Divorce is a result of sin. Sin hardens the heart. Ezekiel chapter eleven verses nineteen through twenty tells us about our hard hearts. He shares how God wants to give us softer hearts instead of hard ones. God wants His children to be kind, loving, compassionate and obedient to do what He has called us to do in our marriages. Hard hearts are the reason we have divorce. In the Bible, Jesus told the people who asked about divorce that it was the hard hearts of the people that led God to allow divorce.

> *Some Pharisees came and tried to trap him with this question: "Should a man be allowed to divorce his wife for just any reason?" "Haven't you read the Scriptures?" Jesus replied. "They record that from the beginning 'God made them male and female.'" And he said, "'This explains why a man leaves his father and mother and is joined to his wife, and the two are united into one.' Since they are no longer two but one, let no one split apart what God has joined together." "Then why did Moses say in the law that a man could give his wife a written notice of divorce and send her away?" they asked. Jesus replied, "Moses permitted divorce only as a concession to your hard hearts, but it was not what God had originally intended.[12]*

Jesus said that divorce was not God's original intention when He created

*A Successful Marriage: God's Way*

the man and the woman. Divorce came because of Adam sinning against God. He was the leader not Eve. When we sin, we are sinning against God. Disobedience is a sin.

Husbands and wives must follow God's commands and love one another. Divorce should not be an option for the believer. God hates divorce. He said so in the Old Testament in Malachi chapter two verse sixteen. The verse says, ""For I hate divorce." says the Lord, the God of Israel." To divorce your wife is to overwhelm her with cruelty," says the Lord of Heaven's Armies. "So guard your heart; do not be unfaithful to your wife."[13] Although this verse is speaking to the husbands, it is equally applicable to wives. As believers, we should hate what God hates. We must heed to God's Word. He commands us not to put asunder or separate marriages. A successful marriage cannot even consider divorce as an option. Marriages that end in divorce are unsuccessful. We must line our hearts up with God and not allow our hearts to be hardened when it comes to our spouses.

We too must understand that choosing to walk with God is just that…a choice. We cannot make people choose to walk with God. If a spouse decides to leave and give up on the marriage then, that is their choice. There are options for the willing spouse. The willing spouse can ask the spouse to stay, pray about restoration of the marriage or let them go. The willing spouse must remember not to carry the guilt of the marriage falling apart. A marriage falling apart takes two parties. It could include one spouse messing up and the other one walking away. It could also include one spouse messing up and the other spouse choosing to remain in the marriage. Each individual case is different. Divorce is not easy. In fact, divorce is like death for some people. His or her desire was to be with a spouse whose desire was to be with someone else. This can be hard for anyone. God is able to help us. However, we have to be willing to receive His help. We all have issues but if we are willing to work at it, God will help us. He will help us to be whole in Jesus name.

We must understand that in order to have victory we need to be ready for an attack on our marriage. Satan is going to try to destroy our marriages. We must prepare to fight him with God's Word. We must stay in God's Word and pray for our marriages. We know that Satan hates us and wants to destroy us. It is death to victory in a marriage if we fail to prepare for war with the devil. We must fight evil and not one another. We must also learn to focus on ourselves instead of our spouses. We must look to see what we contributed to the argument. We are less likely to focus on our spouse when we focus on ourselves. We are wise to follow the instruction of Jesus and deal with ourselves before we try to deal with our spouse.[14]

Perseverance is never giving up on our marriage. No matter how bad it looks, we must never give up. God is faithful and He will keep our marriages together if we stay in Him. We must work hard and never allow the devil to destroy what God put together. We must never give up on the purpose that God has for our marriages. He will not let us down but we must do our part to sustain our marriages. We must keep God first, love each other and strive not to sin against one another. Giving up is different from making a mistake. To give up requires us to choose to do so. Giving up is an act of our will. When we make a mistake, we have not given up but we have fallen. We must never give up on our marriages or ourselves because God never gives up on us.

We find in the following verse some helpful points that will keep us from giving up. According to second Corinthians chapter four verses seven through ten, we find that we are earthen vessels with a treasure inside of us. I believe that treasure is not only life but also the Holy Spirit. The Holy Spirit leads us into all truth about what is on the mind of God. He especially lets us know who we are in Christ Jesus. The excellence we see is not just us but God in us or through us. God does not take His gifts back from us. That is why we see so many talented people using their gifts in a sinful manner. God gave them that gift to glorify Him but they decided not to.

Our marriage must reflect the victorious nature of God. We all make mistakes but we must remember the treasure we have in us. As we find in life, all marriages may encounter trouble at some point. This scripture gives us the "But" clause for any trouble we encounter. The "But" clause will cancel out what was meant for evil against us. The enemy is actually working hard to destroy our marriage "But" we are not distressed or worried because we know that we have victory in Christ. We are perplexed or baffled by the attacks against our marriage "But" we are not hopeless. We have the hope of glory in God working on our behalf. We are persecuted or mistreated "but" not forsaken or deserted by God. We are cast down or wounded "But" not destroyed or even damaged.[15] Let us daily meditate on the victory we find in the Word of God. We can always see what the Lord is saying to us as it relates to marriage in His Word. We all have to crucify our flesh, which means denying our desires to embrace God's desires. We find God's desires in the Word of God. We have victory over the world because we were crucified with Christ.[16] We live because He died. We can crucify this flesh because of His victory over death. Christ was obedient unto death and we must be the same way with God now. Christ died to what His flesh wanted. As a result, we can now enjoy the fruit of His death. He died that we might live. It is the same way in a marriage. We must die to our desires when they conflict with living as God purposed.

You can know this fact: God declared our end from the beginning.[17] There are no surprises to Him because He knows all things. As I die to my selfish ways, read my Bible and develop a personal relationship with Christ I can see the fruit of God in my life. I can see the life of Christ manifesting in me. I do not curse, lie, cheat, steal or fornicate anymore. I do not do those things because I have been made new in Christ. I have many issues. I sin daily just as we all do. However, because I am in Christ I do not habitually sin. I do not plan to sin. I am no longer a slave to sin. We all need the grace of God. Nevertheless, we still have the responsibility to allow the Holy Spirit to guide us away from sin.

We can expect to see the fullest potential of Christ manifest Himself in our marriages. We must never give up on our marriage. They shall live and not die! Our marriages are victorious in Christ. Everything that God created has a purpose in Him. Marriages have purpose too. Couples must be careful not to focus solely on themselves. They must seek God for their purpose in life as a couple. Married couples can bring God glory within their marriages. We must never give up!

We have to ask ourselves what our level of commitment is. For most of us it is, "I am committed as long as they don't do this." This, of course, is erroneous thinking for marriage. Commitment says, "I am committed no matter what." Commitment also says, "I will keep my vows until death do us part". We must establish commitment because conflict is inevitable. Again, it is not a matter of if you will have conflict but how you will handle it when it arises. Two married people are going to disagree at some point. One of the best ways to handle conflict is to know you. You can only control your actions. If we obey the Word we can handle conflict God's Way.

The Bible is God's communication to us. Therefore, His way to handle conflict is communicating. What do I need to communicate? I am glad you asked that question. Handling conflict with communication can go like this…Husbands love your wives and wives submit to your husband in all things.[18] Selfishness (We derive the love of money from selfishness) is the root of all evil.[19] Get self out of the equation and replace it with serving. How conflict is handled can be a determining factor as to whether your marriage will last. When I became a mature adult I put away childish things like screaming, fighting, name calling, etc. The bottom line is, in order to handle conflict we must be committed to maturing in Christ and communicating effectively.

## MARRIAGE LESSONS FROM MOSES

Let us look at how the glory of God applies to marriage. We can define the glory of God as the weighty presence of God. We should all desire to have the presence of God in our marriages. Moses said in Exodus chapter thirty-three verse fifteen, he did not want to go forward if God's presence was not going to be with him. That is how we should be in our marriages. Our daily prayer should include, "God I don't want to go a day without Your presence." Moses had some crazy things happen prior to making the request for God's presence to be with him continually. The history of the text starts with Moses being on the mountaintop with God. The people were impatient and began to worship a golden calf. Moses came down from the mountaintop and saw the people sinning. Moses dropped tablets and took care of the people who were not willing to trust God. Moses and God met to commune again. Although Moses had just recently encountered some conflict, he did not let that conflict deter him from communing with God. We must learn to do that in marriage as well. Conflict should not be able to run us away from our spouse or our God.

Exodus chapter thirty-three verse thirteen shares Moses asking God to show him His ways so that he could know Him. He also asked God to consider the stubborn people of Israel to be His people. This request is fully loaded for marriage. First, we also need to ask God to show us His ways in marriage so we can know Him. Getting to know Him helps us be more like Him. God's truth changes us from the inside out. The more we learn of His ways, the more we respond as He would. The more we learn of His ways, the more we treat our spouses as He wants us to. Secondly, Moses asked God not to cut off Israel. He asked Him to consider them as His people. He therefore was asking God to take ownership of Israel. Yes, they had just made a terrible mistake with the golden calf. However, here is Moses asking God to have mercy upon them. Surely, if Moses can ask God to do this for Israel, then we can do this for our spouses as well. The next time your spouse makes a mistake, you should pray, "Lord, consider my spouse your very own son or daughter in spite of this mistake." I believe this prayer will help the one praying more than anything will. I believe that we will see our spouses through the eyes of God as we pray for them.

God's glory is a product of His presence. It is spiritual but it affects us in the natural. The weight of God's glory will stabilize or neutralize things in our marriage that need it. We have to invite the glory of God into our marriages. When we invite His glory in, it can cancel the negative effects of everything we are going through. The glory of God changes us from the inside out. The presence of God mostly affects our spirit man. God reveals the sufficiency of His glory in a time of need. Your need for God in your marriage is the platform for His glory to be displayed. Let us consider Second Corinthians chapter twelve verses eight through ten, "For this thing I besought the Lord thrice, that it might depart from me. And He said unto me, My grace is sufficient for thee: for My strength is made perfect in weakness. Most gladly therefore will I rather glory in my infirmities, that the power of Christ may rest upon me." As I applied this verse to my marriage, it was more like this for me,

*"Daughter, "My grace, which is My favor and loving-kindness and mercy is sufficient enough against any threat and enables you, daughter, to bear the trouble successfully in your marriage; for My strength and power are made perfect (fulfilled and completed) in your weakness and My Strength is most effective in [your] weakness."*

## MY RESPONSE TO GOD IN THE PRAYER LOOKED LIKE THIS:

*Therefore, I [YaQuanda] will all the more gladly give God glory in my weaknesses and infirmities even in my marriage, that the strength and power and glory of Christ (the Messiah) may rest (yes, may pitch a tent over and dwell) upon my marriage and me. I bow to You, Lord. Have Your way in me and in my marriage.*

This may seem like a stretch sometimes when we are having conflict in our marriages. However, God's Word will always produce in our lives when we believe. The best time to see answers to prayers is when we have a need. By faith, we go to God believing He will answer our prayers.

## GLORY IN YOUR MARRIAGE

In Exodus chapter thirty-three verse eighteen, Moses' request to God was show me Your Glory. We too can ask God to show us His glory in our marriages. Lord, let our marriages reflect Your glory. God's Glory changes us to look like Him. Second Corinthians chapter three verse eighteen says, "The Glory of the Lord … we all … are changed into the same image from Glory to Glory, even as by the Spirit of the Lord". God's glory changes us daily to look more like Him by the power of the Holy Spirit. Situations may happen in our marriages but we can overcome. We can overcome because we are victorious in God. He has promised us that He will take care of us. He has promised us that He will make sure that all things work toward the good of His purpose for us. He will do the same thing in our marriages. His Word is applicable to every aspect of our lives, including our marriages.

In Exodus chapter thirty-four verse six, we learn that God is merciful, gracious, longsuffering, abundant in goodness and abundant in truth. People can see these attributes of God in us. Our spouse should yield the greatest benefit of us looking like God. We can be merciful when our spouse deserves punishment. We can be gracious when our spouse makes a mistake. We can be longsuffering when our spouse is going through something. We can be abundant in goodness towards our spouse when they are acting less than proper. We can show our spouse an abundance of truth by exhibiting the same attributes shown to us by God. We need God to be the very way He helps us to be to our spouse. We did an exercise at my church. A minister asked us to name attributes of God from A to Z. It was a fun exercise as the entire church participated. I came behind him the next week and said now how many of these attributes do you see in your life? Knowing God will cause us to be more like Him. The more God is good to us, the more we should be good to our spouses and others. The more God gives us grace and mercy, the more we should give grace and mercy to others. God sows the seed of His goodness so that the people around us can eat from the fruit of those seeds. We have to be mindful to be a reflection of God in our lives and our marriages. Let us glean some precious jewels of revelation from the acronym **G.L.O.R.Y.**

"**G**" - "Glory changes us from the inside out!" Romans chapter eight verse eighteen says, "For I reckon that the sufferings of this present time are not worthy to be compared with the glory which shall be revealed in us." We see God's glory revealed through us when we come through the sufferings of this life. We all suffer at some point. Allowing that suffering to show forth God's glory in our life and our marriage is an honor and a privilege.

*"L"* - "Long-suffering will pay off soon." Second Corinthians chapter four verse eighteen says, "For our light affliction, which is but for a moment, works for us a far more exceeding and eternal weight of glory;" This verse shows us that we may experience afflictions but they are only for a moment. While this verse is true, when we are going through hardships, it does not feel like it at that moment. Being afflicted and going through troubled times can feel like a very long time. We are wise not to make permanent decisions during temporary situations. I do not need to plan the rest of my life based on some trouble I may be experiencing. In marriage, this is applicable as well. If my husband and I are having a disagreement, I do not need to make a permanent decision based on that disagreement. My husband and I will eventually work through the disagreement. We cannot allow our emotional state to be the basis for our decisions. The same applies to situations we experience. My husband and I have had moments when we had more bills than we had money. We did not make a permanent decision in that temporary situation. We knew that it was an affliction but it did not feel light. We had to believe the Word of God. We believed that it would pass. It did pass. The affliction of not having enough money worked faith in us. We worked the principle of faith and we have never been in that position again. By faith, we do not plan to be in that season ever again. God will use trouble and afflictions to work His glory in us. Glory is spiritual. God in His awesomeness will use a natural situation to work spiritual depth in us. In troubling times, we need to speak the Word of God. The next time you experience an affliction in your marriage do this:

1. Declare that it is a light affliction.
2. Declare that it is temporary.
3. Agree that it will produce a greater glory in your marriage than before.
4. Enjoy the peace and benefits of believing God's Word.

*"O"* - "Only speaking the truth in love." John chapter eight verse thirty-two says, "And ye shall know the truth, and the truth shall make you free." The truth is that God is concerned about us. He is attentive to our marriage. He gave us everything we need to be victorious. He has already spoken that what we do will prosper as long as we follow His statues. We will speak the truth in love when we have been in the presence of truth. The Word of God is truth and it produces truth in us. The Bible is the foundation of all truth. We have to be careful not to speak negative words to our spouses. As we speak only the truth in love, we will see the glory of God in our marriages like never before. Only the truth we know will set us free. As we speak the Word of God, we will see the manifestations in our lives and in our marriages.

*"R"* - "Revealed as glory bearers." "For all creation is waiting eagerly for that …day when God will reveal or release to the public who his children really are."[20] The world is eagerly looking forward to seeing the true sons of God. They are looking for the sons of God that produce the power of God. People are look-

ing for evidence of God's Word. This scripture helps us to see that God uses our marriage to reveal His power. As His children, we are able to do what He does. He heals so we can lay hands on the sick and they recover. He forgives so we can readily forgive each other in marriage. Our marriages reveal God's glory. We understand our responsibility to look more like God as we come to know how important our marital witness is.

"Y" - "Yea and amen!" Second Corinthians chapter one verse twenty says, "For all the promises of God in Him are Yea, and in Him Amen, unto the glory of God by us." All that can be said when we show forth the Glory of God is Yea and Amen. God uses us to show forth His glory. God fulfilling His promises in our lives and our marriages bring Him glory. We give Him praise because we believe His promises shall happen. God's promises include peace, joy, yokes destroyed, restoration, riches, and deliverance. His promises also include power, life, being the head and not the tail, being the lender and not the borrower, prosperity, having healthy kids, generational blessings, all power over the enemy, eternal life, power to get wealth, family unity and total victory in every area of our lives. The Bible is full of promises we can see happen in our marriages to the glory of God.

God gets the Glory when we do what He designed us to do. For example, God created me to write. He gets the glory when I write. God created marriage to be very good. He gets the glory when marriages are very good. We see in Genesis that after Adam and Eve were created God said, "It is very good". Allowing God to get the glory out of our lives is especially important to us as believers. We must do it intentionally and pursue it with passion and commitment.

# *Chapter 11*
# EXPRESSING ANGER POSITIVELY

"I hate you!" Kara screamed at Peter as she stormed out of the room. They had just finished having a heated fellowship of the negative kind. Kara had recently found out that Peter was having improper conversations with his co-worker. Peter yelled back, "I don't especially like you very much right now!" Kara was upset because in addition to what Peter was doing, she was experiencing hard times on her job and her children we acting up in school. Peter was upset because he was remorseful for his actions, but he did not know how to articulate that. Therefore, he quickly found reasons to be mad, too. What Kara and Peter are experiencing is anger.

## UNDERSTANDING ANGER

Having dealt with conflict in the previous chapter, I felt it necessary at this point to deal with anger. Everybody experiences anger at some point in his or her life. Being angry is not necessarily the issue. The issue is staying angry until it matriculates into wrath. Another issue is sinning against someone while angry. We understand sin to be all the bad things we do. We all sin. Anger is a strong passion or a strong emotion due to an implied, perceived or actual injury or insult. Anger can be a proper response when we have been mistreated.

The Bible reminds us that it is okay to be angry. In fact, it almost admonishes us to entertain anger when it is appropriate. The Bible tells us to be angry but not to sin in our anger.[1] God has been angry according to the Bible. The Bible says in Psalms chapter seven verse eleven "... and God is angry ..." This is evidence that getting angry is not the problem. God is a righteous God and He is not walking around Heaven angry all the time. Some people have a warped view of God. They think He is some tyrant in Heaven looking for reasons to pour out His wrath upon them. That could not be further from the truth. They have erroneously ascertained this because it does not line up biblically with God's nature. God is a loving God but He is also a Righteous Judge. As a result of Him being a Righteous Judge, He had to deal with the penalty of sin. The penalty of sin is death. He dealt with it completely when Jesus died on the cross. As a born again believer you will not have to deal with the wrath of God. You will only have to encounter His loving correction. He corrects us because He loves us. He warns us of things that could destroy us. The warning found in the Bible is a strong indication that we can make a bad choice to sin in our anger. We have to choose to sin in our anger. We actually choose to stay angry finding a resolution, which is always the best resolve.

Remember, anger is an emotion. Emotions are excellent followers but they are horrible leaders. We cannot allow our emotions to dictate our actions.

This is detrimental to any situation. For example, I tripped over my husband's tennis shoes because he forgot to put them in the closet again. At that moment, I felt anger. I felt like he had done something wrong to me. I had to make a choice: I could follow my anger and speak negatively to him in a loud tone or I could speak in a gentle tone and turn away my own wrath. The Bible says that a gentle answer can turn away wrath.[2] I believe we have to apply that to ourselves as well. If I follow my anger, it will lead me to sin. I will share another example. I was driving down the road. I knew I was not speeding, however, the cop insisted I was. At that moment, I experienced anger because I felt like the cop was doing something wrong to me. I had a choice: I could follow my anger impulses, call the cop a liar and say some choice words about his badge or I could also speak in a calm tone to myself, calm down and speak to the officer like a sensible human being. The choice is always mine. Let me reiterate that if I follow anger in this example I will experience unnecessary consequences. The bottom line is that we have a choice. We are smart to choose wisely. To choose not to follow anger is a wise decision especially in marriage.

    I want to reiterate that emotions or feelings are good supporters. If I get a nice gift for my birthday then the feeling of happiness is appropriate. If I lose my dog then the feeling of sadness is appropriate. I should not allow my sadness to lead me down a path towards depression. Life will afford us many opportunities to get angry. We have to be wise enough to make good decisions during those moments. We usually spend more time with our spouses than anyone else. If we cannot control our anger, then our spouse is the one who suffers the most. Marriage affords us the most opportunities to get angry. In marriage, we experience disappointments, disagreements, frustration, rejection, unmet needs, hurtful words, lack of empathy and a host of other things. We must learn to direct anger at the situation and not necessarily the person in order for us to handle it properly. I have a T-shirt that my husband purchased for me. It says, "Hate the game not the player". That is relevant because remaining angry with the person is futile. We need to redirect our anger to the situation. We can change the situation sometimes, but we cannot change our spouses.

    I have also come to realize that the T-shirt that says, "Hate the game not the player" can be confusing because the player chooses to play the game. Nevertheless, I cannot change the player but I can definitely choose not to play the game. We have a choice. We have to choose not to allow anger to cause us to act inappropriately. Anger in marriage is not a laughing matter. There is nothing harsher than the consequences of an angry altercation gone wrong. As we mature, we learn to focus on handling situations properly. We seek to rectify situations with the least amount of friction. We learn to speak kind words when it comes to dealing with spousal anger.

    Let us look at this a little closer. If my husband yells at me because he is frustrated from a horrible day at work, I have a choice to make. I can get angry with him and yell back, but doing this will only compound his frustrations. Alternatively, I can direct my response at the situation that is causing him anger with the intent to help him work through it. I direct my response towards the source of his frustration, because we are on the same team. This is not easy but very important to handling anger correctly. Choosing to direct my response to the source of my spouse's anger empowers me to make suggestions as to how to rectify it. Spewing out negative comments to my husband about his anger will not diffuse the situation at all. This is something we all have to work on.

## THE PURPOSE OF ANGER

God is a holy God. Seeing as He did exhibit the emotion anger, we know there must be some good to it.[3] What does that mean to us? It means that there is a thing called righteous anger. If someone is mistreated then he or she has a right to be angry. Anger at this point is an indicator that something is wrong. Anger can be like a fever, sometimes. A fever lets me know that something is going wrong in my body. Anger can be a God-given emotion that tells us that something unrighteous has transpired. The issue here becomes that as a fallen people we have trouble depicting what is unrighteous and what is not. Selfishness has thwarted the original purpose of anger. Sin has set in and contaminated our anger gauges. Instead of seeing things through God's eyes, we deem anything contrary to what we desire as unrighteous.

## EXPRESSING ANGER CORRECTLY

Morally speaking we have seen a decline in our current generation. From the lyrics of songs to the pushing of the homosexual community, we see a decline in morale. There was a time when morality was high in our nation. Children were taught to respect adults and their peers. With bullying and sexual immorality on the rise, we can see the decline in our respect for one another. This relates to marriage because if I perceive my spouse to have hurt me, I will naturally respond sometimes in anger. Anger is a feeling. As a result, even if that feeling comes from an erroneous perception, I will still feel anger. Thus, anger management is a key to overcoming improper impulses of anger.

I had to learn how to handle anger properly. I was an angry person growing up so this process was long and tedious for me. I realized later in life that I was angry because I felt like life treated me unfairly. Being a child, I did not learn how to express anger in a proper manner. As a result, I spent much of my childhood and college years fighting. I fought people who looked at me wrong, said something wrong to my friend or tried to take my boyfriend. (They were unsuccessful, I might add) I was redirecting my anger at situations I could see. I was redirecting my anger at people I could punish. That is something we must be aware of in marriage.

Sadly, if my boss makes me angry, I may take it out on my spouse. Why would I do that? I would do that because I can redirect my anger at my spouse and get some satisfaction from it. I know this saddens you that we can be so heartless. Well, welcome to life. We can be a selfish people at times. That is why we must intentionally learn how to serve our spouses. We have to learn how to honor and respect them. We cannot trample upon the trust of our spouse because we fail to learn anger management. I am speaking from experience. Before I learned to control my anger, I would smash things around the house when my husband made me angry. I am much better now. Actually, I started out first trying to smash him. I am sad to have to share this about myself. However, the mirror I look in now reflects a better person.

When my husband and I were first married, I was still very angry. I had learned how to redirect that anger in so many creative ways. I usually overacted to situations. The source of my overreactions was the anger hidden in my heart. The Bible shares with us a song that says, "Thy word have I hid in mine heart, that I might not sin against Thee.[4] Unfortunately, the song I used to sing was, "Anger have I hidden in my heart, so I will more than likely sin against thee". It is comical now but it was horrible then. My anger controlled me daily. I still have to remind myself to keep my hands to myself when I get angry. My carnal mind has not forgotten the power of anger. When we cannot remember something, we usually have not forgotten it. The mind just cannot seem to access it. My carnal mind seems to have no problem remembering the wrong things. That is why having a mind like Christ is so important. Allowing the Word of God to renew our mind is imperative.

If we are consistently angry then we have to work on it daily. We owe it to our spouse to do our best to control our anger. I knew I needed help when I saw my son display the same anger tendencies I had before. We teach our children how to respond in life. We can teach them negatively by default or we can teach them positively on purpose. I have been working with my son to master his anger. His wife and children will thank me immensely when he grows up. I will share with you some of the steps we have taken to exhibit anger management on a consistent basis.

## STEPS TO OVERCOMING ANGER

The first step I had to learn was not to suppress my anger. I had successfully redirected my anger as a young person. However, as I matured in my relationship skills I started suppressing it. I would get angry and act as if I was not. I would bottle that anger up. The only problem was that it was not long before I exploded as a popped soda can.

The second step is acknowledging to myself that I am angry. I can usually tell when I am about to get angry. That undeniable feeling comes up in the pit of my belly. If I do not take control at the moment then I will more than likely submit to anger. I feel that feeling diminish when I say I am angry. I may say to myself that I am mad because what he said was wrong. I acknowledge my anger so I have no excuse to allow it to overtake me.

The third step is doing my best to convey the message to my husband that I am angry. We feed off each other. Therefore, if I get angry he sometimes responds in the same way. At this point, my main goal is to calm down and speak without making him angry.

The fourth step is then to either talk with my husband or get by myself to see what the root of my anger is. If I need to get by myself, I need to share with my husband that I need a moment. This step can be a bit difficult sometimes. My husband does not like to leave things unresolved. Therefore, he usually tries to get me to deal with the issue right then. The conversation goes like this,

> Me: *"Honey, I am upset right now. I need a moment."*
> Him: *"Why do you need a moment? We are two adults. Why can't we just talk like two adults?"*
> Me: Option 1: *"I said I was angry! Now leave me alone so I can think. Goodness Gracious! This is not what you want!"*
> Me: Option 2: *"I know you want to deal with this now. However, I am feeling like I am not going to have anything positive to say. I do not want another outburst like before."*
> Him: *"Okay, I still don't see why we can't talk about it now."*
> Me: *I just walk away for the sake of peace.*

There is nothing easy about learning a new way to respond to anger. It requires time and a lot of grace. I have recently put up a sign that my entire family can go get off the refrigerator that says, "I AM ANGRY. PLEASE GIVE ME A FEW MINUTES TO GET OVER MYSELF." You may want to try this in the beginning.

The fifth step is dealing with the root of my anger with the intent to eradicate it from my life. I need to know the source. I dealt with strong feelings of rejection most of my life. That added fuel to my anger as well. I found that most of the time I was angry with my husband because I perceived him to be rejecting me. I begin to pinpoint that fact when I stopped and pondered why I was so angry. If he said that the kitchen was a mess then I would get angry. I would get angry because I heard him saying through my rejection filter that I was incompetent at keeping the house clean. In actuality, he was talking about an isolated moment. Figuring out the root of our responses can be painful. They can be painful because we may not be ready to deal with what we see.

## THE ANGER MANAGER AND ROOTS

The Holy Spirit is the "Agent of Anger Management" and He wants to work with us. He reveals issues to us that need to be rectified. He always makes sure we have the love, power and grace we need when He leads us to a difficult place. I have had some low moments when I realized how terribly I responded in my anger. Because of my lack of self-control, I was not able to help myself, as I desired. The Holy Spirit was there to assist me. If I beat myself up then He would encourage me. If I got depressed then He would remind me of the joy of the Lord. The Holy Spirit is the main key to unlock the door to true anger management.

Most people that deal with anger can trace the root of the issue. Some of the roots that I have found are rejection, fear, low self worth and condemnation. We soon realize that these roots have produced fruit in our lives. Rejection as the root of our anger will cause us to perceive every comment contrary to ours as rejection. Instead of people being able to share what they really feel, they have to sugar coat everything they say. My husband had to walk on eggshells when he spoke to me about certain things. It was unfair for him. He does not really care for conflict so he would not want to say anything to upset me. The only problem was that there was no way for him to really know how I would respond to anything he said. I was very unstable in the beginning days of our marriage. He has watched me go through a Holy Ghost makeover from the inside out. One day I released him and told him he needs to say how he feels and let me deal with my issues. He was overjoyed because he really wanted to alleviate angry outburst stemming from conflict. I can imagine it was a load off his back. Who wants to walk around the house everyday wondering if their spouse is going to blow off the handle?

Fear as the root of our anger is nothing short of torment. The Bible shares that fear causes torment.[5] We have a common saying that fear is False Evidence Appearing Real. The sad thing is that whether the fear is false or real, it will still produce a response. If we feel fear that someone will hurt us then we may respond in anger. Again, being angry is not a sin. Allowing anger to promote us to sin is the concern. If I entertain the fears of my heart about my spouse, then I am constantly going to be angry. If I fear that Tommy is going to cheat on me then when something looks like that I am going to get angry. Fear can be the source of anger. However, it is as real to me as burning my finger on a hot stove. The fear is false but my anger is real. Therefore, I must deal with my fears to control my anger.

What can I do to control my fears? I can speak the Word of God whenever I feel the feeling of fear. Fear and faith cannot coexist. As I speak the Word, fear must diminish. Faith comes as I hear the Word of God.[6] I believe that God loves me by faith. Faith cancels out fear. We base our faith on the Truth of God's Word. God's Word will never return void. His Word will always do just what He sent it out to do.[7] God has given us the power to speak the Word of God and see results. When anger comes from fear, we have the Word of God to combat the root and change the fruit. We can control our anger when we speak the Word of God.

Low self-worth or self-esteem is definitely a root worth mentioning. Many people deal with low self-worth but they mask it with other things. They mask it with success, empty complements, dead-end relationships, drugs, alcohol and sometimes anger. Self-worth is something that is not contingent on what other people think. We should base our true self-worth on what God thinks.

What God thinks is what God said in His Word. If I allow the Holy Spirit to reveal my true self-worth based on the Bible then I will not easily allow anger to control me. I will know who I am in God. I can respond differently to perceived or genuine negative situations when I know who I am. The Bible gives me many clues as to my worth in God through Christ Jesus. He created me in His image. He loves me in spite of me. He chose me. He prospers me. I am the apple of His eye. I am His child and His delight. He wants to bless me. He will protect me. He will provide for me. He will lead me. He sanctified me. Surely if God thinks highly enough of me to do all these things and more for me, then I should have a high regard for myself. My self-worth is really my God worth. God loved me enough to send Christ to die for my sins. There is another truth to depict further my God worth. If I was the only sinner on the planet and everyone else was righteous. Christ would have still died just for me. He would have suffered the cross just for me. That is enough to hug myself. Sadly, lies have robbed us of realizing and enjoying some of the benefits of being a child of God. What I did in the past does not negate the love that God has for me. I cannot truly extend grace to my spouse until I have believed and received true grace from God. He loved me in spite of me then. He loves me in spite of me now. He will always love me in spite of me. Applying this same love in marriage causes marriages to grow and thrive as God declared in His Word. Love is the foundation of an abundant life. We can have abundance in natural things and abundance in spiritual things too.

    Condemnation is also a root of anger. We define condemnation as division or separation from God as a judgment.[8] Sin can separate us from God. However, when we accept Christ as our Savior we do not have to fear judgment anymore. Jesus Christ paid the cost for our sins when He died on the cross for us. Condemnation is a lie that comes in the form of overwhelming guilt. Yes, we are all guilty of sin. However, because Jesus died for us on the cross we no longer have to bear that tag. We can boldly declare "Not Guilty" by way of the Blood of Jesus. He died for us to be free from the penalty we owed. The wages of death is sin but the gift of God is eternal life through Jesus Christ our Lord.[9] We owed a debt we could not pay. Jesus paid a debt for us that He did not owe. He died so that we could have life. Abundant life starts now. Sometimes, people will try to condemn us for desiring nice things while we are here on earth. Having nice things is not the problem. The problem sets in when we want things more than we want God or our family. The cost of anything should never outweigh the value of it. Psalms chapter eighty-four verse eleven says that God wants to bless us. It actually says, "… no good thing will God withhold from them that walk uprightly." Christ has given us the power to walk uprightly. We do not have to live in condemnation. The Bible says in Romans chapter eight verse one, "There is therefore now no condemnation to them which are in Christ Jesus…" This is good news. As we conquer the fear of condemnation, we are in a place to manage our anger more effectively. The process is tedious and requires effort on our part. Nevertheless, with God all things are possible.[10] including overcoming the negative effects of anger.

## THE SIXTH STEP

The sixth step is dealing with the matter that sparked the anger. When we deal with the root in an assertive effort, we are able to resolve the conflict. I searched myself to find the root of my anger. I found that I needed to allow the Word of God to speak louder in my mind and heart than my fear of rejection. God is faithful. I begin to hear what my husband was actually saying instead of assuming the worse. I found that I was filtering his words through my filter of rejection. I changed the filter to the Word of God. It was not easy at first. I had become a professional at finding rejection in almost any comment my husband made. He would respond explaining that he was in fact not saying what I heard at all. Eventually, I found myself learning to hear his love for me. It was humbling for me. I am not even remotely saying that this is easy. It may be difficult at first. However, it will be worth it when you no longer go off the handle as much or shut down completely. Some people shut down when they get angry. Whether the response is external or internal, it needs to be controlled.

In this step, I suggest you go over what your spouse said or did that caused you to get angry. Find out what the thought was that sparked the anger. Here is an example. My husband said to me, "Why can't we talk like two adults." but I heard him say, "You are so incompetent that we can't even talk like two adults". As a result, I got very angry. I went back over the conversation. I responded to him the correct way in his absence. I said, "We can talk like two adults when I calm down". It may seem silly at first to talk to your spouse in their absence. However, once you speak it out of your mouth it is actually easier to say it to your spouse. We can display anger in such disrespectful ways. We have to be intentional and careful when we get upset. There is no excuse for us to disrespect our spouse.

This step is important because it includes humbly going back to your spouse. It can be overwhelming because the last thing we want to do is get angry all over again. Again, anger is not the issue. Not being able to control our anger is the concern. You may not need to go through all of these steps. It depends on the intensity of your emotions. These steps can help you learn to deal with the root of your uncontrollable anger. Uncontrolled anger robs us of opportunities to be loving, giving, kind, empathetic, and gracious to our spouse. Learning to control our anger is very important to having a successful marriage.

## LESSONS FROM A.N.G.E.R.

Uncontrolled anger can be one of the most erroneous ways used to handle conflict. We know we can get angry because it is an emotion. We must keep anger under control because it is a dangerous emotion. The Word and the Holy Spirit are the best ways to handle and control anger. When we study more about the emotion called anger, we will find it relates to hurt feelings, a desire to seek revenge, disappointments, failed expectations, fear of something and/or simply being frustrated about something. The marriage environment is the place where each component can happen at some point. Learning how to respond correctly to hurt feelings, disappointments, failed expectations, fear and frustration can be challenging. Nevertheless, it is possible. I want to use the acronym A.N.G.E.R. to expound on handling anger properly in your marriage.

A – "Admit it" We must resist the urge to pretend that we are not angry. Somewhere in life, someone erroneously taught us to act as if everything is okay even when it is not okay. We have become great pretenders at appearing as though we have it all together. We miss a chance to have victory over our emotions when we hold our anger in. We do not have to be disrespectful or rude when we admit we are angry. However, we do need to admit to ourselves and sometimes to our spouses that we are angry. If we never admit it, we rob our spouses of a chance to help us. Acting as if we are not angry is not a good idea. Anger is a fact and the worst thing we can do is hold our anger in. Holding things like anger, unforgiveness and bitterness in becomes toxic like cancer. It begins to eat away at you and to seep into every aspect of your life. Anger will control your thoughts and words. Yes, it is dangerous to hold anger in and not express it in a healthy manner. I have learned that anger aimed toward myself becomes depression and anger aimed towards others becomes control. It is evident that we must pull away and allow our feelings to simmer under the presence of God and then go to our spouses and talk about the issue at hand. Changing my mind will always change my actions.

N – "Never let anger control you." We all have seen someone lose their cool because they were angry. When it comes to dealing with uncontrollable anger, we know ourselves better than others do. We have to make a concerted effort to make sure that we never allow anger to control us. Uncontrolled anger is like lava pouring out of a volcano. It can destroy everything in its path. There are couples who allow anger to control them in a manner that pushes them to shut down on their spouses. They secretly brood over what happened to them. They explode internally instead of externally. Many times, they never share their feelings with their spouse in the proper manner so their spouse feels disconnected to them. Whether you explode externally or internally, uncontrolled anger can be detrimental to any relationship. Let us work on controlling our anger to the benefit of all those around us.

G – "God will help you" I find that one of the most difficult issues to deal with is guilt once we have allowed our anger to explode. God is there to help us work through our anger. He wants us to live a peaceful life. Unfortunately, uncontrolled anger robs us of that peace. Allowing God to help us work through our anger is a key to victory over improperly handling it. We must be real with God and tell Him about our anger. We must willingly allow Him to deal with us about ways to overcome our fleshly desire to take revenge against our spouses. This behavior modification will require the Holy Spirit. God will vindicate us at all times. He will help us if we yield to Him via His Word and His Spirit.

E – "Everybody gets angry" Anger is not a sin and it is very important for us to understand that. It is an indication that something is wrong. We get angry when we see a little old lady get beat up by a huge man. We get angry when we see a parent beat a baby with an extension cord. Anger is a proper response to unrighteousness, but we must handle it the right way. We do not have to make up excuses because something or someone made us angry. We just need to make sure we express our anger appropriately at that time. Although everyone gets angry, not everyone mishandles it. If we find that we have challenges in this area, we must allow the Holy Spirit and this chapter to help us in the future.

It is not wise to let anger linger and fester. Anger can be like pus seeping out of a wound. We must deal with it and resolve it or it will cause even more infection or harm. God was very specific in letting us know that the sun should not go down on our anger. We must adhere to the instructions of God so that anger does not destroy what we have spent precious time building together. We make no room for the enemy when we deal with anger in a way that is pleasing to God. I admonish you to deal with your anger today.

R – "Root and fruit". If we are going to properly deal with anger then we have to realize that anger is only the fruit of a greater issue. We need to address the root. We have to deal with the root so we can change the fruit. Taking time to see why we were offended in the first place is valuable. Upon figuring that out, we can then work to apply the Word of God. The Word of God will always produce good fruit. We are wise to speak the Word over our lives. We will see the fruit of the Spirit when we sow the Word of God into our lives and our marriages.

## PROPERLY HANDLING ANGER

We must properly handle anger or it will affect our relationships and us in a negative manner. Marriages can become a constant battleground if we cannot handle conflict properly. Two adult people living together and spending a lot of time together can become a breeding ground for conflict. How we handle conflict is an indicator of where our marriage really is and whether or not it will last. If two angry people keep lashing out at one another then it will not be long before success in that marriage begins to decay. If we allow anger to control us, we open the door for hurting our spouse.

Anger does not have to be explosive. The term exploding comes to mind when I think of my battles with anger. I would explode and negatively affect my atmosphere by spewing out negativity like a torch blower. The hard thing was coming down from that anger and having to deal with the repercussions of my actions. It was never a pretty sight. Truthfully, the last time I exploded was over a year ago and in my anger, I broke the television. He definitely had to conquer some anger issues at that moment. I don't know if my husband was more upset because of my anger or because I broke his T.V. The television being broken was not what caused me to seriously deal with my anger. The fact that my son, who battled with expressing his anger correctly, heard me break the television is what made me realize that this time I had to deal with my anger issues for real. He asked what happened and I had to tell him the truth. It was hard because here I am disciplining him for his angry outbursts and I cannot control my own. My son and I both went to the altar in church that following Sunday. We have both been doing much better. We are not doing better simply because we went to church. We are doing better because we want to do better and with God's help, we will continue to do better. We are doing better because we are willing to do what it takes to conquer anger's grip on our lives. Faith does not alleviate my responsibility to do my part to see things change in me or my marriage.

Love will combat anger if we allow it. Love will teach us how to walk in victory over anger. If you are like me, you may be wondering how. Love is patient and kind.[11] Uncontrolled anger can be impatient and unkind. If we learn how to walk in love then we can overcome the temptation to be mean or disrespectful. Love will teach us how to act. The Bible says, "God is love."[12] God being love shows us that as we grow closer to God we will see His fruit in our lives. Love is a fruit of the Spirit.[13] As we seek God to teach us how to love Him; we learn how to love our spouse. Love brings healing and if I believe that God loves me in spite of me then it is easier for me to love my spouse in spite of him. The love of God heals me from my mistakes. My love for God helps me to heal quicker from the mistakes of my spouse. The people who are closest to us are the ones we generally hurt the most. Learning how to deal with that hurt requires us to be intentional. I must first realize that my spouse is not my enemy. He is my friend. You must realize your wife is not the enemy of your marriage. Your spouse should be your best friend. Remembering that my spouse loves me helps me to deal with the hurt he causes me. I wish I could say that there is a way that we will never have our feelings hurt. Since we cannot control others, then not having our feelings hurt is just not possible. Many times people hurt us unknowingly. Anger is generally a response to the fact that we have been mistreated. How we handle that anger is the key to victory in our personal life and relationships.

## THE KEYS OF COMMUNICATION

Communication is the key to properly handling anger. Just being able to share what I am feeling can sometimes cause the uncontrollable anger impulses to subside. It does not help if I try to explain and my spouse ignores me. Couples have to learn how to serve. We have to learn how to listen to the heart of each other beyond the display of anger. In fact, if I see my spouse is angry then at that moment I should be praying for a kind word to speak to him to turn that anger away from me and back to the source. Locating the source of anger is very important to handling it correctly. I have to learn how to redirect my anger from my spouse and to the situation. I have to focus on the real issue. Generally, the real issue is how it made me feel. As we learn how to express how we feel without negative responses from our spouse, we can see victory.

Handling anger properly requires two cooperative spouses. As we establish an atmosphere of being loving, kind, fair and peaceful we can see breakthroughs in handling anger correctly. Granted, not everyone mishandles anger consistently. However, as married couples we have to learn how to handle anger before it gets out of hand. We must control our emotions before they control us. One way I can do this is by seeing myself. I like this little saying, "Seeing me before I see you keeps us from I C U". Several marriages are in the Intensive Care Unit because the husband continues to blame the wife and vice versa. If I can learn to see my need for grace and myself then I can give you the grace that I know I need. Marriage is teamwork and we have to learn how to work together.

Learning how to process anger in a positive manner can be challenging if we have not ever attempted to do so. We have to know ourselves and pay attention to potential situations that could anger us. Learning how to redirect negative feelings from people to how it made us feel is a key. For example, if my husband says something mean to me, I have to learn how to say that hurt my feelings but I am not going to be angry with my husband for saying it. I am going to find out why he said that and help him work through whatever he is going through right now. I know that seems unrealistic for some of you reading this. However, marriage is supposed to be a safe place. Therefore, if I mess up at home then my spouse should help me get it right in love. That requires us to take the focus off ourselves. A famous saying is, "If a person angers you then that person controls you". There is so much truth in that. We have to learn how not to allow anger to be a consistent response to uncomfortable things going on in our marriage.

Anger can be like fire and we have to treat it that way when we see it getting to a place where we cannot control it. Stop, drop and roll. Stop the anger from spewing out venom. We must practice being quiet until the anger subsides. Drop the anger by not holding it as your own. Do not claim it as "my anger". Roll away from the situation that is causing you anger until you can deal with it properly.

I have recently learned that we can conquer anger by forgiving our spouses before they ever do anything. This is not the easiest thing to do but it is definitely worth the try. What we have to do is in these following suggestions:

1. Daily acknowledge that you can be content beyond the actions of others.
2. When you are tempted to be angry in a negative manner, say to yourself that you can be content without getting the thing you want.
3. Stop making declarations that you will not be able to be content if a particular thing happens or does not happen.
4. Live a life that operates independent of getting angry because people are not giving you what you desire.

These suggestions will take time learning. Nevertheless, we can handle anger successfully. Learning how to stop playing the blame game makes things easier in marriage. Removing blame from others takes the control out of their hands and places it back in yours. Instead of saying, you made me feel this way. We need to learn to say I chose to feel this way. Emotions can be extreme at times. However, for the most part, if we keep a daily atmosphere of love, joy and peace we can be victorious over extreme emotions including uncontrollable anger. We must forgive in order to live in the fullness of peace. We must release our anger to God. We must allow God to minister to us about us. We are not only hurting ourselves when we hold back forgiveness but we are also hurting those that love us dearly. We all need forgiveness on a daily basis. We must follow Christ and readily forgive others when they make us angry. Jesus gave us an example of how to handle anger in a righteous way. He got angry but He did not sin. He conquered His emotions before they conquered Him. We are very wise to follow His lead in all areas of our lives including how to deal with anger.

# Chapter 12
# THE NECESSITY OF FORGIVENESS

"I will never forgive you!" screamed Andrea as she ran out the front door. She was angry and her words were spewing out venomous poison that could destroy any relationship if left unhandled. Andrea was accusing Sean of lying again about his business trips. He could not understand why his wife did not believe him. He had made a mistake on one occasion. He mistakenly told her he was going to Alabama but actually, he was traveling to Arkansas. It did not help that his high school sweetheart lived there. When Andrea found out, she was livid. She cried for days and she would not talk to Sean. She called him names and she would not let him touch her in any way. Sean was getting a frustrated. He tried to forgive her for being so accusatory but he was starting to feel very bitter towards her. He had not cheated on her or anything like that. After talking calmly one night, Sean found out that Andrea had never forgiven him for not being there for her when her sister died. He had a business trip that he could not change. He felt horrible but could not risk losing his job. He had three children and a wife to take care of. After talking through some things, they both realized they needed to forgive each other.

## PRINCIPLES OF FORGIVENESS

We have to guard our marriages from bitterness, unforgiveness, and resentment. Guarding our heart will help guard our marriage as well. Forgiveness is important in a marriage. If either spouse has unforgiveness in their heart, then there is a place for discord. Unforgiveness is a seed that brings forth fruit. This fruit can be rage, lack of trust, hatred and vengeance. God is a forgiving God. As He forgives us for our sins, we must forgive others. Marriages that experience the negative effects of unforgiveness often allow the enemy to destroy them. The spouse that refuses to forgive is saying, "God forgives me but I do not have to forgive the person who hurt me". If God readily forgives, then we should not withhold forgiveness from someone else. We will notice changes when we have truly forgiven our spouse. We will pray "love prayers" for our spouse instead of praying, "Get them, Lord". We will cast our spouse's mistakes into the same sea God casts our mistakes. We will keep our spouse's mistakes to ourselves and not expose them to others. We will extend the same grace to our spouse that God extends to us. We will pray for God to have mercy on them.

We are wise to forgive others, as we desire God to forgive us. Unforgiveness has no place in a successful marriage. Rage can be a result of built up anger for things people have done wrong to us. It is hard to be trusting when we have unforgiveness in our hearts. We are always expecting someone to hurt us just like the person we will not forgive. Hatred can be the fruit of unforgiveness in that it stops the flow of love in a marriage. God said that we should not try to get revenge on people but that we should let Him handle it.[1] Married couples must learn to be free and forgive. Couples bound by unforgiveness hurt one another by not forgiving. Being free entails forgiving others as Christ forgave us.

Bitterness eats away at the marriage like acid. Bitterness can cause many problems between spouses and can be the result of unforgiveness. It includes having a strong negative feeling about a person. Unresolved bitterness is a result of not communicating. Sometimes spouses get upset with the other spouse and the spouse does not have a clue as to why they are upset. Couples who desire successful marriages must find the root of the bitterness and pluck it up. God is not bitter towards us. We were responsible for His Son having to die on the cross and yet He still chooses to love us. Married couples have to be mindful of how bitterness zaps their joy and minimizes their chances of a successful marriage. Let us look at Job. He had the right to be bitter as far as he was concerned. We have not suffered nearly as much as Job. Nevertheless, at the drop of a dime we get mad and hold bitterness in our hearts towards our spouses. Bitterness is wrong and it gives place to the enemy in the marriages. The enemy uses bitterness to destroy marriages.

Job chapter seven verse eleven says, "Therefore, I will not refrain my mouth; I will speak in the anguish of my spirit; I will complain in the bitterness of my soul." Let us look closely at this Scripture. Job had suffered great losses and he was overwhelmed with bitterness and grief. He knew that God had the power to help him. Job thought that he had lived so holy that he could not have possibly deserved what he was suffering. That is what happens in the marriage. The spouses that are hurt feel like there is no possible way that they could deserve what has happened to them. These spouses are mistaken because if God lifted His grace they would suffer more than what they are going through. It is by God's grace that we are yet alive. Not affording a spouse that same grace is dangerous. God does not forgive us when we do not forgive others. We must look at all we have done to our God and forgive what the person did to us. Job had the nerve to speak out what he felt towards God because he felt like he was so righteous. That also happens in marriage. The spouse that was hurt speaks out and says things that they regret later. Speaking out of anguish is not a good idea. Remember it is not getting angry that is the sin. It is what we say or do because of the anger that can lead to sin.

Job decided to complain about what happened to him. That happens in marriage too. The spouse that was hurt sometimes will complain about the other spouse. In that complaining they call out everything the other spouse ever did that they did not like. Those words hurt the other spouse who probably already feels guilty about what they did. Following in these steps of Job is not always a good idea. We complain against our spouses as though we have done everything right. We all have sinned against God and must extend that same forgiveness to our spouses that He so graciously bestows upon us. Unlike Job, we must not speak out of anguish nor complain out of bitterness. We must look to God for strength and forgive our spouses for what they have done. Job wanted to die and as a result, he spoke out in bitterness. If couples want their marriage to live, they must not speak out against their spouse. Wise couples know the power of forgiveness and the power of the tongue.

Forgiveness will cancel the hold that bitterness has on the marriage. Forgiveness opens the marriage up for God to bless it. God commands us to let bitterness go in Ephesians chapter four verse thirty-one, "Let all bitterness, and wrath, and anger, and clamour, and evil speaking, be put away from you with all malice." God is serious about not walking in bitterness. He commands us to put it away from us. We must make the effort to rid our marriage of bitterness. If we allow it to take root in our marriage, it will produce the bad fruit. The Holy Spirit will always be there to help us do the right things. We must forgive so our marriage can live.

We ask God to give us more blessings. However, with more blessings comes more responsibility. If we are not able to handle offenses in a mature manner then we forfeit our opportunity to get more blessings. Marriage is a blessing. How we treat our spouse is evidence of how much we agree with God. After God made Adam and Eve He said, it is very good.[2] Marriage can be very good but it requires us to forgive as God does. To hold on to the offenses of my spouse is to let go of the blessings God has for me. I cannot hold on to hurts and hold on to the blessings God wants to give me at the same time. I must be willing to let go of the offense to be open to receive from God.

The first step towards learning how to forgive is acknowledging that I need faith to forgive at the level God requires of me. Let us consider a passage of scripture that validates this point. First John chapter one verse nine says, "If we confess our sins, he is faithful and just to forgive us our sins, and to cleanse us from all unrighteousness." First, we must believe that God is real to confess anything to Him. It takes faith for us to believe that God will forgive us for our sins when we confess them to Him. Then we must have faith that He is faithful and just to forgive us and cleanse us. That same faith is necessary in order for us to forgive someone else including our spouses. The Bible also says in Matthew chapter six verse fourteen, "If you forgive those who sin against you, your heavenly Father will forgive you. But if you refuse to forgive others, your Father will not forgive your sins." The same faith we have that God will forgive us is the foundation for us to forgive others.

Can you honestly say to God, "Lord, treat me like I treat my spouse"? That could be scary for some of us. I remember a time I hung up on my husband and preceded to speak negative things about him. In that moment, I started to feel bad. It was a teaching moment that I will never forget. I could sense Holy Spirit sharing with me that I would not talk to God like that. I eagerly agreed. I knew that meant that I had disrespected God when I disrespected my husband. God gave me my husband. He set the order in the marriage. When we buck up against what God orchestrates it is a bad idea and it does not feel good. I called my husband and apologized. I am much better at respecting the head of my family. Sometimes my spouse does not necessarily deserve to be treated good based on his actions. However, when I put the mirror up I see the same thing for myself. I respect his God-ordained position as the head of our house. I am honoring God as I honor him. We love because God has loved us and we forgive because God has forgiven us.

Forgiveness is necessary and required in any relationship. We find that forgiveness entails giving up resentment, granting relief from payment and ceasing to have resentment against the offender. Synonyms for forgiveness are to acquit; clear; exculpate; exonerate; vindicate; remit; shrive; absolution; pass over; discharge; liberate; redeem; release; unburden pardon and mercy.[3] Let us apply a few of them to specific situations. If Sam forgets to pick Kelly up from work, she can choose to release him from owing her anything beyond an apology. In fact, we can release the offense to God even if the offender does not apologize. Forgiveness says even though you are guilty of hurting me I will acquit you. If Amanda refuses to cook for Alex, he can pass over the incident by faith as he goes downtown to pick up some fast food. Forgiveness cuts the cord of someone owing us something. Romans chapter thirteen verse eight reminds us to, "Owe no man anything but to love one another. Loving people will encourage us to treat people the way we want to be treated. Forgiveness as a vindication is powerful. It does not mean in this instance that I defend you or your actions. However, it does mean that I free you from the penalty. I free you from constantly blaming you. I pardon you from owing me anything. If Peter forgets to pay the light bill and the utility company cuts the lights off then Pam can have mercy on him. She can refuse to lash out at him for his mistake.

Forgiveness does not mean you condone what they did, disregard how it made you feel, make excuses for the person who hurt you, ignore what happened to you or shrug it off without dealing with it. Forgiveness is not necessarily forgetting what happened to us. Our carnal mind generally holds on to things that we would rather forget. Remembering what happened to us is not the main issue. How we respond to that memory is more important. Asking God to help you forgive is not a bad idea. He is faithful. Choosing to forgive and allowing God to strengthen us is a sign of maturity. We will use the acronym F.O.R.G.I.V.E.N.E.S.S. to expound further on forgiveness.

## LESSONS FROM F.O.R.G.I.V.E.N.E.S.S.

F – "Faith" Let me reiterate that forgiveness is not natural; it is spiritual. To release someone from something when we feel he or she owes us can be almost impossible. Anger massages unforgiveness when we feel as if someone has treated us unfairly. Anger is an emotion that sounds the alarm that we have been mistreated. Experiencing anger based on a real incident is understandable to most. However, sometimes we experience anger based on something we perceived to be a wrong done to us. We can be very selfish. Therefore, we have to learn to let stuff go. Learning not to sweat the small things is a key to living while experiencing the peace of God, which passes all understanding. In Luke chapter seventeen, Jesus was talking to the disciples. He talked to them about offenses. He really helped us understand that opportunities to be offended will come. Then He went on to give us insight about how the offender should reconsider offending God's children. Let me quote verses three and four, Jesus says, "... If your brother or sister sins against you, rebuke them; and if they repent, forgive them. Even if they sin against you seven times in a day and seven times come back to you saying 'I repent,' you must forgive them."[4] That scripture is plain enough for us to comprehend. Jesus is telling us that we need to forgive. What the disciples said following this instruction is a key to understanding that we need faith to forgive. "The apostles said to the Lord, "Show us how to increase our faith."[5] We too can ask the Lord to help us increase our faith to forgive our spouses.

    O – "Ownership" All of us have sinned. All of us need forgiveness from God. We are wise to forgive because we need God and others to forgive us. We have to take ownership of the fact that we sin and need God's forgiveness on a daily basis. Refusing to forgive our spouses will cause us to be in violation of the Word of God. There is wisdom found in us asking God to help us forgive. As we accept ownership of our need for God to forgive us, we will find that it is easier to forgive others.

    R – "Repentance and confession" First John Chapter one verse nine shares that when we confess our sins to God He forgives us and cleanses us of other things we did wrong. Confession means to agree. When I confess my sins to God, I am agreeing with Him that what I did was wrong. After I confess that I have sinned then I should repent. Repenting includes turning away from the behavior that we confessed was wrong. God will give us the strength to stay turned away. God made us in His image. That means that with His help we can do as He does. Jesus said in Luke chapter seventeen that we have to forgive our brothers and sisters when they repent to us up to seven times a day. That is definitely applicable to our spouses.

    G – "God is a giver" For God so loved the world He gave His Son to die for an unworthy world. We may not think our spouses deserve forgiveness. However, like God we are to give forgiveness. We learn to forgive beyond our limited understanding of what someone deserves. God saved us when we were not deserving of His forgiveness. Romans chapter five verse eight shares that while we were sinners, Jesus Christ died for us. He did not wait until we got ourselves together. He knew we could not get ourselves together without His help. We must follow suit and give as God gives us.

    I- "Intentionally" Forgiveness must be done on purpose. Forgiveness requires us to be intentional about it. We must deliberately forgive others. We do not forgive by happenstance. In order for me to forgive, I have to choose to forgive. Forgiveness is not a default. Even when I know I need to forgive, I can have difficulties doing so. The Bible shares in Matthew chapter twenty-six verse fourteen, "…the spirit is indeed willing but the flesh is weak." Our spirit man knows we need to forgive, as Jesus requires. However, our carnal man does not always comply. We have to be intentional about forgiving our spouses.

V – "Vocal Victory" The words we speak can be like the words Christ spoke. They can be spirit and life if we allow God to use our vocal cords to release His Word. We eat the fruit of own lips. That means what we speak to someone else will produce in our lives too. I remember an incident where a young man spoke death over another person. Before the month was out death was knocking at his door. He found himself laid up in the hospital barely holding on to life. We have to use our words to edify. When we forgive, we show forth the nature of God. Let us use our vocal cords to speak victory in our marriages. Let us forgive. Saying I forgive you is an example of vocal victory. Try it today, my friend.

E – "Empathy" We have to learn to ask ourselves, "How would you feel on the other side?" We would want the person we hurt to forgive us. We have a chance to when our spouse makes a mistake or hurts us. Ephesians chapter four verse thirty-two reminds us that we should be kind and forgive one another. It also reminds us that we forgive even as God for Christ's sake has forgiven us. God honors Christ's payment for our sins on the cross. We should do the same thing with our spouse. Empathy is having understanding for another person's feelings. As believers, we are reminded in Philippians chapter two verse three, "Don't be selfish; … Be humble, thinking of others as better than yourselves." Having a mindset of selflessness and humility will help us think more of our spouse than ourselves. We can do this. Yes, we can.

N - "Not a feeling" Feelings are fickle. Our feelings can be up today and down tomorrow. What makes me happy today can make me sad tomorrow. Forgiveness is a choice we make beyond our feelings. Forgiveness is a fact. We must not allow our feelings to rob us of opportunities to forgive our spouse. We must press past our feelings.

E - "Everyone makes mistakes" We must learn to love our neighbors as we love ourselves. Jesus talked about a man that had fallen amongst thieves.[6] A thief robbed, beat and left him for dead. Several calibers of people came by him. The ones we thought would have helped him kept on walking right by him. The person we thought would not help was the one that helped. Regardless of what we think about people, we all make mistakes. We will all eventually need forgiveness. As Jesus shared with them about loving their neighbor someone asked, "Who is my neighbor?" Being a neighbor is not indicative upon someone having the same faith. Being a good neighbor is an act that God could use to draw an unbeliever to the faith. Surely, our spouse is included as a neighbor. Forgiveness is an expression of being godly and neighborly.

S – "Sacrifice" Jesus was a living sacrifice for us. He paid a debt He did not owe. We owed a debt we could not pay. There will be times we have to sacrifice our feelings to forgive and obey God's command.

S – "Success" We are successful when we forgive. Success is gaining a desired outcome. We get what the Word promises when we do what the Word says to do. The Bible instructs us to forgive. I cannot base forgiveness on how I feel. I must choose to forgive. When I forgive, I refuse to allow what happened to me to continue to control my actions. I need to release what happened to me to God. I have to let it go. Even if I speak to my spouse about the incident, I must make sure I have released it to God first and allowed His healing to flow. Some of the worse things we say come when we speak out of our hurt feelings. As I forgive my spouse, I am able to come up with creative ways for us to move forward. Forgiveness gives me hope for success in my marriage. Hope helps me be creative. Hope energizes me with zeal to create a positive atmosphere of love and growth in my marriage. Success is inevitable when I follow the Word of God wholeheartedly.

## FORGIVENESS SESSIONS

As a marriage counselor, I often have to orchestrate forgiveness sessions. I set a few rules and allow the couple to communicate about incidents that they need to forgive their spouse for. I give them the liberty to discuss the incident(s) in detail. I explain to them what forgiveness entails. I use the acronym F.O.R.G.I.V.E.N.E.S.S. or another method that communicates what forgiveness really is. Then I ask Spouse-1 to describe the incident. I remind them not to speculate or accuse but just state the facts. The reason I do not allow them to speculate is that they do not know why their spouse did what they did. They can assume but that assumption comes from where they are standing. I do not allow them to accuse each other because that causes Spouse-2 to feel the need to be defensive.

I then ask Spouse-1 to describe how it made him feel. I attempt at this point to see if there is a root that is being used a as a filter. If there is a root issue present then we see things through that filter. If I have a root of rejection then I filter situations through that filter of rejection. That can include hearing rejection messages throughout the day. For example, if my husband says he does not like the way the living room looks, I will hear rejection. I may hear that he does not think I am competent enough to decorate the living room. He may simply be sharing his opinion about something that has nothing to do with me. I ask a few questions to find out what the root is. I have found several roots including rejection, fear, low self-esteem, low self-worth, distrust, hurt, unforgiveness, bitterness and others. At this point, I do not place much emphasis on the root because I do not want to minimize what Spouse-1 is experiencing. We will deal with the root later.

At this point, I ask Spouse-2 to share from her point of view. I ask for no excuses just explanations when necessary. Excuses are attempts to justify our behavior. If what we did hurt our spouse then we should apologize for what we did. We apologize even if we did not intend to hurt them or mean it the way they took it. The fact that our spouse's feelings were hurt is the focus. Explanations describe the facts. Discussing the facts is vital to getting to a solution. I admonish

Spouse-2 not to fall into the trap of trying to blame Spouse-1 for their actions. I ask them to explain what happened. I lead Spouse-1 in saying; I forgive you because God forgives me. I teach them to deal with today's issues today. I remind them not to let the sun go down on issues without dealing with them. I attempt to get them to appreciate that tomorrow is a new day. So, let us deal with today's issue on today. This goal is not always possible when emotions are high. Wisdom will always lead us to table situations until a better time. We do need to learn how to deal with today's concerns on today. Everyone enjoys starting the new day with a clean slate of new mercy.

Here is an example of a forgiveness session. Jenny describes the incident as Bobby saying mean things to her. She describes one of many incidents in detail to the point of where it happened, what he said and how she responded. I ask her to tell me how that made her feel. She shares that it made her feel like she was nothing to him. She does state that it has been hard to forgive him. She shares that she has not wanted him to touch her because she feels like he does not love her. I asked Jenny about her childhood. I ask her how she feels about herself. I find out that Jenny deals with fear of rejection as I inquire more about her past relationships and other inspired questions. We table that portion to deal with later in the session. I acknowledge that I can see how Bobby saying mean things would hurt Jenny. This gives Jenny permission to feel and to respond to what she deems as something painful. This is not the time to tell Jenny to grow up and get over it. That would only cause her to repress or deny what she is really feeling. That is not a good idea if we want to see lasting change take place.

I now ask Bobby to share from his point of view. Of course, he is still a bit defensive. I remind him to share what happened without blame or excuses. He shares that he did not say anything mean but he may have said it in what Jenny calls a "mean tone". He apologizes for saying it in a mean tone and he affirms that he does love Jenny. I can detect that Bobby is upset by the way he says he does love Jenny. I lead Jenny in the statement that depicts Jenny's choice to forgive him as God forgives her. Now I deal with the reason and root of how Jenny could say her husband does not love her because he said something in a mean tone. We go into that and it gives Bobby a chance to comprehend why she felt that way based on something he deemed as minor. We work through that rejection. Bobby and Jenny spend several weeks working on helping Jenny change her filter from rejection to love. Having a willing husband was essential in this process.

I used an example from a session that would show the truth of how we filter things through experiences, pains and hurts. Saying mean things or using a mean tone may seem trivial. However, the negative feelings that arise are not so minor, especially when we allow them to fester. Forgiving each other is vital to having peace in any marriage. I have conducted several forgiveness sessions with several couples. We have worked through adultery, lying, verbal abuse, physical abuse, sexual frustrations, anger and much more. We can do forgiveness sessions at home. I suggest you try it together. It is essential to stick to the boundaries.

*A Successful Marriage: God's Way*

## WHAT FORGIVENESS INCLUDES

Forgiving my spouse does not mean I will forget what happened. Forgiveness gives me the power to remember what happened and still choose to forgive. Forgiveness does not mean I agree with what happened to me especially if it caused me pain. Forgiveness does not mean that I will not experience anger but it does free me from staying angry. Forgiveness does not mean I act as if what happened to me never happened. Forgiveness liberates me from the need to get back at my spouse. Forgiveness gives me hope that things can be better in my marriage. Forgiveness gives me access to receive the benefit of God's love. One of the benefits is to have fear cast out of my life and my marriage. Perfect love casts out fear.[7] As I forgive, I can see faith conquering fear. Forgiveness helps me learn how to separate what happened to me from me as a person. We become what we behold. If I continue to behold or hold on to what happened to me, it can become a part of me. Forgiveness helps me to have hope that my marriage is not over because of what happened. Unforgiveness robs me of hope. Forgiveness gives me a chance to focus on solutions and things that will enhance my marriage. Unforgiveness causes me to focus on the problem.

Whatever I magnify will grow in my marriage. I can choose to forgive and magnify hope. I could choose not to forgive and magnify hopelessness. Either way, I have to make a choice. Forgiveness is a sign of maturity. When I was a child, if my friends did not play the ball game like I wanted to play it I took my ball and went home. When I became an adult, I stopped acting like a child. Just because I am hurt does not give me the right in marriage to withhold expressions of love from my spouse or leave him. Going through painful situations gives us opportunities to grow. Going through painful situations helps us learn how to move forward and leave the past behind as a marker of how far we have come together. Going through painful situations helps us learn how to communicate with one another. No one should intentionally hurt anyone else. We should strive to treat people the way we want to be treated!

## I KNEW I HAD FORGIVEN

I had to learn to forgive so I could live in peace. I knew I had forgiven when I stopped talking about what happened to me. I knew I had forgiven when I could praise the person who hurt me. I knew I had forgiven when I saw the person who hurt me be praised by others and I did not get mad. I knew I had forgiven when I did not try to make the person who hurt me feel as if they owed me something. I knew I had forgiven when I stopped trying to control the person who hurt me. I knew I had forgiven when I saw the person who hurt me laughing, smiling or just feeling good. I knew I had forgiven the person who hurt me when we got in an argument and I refused to bring up what they did in the past. I knew I had forgiven when even though I did not feel like I forgave them. I knew I had forgiven them because I chose to forgive them. It was a matter of my will and not my feelings. I know that feelings are fickle and I must not depend on them to forgive. I knew I had forgiven the person who hurt me when I prayed and asked God to give me the faith to forgive them and He did. I knew I had forgiven the person that hurt me when I allowed God to heal the memories of the painful incident. As I forgave, God took the venom out of the memories. He healed them so they did not bring me pain.

I knew I had forgiven the person that hurt me when I stopped crying over spilled milk and I drank some power-aid. God had given me His power to aid me in forgiving those who had hurt me. I knew I had forgiven when I let it go and watched God work His power in me to let it stay gone. I knew I had forgiven when I prayed for God to bless the person who hurt me. I knew I had forgiven when I asked God to grant me an opportunity to be a blessing to the person who had hurt me. I knew I could forgive when I realized that forgiveness does not necessarily mean restoration of friendship if the person has not changed. I knew I had forgiven when I realized that forgiveness did not mean what they did to me was right. I knew I could forgive because I realized just how much I need God to forgive me.

Failing to forgive is acting as if we are qualified to sit on God's throne. He is the Righteous Judge. Surely if He has forgiven us of all that we have done to Him then we should be willing to forgive the people that have hurt us. Forgiveness is not natural. Revenge is natural. It is natural for me to hit you back if you hit me. We need God to forgive and we need faith to forgive. We can find forgiveness through first Corinthians chapter thirteen verses four through eight. Love is the root of forgiveness and bitterness is a root of unforgiveness.

## OFFENSES AND THE NEED TO FORGIVE

The enemy will use any tool to move us away from the path set for our lives by God. Offense is a tool used repeatedly in relationships. We have to learn to move past offense. Holy Spirit helps us understand the ways of God our Father. We can offend Him at any given moment because He is holy. Yet, He allowed His Son to die for us so we could fellowship with Him again. We have to do the same in marriage. We have to allow the sacrifice of Jesus to cover each other's faults so we can stay in consistent fellowship and unity. We are in a position to offend God daily. Yet, His grace and mercy retains us and presents us faultless through the sacrifice of Jesus on the cross. We must get to a point in this life that we render our spouses faultless by way of the cross and love them to life. Faultless here does not mean that a person did not do anything wrong. It remits that we have forgiven them for what they did wrong. If I can love you past your mistakes, then I can help you live in the light of Christ's sacrifice. He died because we were at fault. Because of His death on the cross, He presents us before God as though we never sinned. God loves us to life. We can learn to love our spouses to life as well.

Proverbs chapter eighteen verse nineteen says, "A brother offended is harder to be won than a strong city: and their contentions are like the bars of a castle." This scripture shows us how hard we can become due to being offended. Offenses can cause us to disconnect from each other. It may cause us literally to walk away from the divine order set in place by God. When we walk away from the Father, we uproot ourselves from His divine purpose. This is very dangerous indeed. It is dangerous because as a result, we may suffer needlessly causing others pain as well.

First Peter chapter two verse eight says, "… They stumble, being disobedient to the word, to which they also were appointed." We see in this scripture that when we are offended we are really stumbling at the Word of God and being disobedient. We choose to be children of obedience or children of disobedience. God has peace and blessings for the children of obedience. If I obey the Word and choose not to let my heart be troubled and pray for those who offend me then I can reap the benefits of being obedient. Offenses will come but we have a choice. We can choose not to allow the offenses to trouble us. We can choose to forgive the offender, but if I do get off track, I can miss what God wants to do in my life and in my marriage.

I find that when I am offended I misjudge and condemn without fair trial or benefit of the doubt. Offense comes to kill, steal and destroy. In the event that I yield to being offended and thus not giving my spouse grace, I find that things are harder and more difficult to deal with. As a result, of holding on to offenses, I have disobeyed the Word of God, which commands me to forgive others as God so graciously forgives me. Offended people forget just how much we need God to forgive us and so we condemn others for the same things we ourselves have committed.

When I allowed myself to be offended, I could not see the good in my spouse. All I saw was how horrible he was and how badly he had hurt my feelings. Remaining offended caused me to nurse my wounds. I kept the wounds open by continually talking about what happened and thinking about it. As I rehearsed it, all of those feelings kept resurfacing. It was self-torture to keep allowing myself to experience those hurt feelings over and over again. Not once did I consider how bad I had hurt God. No one can hurt me as bad as I have hurt God. Because of offense, I would not adhere or take heed to the Word of God given to me to show me the error of my ways. I just thought that my spouse was being so heartless and cruel not to see my point of view and how hurt I was. I was offended. Therefore, I tried to get people on my side. Thus, I had to exaggerate to make what my husband did to me sound worse than it was. Offense leads to other sins like lying, cheating, stealing and all kinds of unrighteous behavior because we have made room for the enemy by way of being offended.

I cannot walk in faith and offense at the same time. The definition of faith cancels out the opportunity to walk in both at the same time. Faith is evidence and substance that I believe in God. I cannot see God but in faith, I heed to His Word and His way. Yes, offenses will come but I must choose to forgive as Christ has freely forgiven me. Faith says to the offender, "I love you and I refuse to let this come between you and me." God desires for married couples to be one. Offense can divide us. One of us will have to take the high road of humility and go to the other one in love. I was in a situation and I had not done anything wrong (this time) but I got over myself and when to my sister. I went to her in tears and I said, "If I have done anything to offend you I am sorry. Please forgive me because I love you and I need you." That was the Spirit of God working life in that situation and working life in me. Now, that sister respects my authority in the church and most importantly in Christ. God has given us power over offense but we must walk it out. The only sure way not to walk in offense is to walk in faith. When we walk in faith we are saying, "God I yield to Your sovereignty. Father, I yield to Your Word."

It takes a person of character and integrity to go directly to the person and squash the issue that caused the offense in the first place. When we do that, we are bringing it to light and that kills the power of influence by the enemy. When we go to our spouse and say please forgive me, even if we did not do anything intentionally wrong, we are displaying the nature of Christ. We are living as He did. He asked the Father to forgive the people who hung Him on the Cross. We may go through but we will never go through all that Christ went through for us. He was and is the only one that ever walked this earth and was not guilty. Surely, if He can forgive we can too.

God does not even want our gift if we think we have offended our brother or sister.[8] We must allow the Holy Spirit to show us the people we need to go to before we bring God a sacrifice. God does not want it if we do not adhere to His requirement. It is harder to pray and worship God when we are offended. It is harder mainly because we have made place for the devil. The devil desires to steal our prayer life, our praise, and our peace. We must not allow offense to get us off track with God. We do have a choice in that matter. We have to choose to get over ourselves and let it go. God has been and is too good to us to allow something to offend us to a point where we walk away from Him. We must learn not to get offended but allow God to deliver us from that issue that is causing us to stumble. Being offended says more about me than the person that caused the offense. Being offended can render me ineffective for the Kingdom of God. When I allow the enemy to distract me by being offended, I am not furthering the kingdom of God in that situation. Offenses are a hindrance to the divine growth of God's kingdom. In addition, how I handle them shows where I am in my relationship with the Lord. If I am in that place with God where I hear Him and obey Him, then I never have to worry about walking in offense. I will choose daily to walk in faith and total obedience to God's Word, which cancels out being offended.

In conclusion, we must allow the Holy Spirit to help us. He is here to help us. He is our advocate. God sent the Holy Spirit here to guide us into all truth. The first truth He guides us into is about ourselves. He will bring God's Word back to our remembrance when it is necessary. He is our Comforter and

He will comfort us when we have been done wrong. Vengeance belongs to God. We must resist pride and refrain from trying to get revenge on someone for what he or she has done. The Holy Spirit is our Counselor and He will counsel us by way of the Word. He will always teach us the will, Word and way of God. The Holy Spirit is worth keeping and He will keep us from allowing offenses to control us. He is the power we need to forgive those who offend us. He is the power working in us to get us to the point where we have an "unoffendable" heart. Offenses may come but when they do come, they will not distract us because we have sought God for and received that "unoffendable" heart. That is where God is calling us to in the body of Christ. That makes one less way we can get off the path God set for our marriage. Offenses may come but they do not have to come into our hearts. We must guard our hearts and marriages to stay on the right path with God.

In marriage, we will encounter things that can bring division, conflict, disharmony and lack of unity. That is why it is necessary for us to learn how to preserve, protect and promote in our marriages. We can preserve them by forgiving each other the way God forgives us. We can protect our marriages by forgiving each other before bitterness sets in. We can promote unity in our marriages by forgiving each other for our mistakes. Resisting the temptation to blame, condemn, criticize, compare or judge is a key to fostering an atmosphere of unity in our marriage. The Bible reminds us that we should not judge our spouses. It asks us, "So, why do you condemn another believer? Why do you look down on another believer? Remember, we will all stand before the judgment seat of God." [9] You can have the peace you desire in your marriage if you, "Always be humble and gentle. Be patient with each other, making allowance for each other's faults because of your love. Make every effort to keep yourselves united in the Spirit, binding yourselves together with peace."[10] We learn the benefits and the necessity of forgiveness in marriage as we experience altercations, disagreements and different situations that require us to forgive. At the end of the day, we learn that we have the faith to forgive because we have the faith to be forgiven.

# Chapter 13
## LEARNING HOW TO SUPPORT YOUR SPOUSE

"Lord! Help me! I cannot do this!" is all I could get out in prayer one morning. I could not believe what was happening. I knew that God was real but I was struggling in my faith. We had lost everything. We lost the house, the Denali, the money and so much more. I could not help wonder why we were going through something of this magnitude. My husband had made a mistake through his associations with his business partners and I had some hard choices to make. I had to choose whether I would leave or stay. Would I take flight or stay and fight for my marriage? The thought of leaving was outlandish to me because I remembered how much God had forgiven me. I knew my husband needed my support. I could not risk walking away from the best thing that happened to me next to God. It was not easy because giving up seemed as if it would be so much more painless than staying. I loved God and my husband too much to desert purpose because life was uncomfortable. Through our trials, we both grew stronger in our faith and our love for one another. I chose to be a helpmeet to my husband at the lowest point in his life. I knew he would do the same for me. In marriage, we will have many opportunities to support one another. We are wise to make a concerted effort to be there for one another.

## UNDERSTANDING SUPPORT

Support includes bearing, being an advocate, helping, adjusting, maintaining and comforting.[1] Let us apply these components of support to marriage. A wife can support her husband by bearing some of his responsibilities when he needs help. I remember when I went back to school to finish my degree after marrying and having two children. My husband supported me by bearing the responsibility of tending to the children and the needs of house. As an advocate for our spouses, we should be cheering each other up opposed to tearing each other down with criticism. When a wife is an advocate for her husband, she will be there for him even when he fails. I remember a time when my husband was trying to run our three pharmacies. I could not help because I had to be home with the children. My husband would make mistakes and I would be the devil's advocate instead of my husband's advocate. I was a "help beat" instead of his "helpmeet". I have long repented and we have a much better marriage.

When a wife helps her husband with what God has called him to do, she opens the door for him to adore her. I remember a time when I would complain if my husband asked me to assist him or help him with the businesses. He simply wanted me to do what I was good at doing. I had not found my place in Christ, so I could not possibly be happy for him. Here God was blessing us with our own businesses and I was too busy saying he did not spend enough time with me. I refused to adjust what I wanted in order to be there for him. Again, I have repented of my foolish behavior and our marriage is back on track. In order to help my spouse maintain his business, I had to understand that his business meant the world to him. As a result, I had to step over my wants sometimes to help him maintain what he wanted.

When we comfort our spouses, we find that they come to us when they need it. A husband must be able to come to his wife when he is going through a hard time. There were times in my husband's business endeavors when it looked like the pharmacies were going to fall apart. When he came to me, he wanted to hear there are secrets to success found in failures or that the works of his hands will prosper. He wanted to be encouraged. If I had said I told him this whole thing was a bad decision, then he would have retreated. He probably would have thought twice about coming to me when he needed to be comforted. A wise husband or wife understands the power of encouraging and comforting his or her spouse when things are not going well. Supporting one another requires relentless effort but it is a component of a successful marriage. Success God's way includes supporting one another.

Many issues our spouses have can affect the marriage. We will look at some emotional, mental, physical and spiritual issues that can affect marriages. We can allow them to strengthen or destroy the marriage. God is able to take even bad situations and work them out to His Glory.

## EMOTIONAL SUPPORT

We must handle emotional issues correctly or they can disturb the flow of the success in the marriage. Emotions are the strong feelings that can cause a physical reaction. In other words, emotions are feelings that can drive our actions. However, not all emotions are bad. Some emotions include anger, jealousy, envy, powerful, acceptance, worthiness, humility, empowered, hate, unforgiveness, bitterness, depression, shame, fear, rejection, feelings of unworthiness and many more. Some feelings can lead us astray while other feelings should support our faith and obedience to the Word of God. For example, if I get angry with my spouse, I should obey the Word not to sin in my anger. However, if I allow anger to lead me and tell me what to do then I will more than likely sin and cause more damage as a result. Anger can be positive when we use it as an indication of righteous indignation. It is graceful to be angry at how abortion is destroying lives of innocent babies before they are even born. However, we should not allow anger to push us to kill the doctor that performs abortions. The fruits of the Spirit are the remedies to being lead by emotions.

We are wise not to allow our emotions to lead us. God gave us our emotions to help us while we are here on earth. We should not allow our emotions to lead us into sin. Allowing emotions to lead us can cause fears, addictions and weaknesses. The power behind our fears is the feelings we experience when we think of the thing that causes us fear. Some hurtful or shameful experiences in our past can be the source of emotional issues. The power of forgiveness destroys the emotional power that the experience has over us. We can trace almost everything we do back to a particular mindset. The feelings that we experience when we think about the past reflect our mindset. We counteract our faith when we respond to these situations or thoughts about these situations based on our feelings. We cannot base faith on our feelings but on the Word of God. As a result, regardless of what happened to me or what I did in the past, I can declare the truth of God's Word. Declaring God's Word will eradicate the residue of my past.

We will not see results from emotional prayers that are based on our feelings rather than on the Word of God. We must take time to worship the Lord prior to asking Him for anything. As we worship Him, we bring our emotions and feelings under subjection to Him. The fruit of the Spirit will help us combat the temptation to allow our feelings to lead us. Love will always speak on God's behalf and enable us to treat our spouses with kindness and patience. Peace is what we need when our spouses' emotional concerns are stirring us up to respond in a negative manner. We have the power of God through His Spirit to overcome insecurities, frustrations, hurt and being vindictive. One of the greatest tools we can use is waiting before we respond to situations. Emotions like to do and say things in or by impulse. Waiting a few minutes to respond can alleviate a lot of pain. When in doubt, do not speak, just wait.

Emotional issues can also include mood swings, depression, shame and codependence. We have to be very careful not to fall victim to our emotions but walk in total victory over them. Many women deal with emotional issues and we must deal with these before they destroy the marriage. Men can be emotional too. However, statistically speaking, women tend to deal with this more than men do. We must support and help each other have victory no matter what we are dealing with.

We will look at how the Holy Spirit can help us overcome emotional issues with the support of our spouses. We can benefit from supporting our spouses in their quest to obtain and maintain emotional freedom as well. It also benefits them for the sake of the children if they have any. This is relevant because we pass these issues from generation to generation if we do not deal with them properly. God sent His Word to heal us and we must embrace His Word and apply it to our lives. Our words have power! Proverbs chapter eighteen verse twenty-one lets us know that we will eat the fruit of our lips. What we speak will affect our lives because our words are seeds. When we sow seeds with our words, we will have to deal with the fruit that those words produce. If I keep speaking negatively over myself then I will see those negative words produce negativity in my life. With maturity, we learn to pay attention continuously to the things we say. Understanding that our words affect us is helpful in learning how to speak life.

We can help one another by sharing the love of Christ with each other. We can edify each other by spending time in the Word and affirming who we are in Christ. The hold of the enemy will be broken when each spouse believes in who they are in Christ. We can speak life to each other's dreams by allowing each other the necessary room to be ourselves. We build each other up by sharing and showing how much we love and believe in each other's dreams. We must learn to speak words of life and words of encouragement. Each spouse will have higher self-esteem as he or she speaks the Word to one another. We must aspire to do things that give each other joy and hope. Couples must learn to delight in each other. Married couples must know that God's plan for them includes their total deliverance from negative emotions that lead them the wrong way. Studying the Word together and sharing what Holy Spirit reveals will strengthen our marriages.

In supporting one another, we must remember that expressing our emotions is not wrong, but allowing our emotions to rule can lead us to negative results. Emotions are great followers but they are horrible leaders. If we experience a happy situation then our emotions can make that a joyous moment. However, if we encounter a negative situation and allow our emotions to lead us astray, then emotions can rob us of a chance to exercise faith. For example, if my husband makes me angry, then I have at that moment a choice to make. I can allow my anger to increase and speak negative words to him. I can choose not follow my emotions and speak positive words about the situation in faith. We always have a choice.

We can comfort one another by sharing that Jesus Christ knows our pain and our struggles. We must understand that He will forgive us if we will confess and repent. We can speak to the each other in a manner that gives us the joy of being free in Christ. When conflict arises, each spouse must learn how to communicate if something is hurting the marriage. We can express our love based upon knowing what each other likes and needs. Love will cover our sins and that is why love is essential in marriage. We must begin to see each other the way God does. His plans for us are that we live in total victory in Christ.

We can help each other grow in prayer by setting a time to pray together. We can consistently pray for each other's total deliverance. There is power in the petitions of a husband and wife's prayers. When we are consistent in prayer, it causes us to grow tremendously. We can help each other prioritize worshipping God by learning how to worship God in the beauty of holiness together. God has given us the power to call those things that we cannot see as though they already are because the Word said so. For example, I am not pretending that my spouse is not sick when I declare their healing. I am simply commanding his life to line up with what the Word says. The Word tells us that Jesus' stripes released the power of healing for him to be well. Sometimes our prayers are hindered due to a lack of forgiveness. Remember, forgiveness is the key that unlocks the door to every aspect of freedom available. We must forgive liberally. Any issues we encounter are just another name to bow down to the Name of Jesus Christ our Lord. We have to take authority and walk in the freedom afforded us by way of the Cross and support one another.

# MENTAL SUPPORT

Mental issues are those issues that stem from the mind. The carnal mind can control our actions if we allow it to. Our natural mind is always at war with the mind of the spirit. Christ has given us victory over our flesh. If we allow pride to set in then mental issues will play a strong part in our decisions. Pride pushes us to say that we did something that God did. We must humble ourselves before God and give Him the glory for all that He does in our lives. Mental issues affect a marriage because people that are dealing with these issues sometimes refuse to allow God to give them a mind like Christ. That person has not allowed the Word of God to renew their mind. They are obeying the dictates of their carnal mind. This person says, "I know more than God does and I do not need Him telling me what to do." Therefore, that individual blames his or her spouse for everything that goes wrong and takes credit for everything that goes right. Inevitably, any spouse that refuses to let God renew his or her mind will produce the fruits of the flesh. These fruits include stealing, adultery, lying, deceiving, wickedness, blasphemy, pride and foolishness. Mental issues reflect that we are following the flesh. The flesh hates God and does not want to submit to Him.[2] The spouse that will not submit to the will of God is capable of any sin. It behooves couples to pray and fast for total deliverance for themselves and each other.

The mind is where the battle takes place. The mind is important because God addresses it. In Romans chapter eight verse five, we see what the Lord has to say about the mind. "For they that are after the flesh do mind the things of the flesh; but they that are after the Spirit the things of the Spirit." The things of the flesh are worldly things and sin. However, not all things found in the world are sinful. There are probably no Cadillac cars in Heaven so we have to drive them here on earth before we leave. Now, that does not mean we are going to hell over a Cadillac. Just because I desire to have nice things doesn't depict that I am not spiritually minded. However, the mind of the Spirit is more concerned about spiritual things. The flesh does not want to please God but wants to satisfy itself. "So then they that are in the flesh cannot please God."[3] The mind of the flesh cannot please God because a fleshly mind thinks about worldly things and not spiritual things.

If the Holy Spirit dwells in us, then He shows us how to follow God. If a spouse does not have the Spirit of Christ, or is not seeking to have the Mind of Christ, he or she could very well end up following the flesh away from the will of God. Either we are saved and have an "unrenewed" mind or we are not saved at all. Either way the battle for control of the mind is going on. The enemy knows that if he keeps our mind "unrenewed" that we will never walk in the power of Christ. There are many conditions that we need to renew our mind from to be free in those areas. As believers, we should have the mind of Christ.

Upon studying the conditions of the mind, we can apply the conditions found about the mind to marriage. Some types of issues that we may encounter in marriage are being confused, being doubtful, dealing with unbelief, being anxious and being judgmental. The Word deals with these conditions and shows us how they affect marriages.

Spouses struggling with being confused are scattered and mixed up. They are unable to trust God. They are unable to make sound choices about their faith. James chapter one verse eight calls a confused person a double-minded man. "A double-minded man is unstable in all his ways." The confused spouse cannot make a decision because they have not made up their mind about God's integrity. "Without faith it is impossible to please God."4 A double-minded or confused spouse can cause discord in the marriage. Believers must know who they are in Christ Jesus. If there is a confused spouse in the marriage, couples are unable to get on one accord. We have to make a decision to believe God. The confused spouse resists the leadings of the Holy Spirit. The supporting spouse must allow God to speak words of wisdom to the confused spouse. A good witness at this point will give God the opportunity to draw the confused spouse closer to Him. Each spouse will need to study the Word and speak it to combat the confusion.

God is a God of order and when we follow Him, we stay on the path towards victory no matter what happens. This is where being a supporting spouse plays a major role in the survival of the marriage. God has given us the blue print for victory in our marriage in the Bible. The issue is that we want victory without the battle. Fighting for our marriage is always a good idea when we are standing on the Word of God. Do not give up on your spouse but support one another no matter what he or she is dealing with.

Another issue is doubting God. Doubting God includes being uncertain about God. Doubting stems from lack of trust. The spouse that doubts God may step out into the water but doubt that Jesus is God enough to sustain him or her. We see in Matthew chapter fourteen verse thirty-one that Jesus addressed this issue. Peter stepped out into the water but took his eyes off Jesus and began to sink. "But when he saw the wind boisterous, he was afraid; and beginning to sink, he cried, saying, Lord, save me. And immediately Jesus stretched forth his hand, and caught him, and said unto him, O thou of little faith, wherefore didst thou doubt?" Doubt causes us to be negative.

We may have gone through with the wedding but being doubtful that the marriage would work could be problematic when hard times come about. This type of thinking is dangerous because doubt can cause us to miss our blessings. We have to get in a place where we can hear the voice of God. We have to learn that God is always talking to us. He desires that we keep the atmosphere of our lives conducive to His voice. God speaks through revelation of His Word, things we see day-to-day, peace in the midst of trouble, convictions, and experiences. We must learn to obey God as He speaks to us with an eternal purpose in mind. We must be encouraged to get in a committed relationship with God. As we grow more in the ways of God, we learn how to overcome doubt when it comes. We learn to trust God to bring to pass His promises or His Word in our lives. We must continuously pray for each other's eyes to be fully open to receive and obey God. The more we experience God's Words coming to the pass then the less we have room to doubt that God will do as He said in His Word.

Another issue is unbelief because even the disciples dealt with unbelief. As a result, we must address this condition in the light of a believer. The unbeliever is not saved. The believer has confessed Christ and should not be suffering with unbelief but it is possible. If we deal with unbelief and we are saved then we must seek deliverance. We seek for deliverance because the freedom of someone we love is connected to our belief. God uses us daily to affect positively the lives of people around us. Unbelief robs us of chances to show the world that God is all-powerful. Even when Jesus asked the father of the demon-possessed son, did he believe the father said yes I believe but help my unbelief.[5] He knew Jesus had the answer but he doubted when he asked if there is anything He could do. If we deal with unbelief then we must ask God to help our unbelief.

It does not hurt to fast and pray for deliverance as well. Fasting opens us up to hear God more clearly. Life turns up the volume on problems and all the reasons why we should not believe in God. However, we can hear the voice of God clearer when we fast. As we see God move more in our lives, we can increase in our faith. Pride will keep us from asking for help. We can secure all the help we need in Jesus' Name. Jesus can set us free to the glory of God. Jesus said, "If you can believe, all things are possible to him who believes."[6] Having a successful marriage is not hard with God's help but it requires that we believe. We must believe that God is God by faith in order to come to Him on behalf of our spouse, our marriage and ourselves.

Being anxious is another issue we may deal with in being supportive of our mates. Philippians chapter four verses six through eight tells us how to deal with being anxious. He tells us to not to be anxious about anything. However, we must go to God about everything via prayer and supplication and with thanksgiving. We, by faith make our requests known unto God. The Word promises us that the peace of God will keep us beyond our natural understanding. His peace will keep our hearts and minds through Christ Jesus. The Word also tells us to be careful of what we think about. We must learn to think only about things that are true, honest, just, pure, lovely, of good report, virtuous and praise worthy.[7] The Bible tells believers in this Scripture to thank God, pray and allow the peace of God to overtake us.

Worrying about our marriage will not help. Believers must think about the things that will help us. Believers must think about their spouses being true to God. Believers can think about being just and forgiving towards their spouse. The believer can think about how much better their marriage will be as they grow in the Lord. Believers can think about how lovely life will be in the future. Believers can meditate on the good report that their marriage will depict about God and His grace. Whatever believers do, they must not worry or be negative. That requires us to commit to our relationship with God, our spouse and other believers. We need other believers because we all need a level of accountability. Not to mention, we can sharpen one another. Our marriage should not be an island because we need other believers to strengthen us.

Being judgmental is another issue we may deal with. We can erroneously judge others without first looking at ourselves. The Bible is clear that judging others is not our job.[8] We do not want God to bring judgment on us so we should not judge others. If our spouse is doing wrong, then we must take it to God in prayer. We must not judge them or allow pride to lift us up, but we must give them over to God. We can speak to our spouse in love about their issues but we must never condemn them. God the Father will determine where we spend our eternity. We have no room to condemn anyone else because we all need the same grace from God.

Sometimes a spouse will speak to the other spouse about an issue and the guilty spouse may lash out and accuse that spouse of judging them. For instance, if Paul tells Amy that her drinking and smoking is wrong then she may accuse him of judging her. Paul is not judging Amy. However, because she is guilty she finds fault in him because he is doing his best to live according to the Word of God and she is not.

Sometimes we may attempt to correct our spouse in love but they may choose not to receive it. While that rejection may be painful, we must go back to God in prayer. We must resist the urge to nag or lash out at our spouses. God never violates our choices. We too must respect each other's choices. We must be careful to make sure that love is the foundation of all our actions. We are not to insinuate that we are better than anybody else. However, as we follow Christ we will definitely be better off than someone who does not believe. We are not in a place to judge anyone but we can judge his or her actions based on the word of God. As we do that, we must remain in a place of love and support. We can only be vessels that God uses if we have His heart and purpose in mind at all times.

As we support our spouse dealing with mental issues we have to pray, speak the Word in love and live the Word. Darkness produces blindness in people by covering the issues that are destroying them. Each spouse must live a life that the light can shine through for His glory. Faith is required because things may not look good, but in God, they will work out for your good. Holy Spirit is the One that draws people to Jesus. It is not the responsibility of the spouse to save anyone. God is the Author and Finisher of our Faith. To be "Savior" is far too much pressure for anyone. However, the light of Jesus will shine and win if we walk and live the Word. Holy Spirit can use us to draw our spouses when we walk right before God.

## PHYSICAL SUPPORT

Physical issues can be very taxing on couples. These include anything that causes a spouse not to be able to perform something "normally". This can be as simple as having uncontrollable shakes to having a missing limb. Regardless of the spouse's physical limitation, marriage is designed to last until death do us part. There are times when couples get married and they know about their spouse's physical condition. The knowledge beforehand gives the supporting spouse the opportunity to study about the issue and time to prepare their heart. We never really know the fullness of what we have to deal with in situations until we get in the midst of them. It is seemingly easier for a person to marry someone with a physical limitation if he or she knows beforehand. However, there are times when a spouse has an accident or genetic disposition that causes him or her to be limited physically. It is during these times that the supporting spouse needs the support of loved ones and especially help from God.

The marriage vows include in sickness and in health. We must be careful not to break our vows because our spouse develops a physical handicap. One of the more common physical dysfunctions is the spouse's inability to perform sexually. More and more men are dealing with impotence. This dysfunction can cause problems in the marriage. We can handle these problems with love if the supporting spouse is willing to work through the alternatives.

Another physical handicap is having a spouse that experiences any type of ailment that causes them not to be able to do things that they were previously able to do. This could include back problems, head injuries, limb limitations and a host of other things. I dare not go too deep about all the many types of physical limitations, issues, dysfunctions or handicaps. In fact, I mentioned them is to remind you or inform you that Jesus Christ died for you to have victory over sickness and any other physical infirmity. We can appropriate the Word of God that says by Jesus' stripes we were healed. God has already released the healing through believing in His Word. God made our healing available when they beat Jesus with the cat of nine tails thirty nine times. The cat of nine tails that they beat Him with had a piece of glass or metal on the end of each leather strap. Each time they whipped our Lord and shed His blood, it was for our healing. No, we do not have to bow down or tip toe around any sickness! We simply have to take authority over all sickness and allow the Lord's will to be done. He sent His Word to heal us and that same Word is available to you now.

## SPIRITUAL SUPPORT

Spiritual issues can be very detrimental to the growth of any marriage. If one spouse is not saved and the other is saved then the saved spouse has to carry the spiritual weight of the family. This can be very taxing on the marriage. The enemy will consistently use the unsaved spouse against the saved spouse. The greatest thing the saved spouse can do is live a life that depicts the true nature of God. The light of Jesus will shine and the unsaved spouse will either choose to be saved or not. One thing that we cannot do is change the will of someone else. We have authority over evil spirits but we do not have authority over someone else's will. Trying to make someone accept Christ explains why so many spouses find themselves mad at God. While your prayers are essential, you must understand that accepting Christ is an individual decision. As we learn to pray for our spouse, we must learn the Word, will and ways of God. He will never make us accept His Son. Jesus Christ is the best Gift ever given. Nevertheless, that is exactly what He is to us, a Gift. We have to accept Him and obey Him.

There will be times when the saved spouse will make mistakes. Sometimes, the unsaved or saved spouse will use that against the saved spouse. We must all work out our own walk with God and know who we are in Him. We all fall short and we must never allow anyone to dictate our salvation. Salvation belongs to God and Him alone. No one else has a heaven or hell to put us in but God does. In the event that a spouse witnesses a saved spouse sin, the saved spouse must repent quickly which allows the spouse to witness the difference between a sinner and a saint. The saint sins and repents, which includes turning from that sin. The sinner sins and keeps sinning. This point is similar to pigs and sheep. Pigs get in the pig pen and wallow in filth. Sheep get in the pig pen and whine because they don't like being dirty. Get the dirt off friend by walking with God and allowing His commands to change you. We must live a life that lines up with the Word of God.

Saved spouses can support each other maintain spiritual wholeness after they have been delivered by allowing the Holy Spirit to work through them. They can confirm their deliverance in Christ by praising God for it. They can enjoy life with joy by speaking positively about their new life in Christ. They can give each other hope by sharing their new mind in Christ, which is evident by their actions. Couples can teach each other the Word and comfort one another after making mistakes. The act of speaking life and guiding each other into the truth of God's Word can stimulate marital growth. Carving out time to pray and worship God together can further foster the bond between them as husband and wife. Spiritual issues are very important in marriage. God created marriages for His glory and He wants his people to enjoy it. God is a Spirit and married couples must worship Him in Spirit and in truth.[9]

A couple that prays together has a better chance of staying together. If one of the spouses is not saved, then the saved spouse must pray and do what the Word says about winning souls to Christ. They must be ready to share their testimony of salvation with their spouses. They must allow the beauty of the Spirit to adorn them and they must live what they read about in the Bible. In order for the marriage to reach the fullest level of success, both spouses must be born again. The Word of God is for believers. The unbelieving husband cannot love, honor or cherish his wife the way God intended until he has initiated continued fellowship with God through salvation. The love God has for unbelievers is expressed in John chapter three verse sixteen, which states that "God so loved the world, that He gave His only begotten Son, that whosoever believeth in Him should not perish, but have everlasting life". Sinners must believe in Jesus to have eternal life.

God is faithful to provide for us, as we believe Him for total victory in our marriage. There will be times in the marriage that the husband will have to support the wife and vice versa. Marriage is hard work but it is worth it. As we sow into our marriages, we will not be disappointed in the harvest that we will reap. If we apply the principles found in the Word of God, then we will see His promises happen in our marriages like never before.

As spouses support one another, we must be intricately aware that supporting each other is ongoing. Learning how to support one another is a process. The process includes obtaining the desired results and maintaining them upon acquiring them. The difference between obtaining something and maintaining something is in their meanings. My dictionary reports that to obtain is to possess or hold on to and to maintain is to preserve from failure. All that we have discussed and will discuss helps us understand how to obtain and maintain a successful marriage.

Obtaining spiritual freedom requires people to accept Jesus Christ as their personal Savior. They simply travel down the "Romans Road" and follow the directions of the signs. The scriptures of the "Roman's Road" are Romans 3:10, Romans 3:23, Romans 5:12, Romans 6:23, Romans 5:8, Romans 10:9-13, Romans 8:14. These scriptures provide the way to experience salvation. A person has to make the choice to be saved. We find spiritual freedom in Christ, because He is the only way by which we can obtain spiritual freedom. Once we obtain spiritual freedom, we must allow Holy Spirit to work in us to maintain it. Holy Spirit will maintain our faith and He preserves us from unnecessary failure when we follow Him. He works in us to produce the righteousness of Christ. The works of the Holy Spirit are: He bears witness of us in Christ;[10] He leads us into life;[11] He gives us joy;[12] He enables us to abound in hope;[13] He teaches us about the things of God;[14] He comforts and abides with us forever ;[15] He speaks to us and guides us into all truth;[16] He lives in us and loves through us;[17] He helps and teaches us to pray according the mind of God.[18] The Holy Spirit enables us to maintain our spiritual freedom. He works in us and through us to produce the righteous of God in Christ Jesus. The greatest support that a spouse can administer is the support that leads to a deeper walk with the Lord.

The Roman Road leads a sinner to the way of salvation. Please read and meditate on the Romans Road scriptures. Do you see how much God loves you from reading these verses? Are you ready for a new relationship with Him? If you are saved then you will experience a deeper walk with the Lord. If you are not saved, then please contact us at *salvation@ispeaklife2u.com* so we can pray with you.

# Chapter 14
## APPRECIATING THE PROCESS OF VICTORY

"Hurry up and get dressed!" screamed Alexandria. "I cannot be late to the finals Todd!" she interjected with force. "Calm down woman!" retorted Todd. "I am moving as fast as I can!" Todd added. Alexandria and Todd got in the car and prayed as they hurriedly drove to the track field where Alexandria would be running. She was fast and she was favored to win. Alexandria refused to let that go to her head. She told Todd, "People are fickle and they will turn on you quick! I am going to work hard to win this race." Alexandria practiced day in and day out. Her trainer worked with her and Todd cheered for her every step of the process. Winning is intentional. Just as there was a process for Alexandria to win her race there is a process for winning in marriage. We learn to appreciate every step of the process as we learn the value of each experience. Alexandria was favored to win and she won the race. You are favored to win and you too can have victory in your marriage.

## UNDERSTANDING PROCESS

Understanding what is necessary for victory can help us pursue a successful marriage. It is a process, and as we go through this process of victory in marriage, we learn many things about God, our spouses and ourselves. Victory includes understanding that there may be failures along the way, but failure in one area does not equate to utter defeat in all areas. Small victories along the way still results in winning. Everybody loves to win. I don't know very many people who enjoy losing, and I don't know very many people who simply wake up victorious every day. Losing a battle does not mean we have to lose the war. Even talented people have to work towards winning in their expertise or craft. We can look at ESPN and see talent on display. If you interview any of those athletes, you will find out they had to prepare to win. The process of becoming victorious in our marriages requires preparation. No one bakes a cake without making sure she know and have all the ingredients she needs to bake the cake successfully. God has given us the ingredients we need to have victory in our marriage, but we have to do our part as we obey Him and do as the Bible instructs us.

If we want true success in our marriage then we have to be aware of what a good marriage looks like. We cannot obtain something that we do not know about. We can always refer to Adam and Eve in the Bible before they sinned against God. We can refer to God's relationship with His people in the Old Testament. We can refer to Christ's relationship with the Church. We have discussed all three of these throughout this book. All three of these examples include people. People are prone to make mistakes. As a result, it is very important that we have patience when handling the different issues that arise in marriage. God is very patient. He waits patiently on us to listen to His call to salvation. Adam had to exhibit some type of patience as he was naming all of the animals. Eve had to exhibit patience because she had to wait on Adam to do what God had instructed him to do. Jesus Christ is patient as He draws us to accept Him as our Savior. Patience is very important in the process of victory in marriage. Patience includes having the fortitude to wait on your spouse to mature in certain areas. Patience gives us the serenity to embrace the fact that we cannot change our spouse but prayer and God can. Patience includes resisting the urge to complain about each other's faults. Patience is staying power when we feel the irresistible urge to give up. Patience is one of the keys to success in life.

The process of victory in your marriage includes resilience. Resilience is being flexible. In marriage, there will be many opportunities arise that will require flexibility. We do not have the luxury of having our own way all the time. We have to compromise in order for both parties in the marriage to be content. There will be times in the process that we appear to be off schedule towards the goals we set. As we strive to obey God and His Word, we will see that He is well able to make sure we finish the things we need to accomplish in His time. God has a plan for our marriages and He will help us to stay on schedule according to that plan. We don't have to fret because we feel like we won't achieve what we set out to do together. Following God will ensure us that we are continually advancing. We cannot move forward if we are consistently looking backwards. The windshield is huge while the review mirror is tiny. Focusing on our future together will help us use our time wisely. Being overly attentive to things we cannot change robs us of opportunities to embark upon things we can. While we cannot change our past, we can definitely use our energies to create new waves of glory for the future. The glory of God exudes out of our lives when we do what we are good at. If I attempt to play hockey, I guarantee you that God will not get the fullness of glory. However, when I ran track God did get the glory because I was good at it. Make no mistake, just because you are good at something does not mean you should major in it. Having an open relationship with God can help you grasp what you should major in and what you should minor in. I usually say, "Just because you can doesn't always mean you should".

We must expect progress because expectation is significant to having success in any area. As we expect to grow, we will see the benefits of having positive aspirations. Expecting your marriage to develop and mature is necessary. As we expect certain things, we find that we are willing to work towards them coming to fruition. Progressing includes improvement. There is always room for improvement in our individual growth and our growth as a couple. Setting goals is vital to being able to measure success. As we set goals in our marriages, we have to stick to the plan as much as we can. While being flexible is good in certain instances, our day-to-day life needs to reflect order. Systematic order does not squelch creativity. It actually can work to increase it. Learning how to use our time wisely as we aim towards being more productive in our marriage will prove to be a wise decision. Working together to come up with strategies for marital success is a great idea. Marriages are not exempt from needing the purposeful pursuit of productivity. Knowing that our marriages are producing good results encourages us to work harder and more diligently to ensure its success. The process of victory has many components. However, as we strive for success we will realize that we have access to all the tools we need in order to be successful the way God intended.

## LESSONS FROM PSALMS

We strive to have a marriage based on Psalms chapter one verses one through three. This type of marriage includes the components listed in the scripture. "Blessed is the marriage when the couple does not walk in the counsel of the ungodly." If you are having problems in your marriage, it is not wise going to a person that does not love God and ask for their counsel. You must seek godly counsel to ensure the success of your marriage.

"Blessed is the marriage that does not stand in the way of sinners." We cannot stand in the midst of sin because eventually sin will seep into our lives. We have to stand in the way of the righteous. We have to spend time with and fellowship with the children of light. God has called us to be a light in the midst of a dark and perverse nation but we cannot do that if we hang out with them. We must pass through their circle and leave the residue of our prayer life and time in the Word with them. We have to be very careful not to grieve the Holy Ghost by hanging out with and fellowshipping with darkness. Light has nothing to do with darkness but causes it to flee.

"Blessed is the marriage that does not sit in the seat of the scornful." This is so important because we must all forgive. The scornful have decided not to forgive but instead to give into the temptation of revenge. The scornful will use any opportunity to get back at their spouse. The scornful will bring up old stuff that they said they had already forgiven their spouse for. The scornful spouse plays God because He said vengeance is mine in Romans chapter twelve verse nineteen. He meant what He said and we must be careful not to take a seat as the scornful spouse. Christians should be a reflection of Christ. In Him, we find forgiveness instead of fury. If you are a scornful husband or wife, I am begging you to repent and ask God to deliver you now so you have a blessed marriage to the glory of God.

The scripture also reminds us in Psalms chapter one verse two that "our delight must be in the law of the Lord." We must delight ourselves in Him so that He can produce His desire in our marriage. His desire is His nature. God is looking for couples who will willingly yield to His holiness and produce His fruit. He is looking for love, peace, patience, goodness, self-control and all the evidences of His presence in our marriage. In order to see His fruit in our marriages "we must meditate on His law both day and night" because life will cause us to forget what He said. The word meditate is more than just thinking about His Word. It also entails speaking aloud the Word of God. We must learn to speak the Word and cause our lives to produce the fruit of the Word in our marriages. We have to take the Word in and live what we have ingested. God is very faithful to bring His Word to fruition in our lives. We have to do our part and meditate on His Word. God even told Joshua in Joshua chapter one that if he meditates on the Word of God then his way will be prosperous and he will have good success. We too can enjoy prosperity and good success in our marriages if we heed to the instructions of the Word of God.

Verse three of Psalms chapter one gives us hope for our marriages. As we obey verses one and two then we can see the fruit from verse three manifest in our marriages. The Word shows us that "our marriages can be planted like a tree that is rooted near living water." The living water of the Word can cause our marriages to grow beyond measure. However, the significance of this portion of scripture is that we will be planted. Life and problems cannot sway us easily when we are planted. The enemy will not be able to uproot us out of our marriage with various temptations and tricks if we stay rooted in God's Word. Our marriage will be able to bring forth fruit that will be ripe. One of the worst things we can experience is eating fruit out of season. The taste is beyond disgusting because it is not time to eat that fruit. The importance of allowing God to bring forth fruit from our marriage in His time is essential to the probability of the marriage surviving. You see my friend, if we do the right thing at the wrong time it becomes the wrong thing. Timing is essential in the things of God. We must be sensitive to the seasons that God has set for our marriages. There will be times of sorrow, joy, peace, love, rebuilding, tearing down, etc. However, we have to be cognitive of what God is doing in our lives.

The reason "our leaves will not wither" from our marriage is that God will bring them forth at the right time. Jesus said in John chapter fifteen verse sixteen that we shall bring forth much fruit and our fruit will remain. He also spoke in another verse about a fig tree that had the correct leaves but did not have the expected fruit.[1] The process of bringing forth fruit includes the indication that our leaves have done their part. Leaves can tell where we are in the process of our fruit production. Let me dare step into explaining this from the point of view of marriage. The fruit of your marriage could be a successful business. However, the leaves of your marriage are an indicator that you are in the place to bud at the right time. Your faith is equivalent to your leaves. Your faith is your expectation that God will produce His fruit in your marriage. As these leaves (faith) bud, it is an indication that we can expect fruit to manifest. The first sign that fruit is coming can include the finances manifesting for the business. Remember, the business is the fruit but it has to start small and grow. If God gave you the money too soon, you may spend it out of season. If God gave you the money too late, you would have missed a chance to produce your fruit (the business). You see the process is very important and involves the perfect timing of God. If there are leaves (faith) in our marriage but no fruit then we are not successful. If there are no leaves (faith), then there is no expectation of fruit. Remember our leaves in this instance represent our faith. We have to have faith in God in order to see the manifestation of God.

In order for Tommy and me to see the fruit of our marriage, which is a successful business, we have to have faith. Our faith will be the indication that our fruit is getting ready to manifest. In this case, our leaves are an indication of our faith. The leaves are evidence that something is going to happen. Faith is also the evidence and the substance that something is going to happen. When Jesus cursed the fig tree, it was because the season and leaves were in order but there was no fruit. Be careful not to be in this position. Always stay in a place of expectation with God. Our leaf will not whither because our leaf is our faith. Our faith will not whither because our faith is based on the Word of God. In addition, my friend, the Word of God will never fail. After all is said and done, it will be the Word of God still standing. I hope I was clear in explaining the importance of staying in right relationship with God through faith in His Word and His Spirit so you can produce your fruit at the right time. The greatest part of this scripture is that "whatever you do in your marriage will prosper" if you obey the commands of the Lord specified in verses one and two. That is an open door to success in any marriage. Praises be to God for whatever we do in and through our marriages that is in harmony with His Word, His will and His way.

## WISDOM FROM PROVERBS

Every husband must get in a place of being a Proverbs one husband. This husband is a man of divine wisdom. He does not ignore or despise instruction but he embraces the mentorship of his mentor. This husband will not fall prey to the enticement of sin and temptation. God will pour out His Spirit on this husband and reveal His Word unto him. This wise husband will not ignore the voice of God, but he will run to God in total surrender and submission. God will protect this husband and his family from the calamities of this world. Oh, to be a wise husband is the delight of those men who desire to lead their family in the ways of God.

Wives have to work hard and intentionally to become a Proverbs thirty-one wife. For she is not just found but made by God and presented to her husband in the fullness of the God's glory. This wife is priceless and her wealth is beyond measure because God has placed His Spirit in her. She does her work in the spirit of excellence. This wife is the joy of her husband's heart because he can trust her. He knows that she will not do him any evil. He rests in the fact that she is a woman that fears the Lord. This woman is busy but balanced. She takes care of her house but she also works to bring wealth into the house as well. God wants the opportunity to take wives and make them the Proverbs thirty-one women to His glory. We must seek God and allow Him to make and mold us according to His design for our lives. Wives must be seekers of God, willing workers, have integrity, be balanced, givers, honorable, confident, fearless, self sufficient, strong, honorable, able to rejoice, not idle busy bodies, praise worthy and wives that fear the Lord with total reverence for His Word.² God is faithful to present wives to their husbands as virtuous women but they have to be willing to go through the process that He designed.

## BE FREE IN YOUR MARRIAGE

Being free in Christ is a fruit of victory. "Be" is a state of existence. It is who we are no matter the situation. To be means to "remain, stay, exists, live, come to the light or be situated". ³ We remain free. We stay free. We exist as free. We are free to live in Christ. We have come to the light as free people. We do not try to be free because we are free. Being free entails "being liberated, boundless, limitless, released and not in bondage."⁴ Free is an adjective and a noun. It describes what we are. "I am free" is the same as saying "I am a person". There should be no doubt about it. We get a firm understanding that no one can take our place in God when we know we are free. We are His children and we do not have to be concerned about somebody taking our place in His kingdom. We must know who we are in Christ. Knowing who we are empowers us to be an example of God's goodness.

We really need to know what God's Word says in order to see His truth manifest in our marriages. The truth you know is the only truth that can set and make you free. Many people have been set free but they have not been made free. That is why we see people are released from prison but end up right back in there. They have been "set" free but they have not been "made" free. Their mind has not be renewed or changed. No one has taught them how to walk, talk and be free. If we would teach "New Christians" how to be made free in the Word of God, then we could see the results of Jesus Christ in their daily lives. The truth of the Word will set you free from sin and it will make you free so that you never go back into bondage again. John chapter eight verse thirty-six tell us that we shall be free because of Jesus. "If the Son therefore shall make you free, ye shall be free indeed." If the Son sets us free, we are free. If anything outside of Jesus attempts to set us free then we will find that we are still bound. Nobody can make us free but Jesus. The first "free" in the Scripture means, "To liberate or make free."⁵ Jesus will liberate us and make us to be free. The second free in the Scripture means, "to be a citizen or not a slave."⁶ This Scripture is saying that when Jesus makes us free, He liberates us and we are no longer slaves to sin. We become citizens of "free".

The Bible says that whoever commits a sin is a servant of sin.⁷ To live a life of sin is being a servant of sin. That means sin tells that person what to do. Sin becomes the master. The person who follows every lust of their flesh is a servant of sin. This person needs Christ to make them free. Being free relates to a successful marriage because trying is an excuse to fail. We do not try to pray together; we do it. We do not try to treat each other with respect; we do it. Christ did not try to die for us; He did. God does not try to forgive us but He does it. We must not try to live right but we must do it with God's help. Christ makes us strong so we really can do all things by faith. Husbands and wives must not try to be good to one another but they must simply do it. We do not have to try to be successful. We simply have to walk in the success that God has already afforded us. We have victory over sin.

We must be very careful as to what we allow in our homes and in our marriages. The enemy of our soul is cunning and he wants to thwart the purposes of God in our marriages. Steps for maintaining victory in our marriage include:

1. Each spouse must accept Jesus Christ as personal Lord and Savior.
2. Each spouse must take a spiritual inventory of his or her own lives.
3. Both spouses must agree and dedicate the marriage to the Lord.
4. Both spouses must be equipped to fight the enemy with the Word for the marriage.
5. Both spouses must take a spiritual inventory of the marriage.
6. Both spouses must cleanse the marriage of ungodly things.
7. Both spouses must cleanse each aspect of the marriage with the Word of God.
8. Both spouses must consecrate the marriage for the work of God.
9. Both spouses must fill the marriage with the glory of God.
10. Both spouses must work to maintain spiritual victory in the marriage.

These steps are ways in which married couples can get keep their marriage victorious. Being free includes not walking in darkness. The Bible speaks of men loving darkness more than light.[8] The marriage that is free in the Lord will continuously seek God's light in His Son Jesus for their marriage. Getting rid of the darkness is the beginning. However, keeping the darkness out requires intentional efforts on the parts of the married couple. God's Word will always lead us to total victory in Christ Jesus.

Galatians chapter two verse twenty is a Scripture that strongly applies to marriage. It says, "I am crucified with Christ: nevertheless I live; yet not I, but Christ liveth in me: and the life which I now live in the flesh I live by the faith of the Son of God, who loved me, and gave himself for me." Being crucified with Christ can entail the suffering we endure in our marriages. The things that cause one person to suffer may not be the same as what causes someone else to suffer. The Scripture says "I" am crucified with Christ. That also entails that "I" have crucified my flesh. "I" have died to the old man in me who wants to do my spouse wrong. Nevertheless, just like Jesus "I" am alive. "I" live in the freedom of God. "I" live in the freedom of Holiness. "I" live in the freedom of the Spirit of God leading us. "I" live but it is not me it is Christ who lives in my heart. "I" walk in righteousness but it is not me it is Christ because my righteousness is filthy before God. Jesus Christ lives in my heart so "I" can live this life on earth by faith knowing that He will enable me to do everything that God has purposed me to do. "I" live by faith and not by sight because it is Christ who makes me just. Christ loved me and gave His life for me. "I" must live in Him. "I" must be who

He has made me to be. We all must give an account of "I". We must work out our own salvation and make sure that our "I" looks more like Christ every day.

There are many benefits to being free and walking in that freedom in a marriage. Psalm chapter one hundred and thirty three reflects some of our benefits. A marriage that has two people walking in the freedom of Christ can experience God's blessings. They can experience and enjoy the benefit of forgiveness. Jesus forgives us and we should forgive our spouse. To be free entails that God heals all of our diseases. We can walk in divine health when we walk with Christ Jesus. God will redeem the marriage that is under His protection from destruction. The enemy hates marriage but God will deliver the marriages submitted to Him. He will crown each spouse with loving-kindness. He will open up each spouse to give each other tender mercy.

God is good and worthy to be praised for what He wants to do in our marriage. God is the Key ingredient for a successful marriage. There is nothing too hard for God. Married couples must learn to submit to each other and to God's Word. We find the best devotionals for married couples in the Word of God. A wise couple will see to that they feed their marriage the Word of God, which is the bread of life. In addition, they must give their marriage the living water. God is a Spirit and the marriage that worships Him must do so in Spirit and in Truth.[9] The purpose of your marriage rests upon God getting the glory out of your union in spite of your flaws. As you continue to reach towards victory in your marriage, you will find out more and more about God's purpose for your marriage. As you appreciate the process of victory, you will reap the rewards of not getting weary. I know you are successful. I believe in you! You have many tools now to help you have a Successful Marriage: God's way… It is up to you friend! Your marriage will never be the same again and neither will you.

## UNDERSTANDING VICTORY

The process of victory also includes being viable. When we are viable, we are capable of operating and developing as a marital unit. Being viable includes having a greater quality of marriage. We are able to function and work together adequately because we embrace the process of victory. This process can be likened to preparing for the Olympics. It includes many different aspects of preparation that are similar to the process of victory that we experience as couples endeavoring for success in our marriages. Another ingredient of victory is increase. As we grow together, we increase in value and effectiveness. Our significance intensifies and escalates in leaps and bounds when we walk according to the divine plan of God. Married couples that honor God in their lives will see their territories enlarge. As they show they are trustworthy, God gives them more because they are good stewards of His blessings.

Confidence is a factor of victory. Confidence includes having faith in your marriage and your spouse. When we are confident, we become more trustworthy. We also show more support for our spouses and remain loyal to the marriage vows. When we are certain that our marriage is going to be victorious, we are assertive in the areas that we know we need to improve. Confidence includes knowing by faith that your marriage will work out and will be successful. Tenacity is part of being victorious. There will be times when we experience feelings that are contrary to those good for a marriage. Resisting the urge to give up on our marriage is the fruit of tenacity. Since trouble is a natural part of life, we have to be insistent and steadfast to believe that we will make it through. Remaining obstinate in the face of devastating circumstances will help ensure success. Married couples need to have a persistent, dogmatic determination not to be easily pulled apart by anything they encounter. They have to be persistent in maintaining the value of their marriages. There may be times in a marriage that we have to put in overtime. That can be equivalent to having to deal with a situation longer than you had not planned on dealing with it. We all have to make sacrifices in marriage. Refusing to throw in the towel during hard times is required to see true victory. Resilience is a vital aspect of victory. It is the ability to recover from unexpected changes and overwhelming situations in a manner that causes the marriage to thrive and not simply survive.

Taking hold to the fact that victory is your portion is the prelude to continually experiencing it in your life. The Bible shares many promises that are ours if we do what it takes to secure them. A successful marriage does not fall out of the sky. They come with hard work, sacrifice, commitment and willingness to do whatever it takes to win. You are a winner. In God, we always win. We always win because He makes sure that everything works toward the good of His purpose He has for our lives. I instruct couples to look again when it looks like they have utterly failed. I know that when they look again, they will find educational lessons that will inform them how to find the success they are searching for in their marriages. You too, my friend, can have the successful marriage that God has for you as long as you are willing do what you need to do by any holy means necessary. Success is yours if you are willing to bequeath it. Remember, you always win!

# BIBLIOGRAPHY

## INTRODUCTION
1 Merriam-Webster
2 Matt. 14:30
3 Heb. 13:8
4 Matthew 7:1
5 Romans 3:23
6 Ephesians 2:8
7 John 3:16
8 Romans 6:23

## CHAPTER 1
1 Matt. 7:24-25 NLT
2 Eccl. 4:9-10
3 3 John 1:2 NKJV
4 Ps. 1:3
5 Merriam-Webster
6 Matt. 18:19
7 Hab. 2:2-3
8 Rom 5:8
9 Gal. 5:21
10 1 John 4:10
11 John 10:17-18
12 1 Peter 4:13
13 Psalm 34:19
14 2 Cor. 4:8-9
15 Ps. 84:11
16 Deut. 8:18
17 Merriam-Webster
18 Strong's (success-7919)
19 Luke 22:42
20 Prov. 23:7

## CHAPTER 2
1 Is. 46:10
2 Merriam-Webster
3 Heb. 12:1
4 Is. 6:5
5 Gal. 3:11
6 1 John 1:5
7 John 8:12
8 John 8:34
9 John 8:31
10 Col. 3:8-9
11 Col 3:5
12 Matt. 19:17
13 Rom. 8:5 NCV
14 Rom. 15:2-3a
15 1 John 5:4
16 2 Cor. 4:3-10
17 2 Cor. 10:4-5
18 Gal. 5:22-23
19 2 Cor. 10:4-5
20 Rom. 3:19-28
21 Rom. 7:21-24
22 Rom. 7:25
23 1 Cor. 10:12-13
24 Luke 22:46

## CHAPTER 3
1 Phil. 2:3 NLT
2 Col. 3:23 NLT
3 Listed from Warren, Rick Purpose Driven Life. Grand Rapids, Michigan: Zondervan 2002
4 John 5:6
5 Mark 9:23
6 John 3:16
7 Matt. 22:35-38
8 Matt. 22:39
9 John 13:34-35
10 Gen. 2:25
11 Merriam-Webster
12 Gen. 3:8
13 1 Thess. 3:10
14 1 Tim. 5:8
15 Eph. 5:25-33
16 Adapted from Ps. 1 NKJ
17 Gen.2:23
18 Eph. 5:23
19 Eph. 5:24
20 John 17:12
21 1 Pet. 3:7
22 Eph. 5
23 1 Pet. 3:7
24 Eph. 5:22-24
25 Prov. 12:4
26 Eph. 5, 1 Pet.3:3-4
27 www.Bible.org/who-doeswhatquiz
28 Eph. 4:7
29 Col. 4:6
30 Prov. 1:7
31 Jer. 3:14
32 Eph. 5:25

## CHAPTER 4
1 John 8:38
2 Merriam-Webster
3 Deut. 8:6 NLT
4 Deut. 10:12 NLT
5 Deut. 11:22 NLT
6 Deut. 30:16 NLT
7 Ps. 25:9 NLT
8 Ps. 18:21 NLT
9 Ps. 27:11 NLT
10 Ps. 128:1 NLT
11 Prov. 4:7
12 Merriam-Webster
13 Luke 6:38
14 John 15:17
15 Rom. 8:37
16 Gal. 5:19-20
17 Gal. 5:24
18 Gal. 6:8
19 1 Pet. 3:7
20 Mark 7:21-23
21 1 John 2:15-16
22 Job 31:1 NLT
23 Prov. 14:12
24 Prov. 3:5-7
25 Jer. 29:11
26 Rom. 8:28 NLT
27 Phil. 1:6
28 Matt. 19:7-8

## CHAPTER 5
1 Merriam-Webster
2 John 10:18
3 John 15:13
4 Titus 2:4
5 Strong's (Philandros-5362)
6 Strong's (Agape-26)
7 Merriam-Webster
8 Eph. 5:25
9 1 Pet. 4:8
10 Is. 53:5
11 1 Cor. 13:4-8

12 1 John 3:1
13 1 Pet. 3:7
14 1 John 4:8
15 Isaiah 64:6 .
16 John 3
17 Song. 2:15
18 1 John 4:13
19 1 John 4:17
20 1 John 4:18
21 John 11:25
22 Heb. 11:6

## CHAPTER 6
1 Jude 24
2 Jer. 33:3
3 Heb. 8:25
4 Rom. 8:31
5 Is. 54:17
6 Gen 3:9
7 Gen 3:10
8 Gen 3:11
9 Gen 3:11
10 Gen 3:12
11 Strong's (Phileo-5368)

## CHAPTER 7
1 Strong's (Aheb-157)
2 1 Cor. 7:5
3 Gen. 24:67
4 Gen. 29:20
5 Gen. 29:32
6 Gen. 2:18-19
7 Rom. 8:7
8 Gen. 2:23
9 Heb. 13:4
10 Prov. 5:15-23

## CHAPTER 8
1 Ps. 37:4
2 Matt. 19:7-8
3 Phil. 4:19
4 Eph. 5:22
5 Eph. 5:28

## CHAPTER 9
1 Phil. 2:3
2 Merriam-Webster
3 Merriam-Webster

4 Applied from www.Bible.org/whodoeswhatquiz
5 Eph. 5:24
6 Eccl. 10: 19
7 1 Cor. 14:33

## CHAPTER 10
1 John 1:36
2 Rev. 5:5
3 Merriam-Webster
4 Rom. 5:8
5 Eph. 6:12
6 Eph. 3:20
7 Matt. 19:4-5
8 Matt 19:6
9 Eph. 5:21
10 Eph. 5:22
11 James 4:7
12 Matt. 19:3-8
13 Mal. 1:16 NLT
14 Matt. 7:1-5
15 2 Cor. 4:7-10
16 Gal. 2:20
17 Is. 46:10
18 Eph. 5:24
19 1 Tim. 6:10
20 Rom. 8:19 NLT

## CHAPTER 11
1 Eph 4:26
2 Prov. 15:1
3 Ps. 7:11
4 Ps. 119:11
5 1 John 4:18
6 Rom. 10:17
7 Is. 55:11
8 Merriam-Webster
9 Rom. 6:23
10 Matt. 19:26
11 1 Cor. 13:4
12 1 John 4:8
13 Gal. 5:22

## CHAPTER 12
1 Rom. 12:19
2 Gen. 1:31
3 Merriam-Webster
4 Luke 17:3-4 NIV

5 Luke 17:5 NLT
6 Luke 10:36
7 1 John 4:18
8 Matt 5:23-24
9 Rom. 14:10 NLT
10 Eph. 4:2-3 NLT

## CHAPTER 13
1 Merriam-Webster
2 Rom. 8:7
3 Romans 8:9
4 Hebrews 11:6
5 Mark 9:24
6 Mark 9:23
7 Phil. 4:8
8 Matt. 7:1
9 John 4:24
10 Rom. 8:16
11 Rom. 8:5-11
12 Rom. 14:17
13 Rom. 15:13
14 John 14:16
15 John 14:16
16 John 16:13
17 Rom. 5:5
18 Rom. 8:26-27

## CHAPTER 14
1 Josh. 1:8
2 Prov. 31:10-31
3 Merriam-Webster
4 Merriam-Webster
5 Strong's (free-1659)
6 Strong's (free-1658)
7 John 8:34
8 John 3:19
9 John 4:24

# ABOUT THE AUTHOR

Dr. YaQuanda Payne-McCall is a woman of character and integrity. YaQuanda's testimony is truth that Christ can make sure you don't look like what you have been through! That is why the heart of God coupled with the power of God can be conveyed to destroy yokes in the lives of all she comes in contact with! Dr. McCall believes: "My past does not dictate my destiny!"

Her no nonsense approach to mediocrity is a commanding force behind her vision. YaQuanda is a compassionate, loving and warm woman of God that seeks to please The Father. YaQuanda is filled with the Holy Ghost with signs and wonders following her ministry. YaQuanda is married to Minister Tommy McCall. He is a wonderful, God fearing and intelligent entrepreneur. Together they have established several successful businesses including three pharmacies and a pharmacy consultant company called Pharmacy Solutions. The McCall's have five children. YaQuanda is the daughter of Fred Payne and Vanessa Williams. YaQuanda has one younger brother Fredrick Payne and two older brothers, Junious and Tony.

YaQuanda is a licensed, ordained and confirmed minister of the Gospel. She has served in the capacity of Associate Pastor. She also travels preaching the Gospel. YaQuanda supports missionary and Kingdom work worldwide. YaQuanda will soon be gracing foreign soil to preach the Good News of Jesus Christ Globally! Dr. McCall speaks life and lays hands on the sick and they recover. She has prayed for countless people in person, over the phone, via a letter in the mail and she has seen the power of God pulverize every evil force. Dr. McCall walks in the authority of God, the power of God and in an undeniable degree of Glory that commands change in others! YaQuanda is known for teaching and preaching with simplicity and revelation power. She currently serves in ministry with her husband at Truth Gatherers Community Church in Tallahassee, Florida.

Dr. YaQuanda Payne-McCall is a woman after God's own heart. Above all else, she desires to please The Lord and lead His people out of Mediocrity. YaQuanda is the author of A Successful Marriage: God's Way, along with several other books and workbooks. She is a college professor, seminar instructor, seminar facilitator, speaker, preacher, teacher, worship leader, songwriter, dancer, dance instructor, flag choreographer and she possesses several other talents that the Father has graciously bestowed upon her. Ya-

...a is known for her ability to shift any atmosphere into one of power ...nointing. She is sought after for her ministerial enhancements, phe-...enal plays, creative life speaking ability and her dynamic yoke destroy-...g personality. YaQuanda recently co-wrote, co-produced and played the ...ading role in her first major play: "I'm Gonna Make It". The play was featured on the local news due to the Positive impact it had on the community. YaQuanda makes the Gospel plain but has a no nonsense attitude towards mediocrity and sin. As a result of God's favor, YaQuanda has had many opportunities to be an empowering voice at several life enhancing conferences, business seminars and educational forums.

Dr. McCall graduated from Florida A & M University with a Bachelors degree in Computer Information Systems. She also graduated from Jacksonville Theological Seminary with a Masters degree in Christian Counseling. YaQuanda received her Doctorate in Biblical Studies from Truth Bible College and Seminary. YaQuanda completed the School of the Prophets, School of the Prophetic and School of Prayer. Dr. McCall is a student of the Word endeavoring to teach others about The Way!

Above All else, YaQuanda loves the Lord. She has yielded and dedicated her life to the Father's purpose and commands. The world will continually be blessed by the encouraging, life changing and life speaking nature of Dr. YaQuanda Payne McCall.